The Law and
the Treatment of Drug-
and Alcohol-dependent
Persons

The Law and the Treatment of Drug- and Alcohol-dependent Persons

A Comparative Study of Existing Legislation

by

L. Porter
*Attorney-at-Law,
Washington, DC,
USA*

A.E. Arif
*Senior Medical
Officer in charge of
Drug Dependence
Programme,
World Health
Organization,
Geneva,
Switzerland*

W.J. Curran
*Frances Glessner
Lee Professor of
Legal Medicine,
Harvard Medical
School, Boston,
MA, USA*

World Health Organization
Geneva
1986

ISBN 92 4 156093 2

PRINTED IN ENGLAND

85/6586–Clays Plc–4500

Contents

Preface

This publication forms part of the World Health Organization's continuing review and analysis of legislation on health matters that are likely to be of interest to Member States. It aims to assist all those concerned with the legal aspects of programmes designed to control and prevent health problems related to alcohol and drug abuse, and to inform workers in both the health and legal fields about relevant issues, problems, and opportunities for research, training and action.

During the preparation of this book, governments of 42 countries and one territory (Hong Kong) were consulted and provided information. Guidance on the content of the study was provided by members of a special advisory group (listed in Annex 1), and experts from over 20 countries provided suggestions and comments. On behalf of the World Health Organization, I thank all those who contributed to this work, and especially the authors, who had the daunting task of bringing together all the information. It is my sincere hope that the collaboration established in the course of this study will continue in the future. I also gratefully acknowledge the support of the United Nations Fund for Drug Abuse Control, without which it would not have been possible to conduct the study in the limited time available.

N. Sartorius

Director, Division of Mental Health, World Health Organization, Geneva, Switzerland

1. Background

1.1. Introduction

This book is concerned with ways in which the law can serve to create and maintain effective programmes of treatment for both drug- and alcohol-dependent persons. It contains the results of a comparative study of relevant legislation, guidelines for assessing how existing legislation functions, and suggestions for alternative approaches to the development and review of national legislation in this field. It is concerned primarily with how legislation promotes the treatment of persons who are dependent on either alcohol or drugs, or both, and concentrates on an analysis of the legal provisions governing treatment programme administration. It is anticipated that, through comparative review of the legislative provisions, countries will be able to determine more effectively what changes, if any, are needed in their approach to such questions.

International efforts to control the illicit traffic in drugs have been significantly strengthened during the past 25 years with the entry into force of the 1961 Single Convention on Narcotic Drugs and the 1971 Convention on Psychotropic Substances, and their amendments. National governments, partly in response to such international conventions and partly as a result of increasing abuse of drugs in their countries, have enacted legislation designed to curb illicit drug traffic. Regional agreements, such as the South American Agreement on Narcotic Drugs and Psychotropic Substances, which came into force in March 1977, have also been drawn up in response to the need for multinational collaboration. Both the two international conventions and the regional agreements on drugs contain provisions on the treatment of drug-dependent persons. Treatment is seen as one of several ways of controlling the demand for illicit drugs since it should reduce the number of people abusing such substances.

Alcohol and substances liable to abuse other than drugs are not the subject of international agreements or conventions, except for a 1919 convention relating to liquor traffic in Africa (*1*).

Because the present publication is concerned with the treatment of drug- and alcohol-dependent persons, it does not cover legislation on drunk driving.

Legislation on drugs and alcohol has many objectives, some of which may be in conflict from time to time. For example, the aims of law-enforcement agencies, public health and welfare institutions, and mental health departments are not always in harmony in a given jurisdiction, although each has a legitimate interest in the treatment of drug- and alcohol-dependent persons. Over several decades, WHO has paid increasing attention to the role of legislation in public health policy development, programme planning, and implementation, and WHO expert committees have made recommendations regarding legislation in these areas. Law, whether in the form of statutory enactments and regulations for implementing them or of judicial decisions, is playing an increasingly important role in public health matters. This is particularly evident in the planning and delivery of treatment services, including those for drug- and alcohol-dependent persons. It is therefore useful to compare the approaches that different countries have adopted in their legislation in these areas and to determine whether or not particular items of legislation will facilitate treatment programmes.

1.2 Purpose and scope of the study

The purpose of the study reported here was to analyse existing legislation on the treatment of drug- and alcohol-dependent persons in selected countries in order to assist countries in reviewing their own legislation and in determining whether it should be revised.

A review of legislation involves two tasks. Firstly, the text of the law must be carefully examined to determine its literal meaning and its legislative history. Statutory definitions and the legislative meaning of terms such as "drug dependence", "alcoholism", and "treatment" are important in this respect. Secondly, it is important to determine whether or not legislation facilitates treatment and how it is perceived to operate by the public and by those who administer programmes set up under the legislation.

A comprehensive review of the national and subnational legislation and their specific provisions in many countries was thus undertaken. The results of the comparative legislative analysis are given in Chapter 4 of this publication.

In order to make the study useful on a comparative basis, attention was focused on several legislative trends in the countries surveyed. The first concerned new national legislation and initiatives to change legislation on the treatment of drug- or alcohol-dependent persons. The next area of inquiry concerned the legislative systems of the countries surveyed. Where were treatment programmes found in a federal system and how were different national and subnational laws reconciled? What was the effect of the international conventions and regional agreements on treatment efforts? Two further aspects of the survey concerned: (a) the role of national advisory or coordinating bodies, such as commissions and boards; and (b) the implementation of treatment programmes, their strengths and weaknesses.

Some countries have approached the treatment of drug- and alcohol-dependent persons through the use of separate specialized laws, others through more general laws and by including the relevant provisions in the mental health or criminal code. The study compares these different approaches.

We were particularly concerned to see whether key terms, including "drug dependence", "alcohol dependence", and "treatment", were defined in the legislation and whether these definitions met current needs. Our final concern was with the various routes of entry into the treatment system and access to services. We therefore reviewed and compared national and subnational statutory provisions governing: (a) compulsory civil commitment; (b) diversion to treatment from the criminal justice system; and (c) the legal provisions governing reporting, central registration, laboratory testing, and community surveillance of drug- and alcohol-dependent persons.

The review revealed a wide variety of legislative approaches to treatment and many different routes of access to treatment services. Coordinating mechanisms for reviewing the legislation were also found to be varied and to have different objectives. There is clearly a need for effective evaluation programmes and for harmonizing such mechanisms.

1.3 Methodology

The survey considered legislation enacted up to 1982. No research was done on legislation received after September 1982. The legislation reviewed was generally found to have been enacted within the past 20 years. Copies of the legislation were obtained from the following sources:

(*a*) complete texts of legislation and summaries of such texts published in the *International digest of health legislation*;

(*b*) complete texts of legislation published by the United Nations Division of Narcotic Drugs (E/NL series);

(*c*) personal communications from professionals in the countries surveyed; and

(*d*) United Nations and national government legislative document repositories.

WHO documents and reports on drug and alcohol abuse were analysed, and United Nations reports and publications, especially on the international drug conventions, were reviewed. Various legal and health agencies and individuals were consulted. WHO collaborating centres in mental health and in drug and alcohol dependence were contacted and consulted. Among others consulted were the United Nations Fund for Drug Abuse Control, the United Nations Division of Narcotic Drugs, and the International Narcotics Control Board. The International Labour Office and other international organizations, including the International Council on Alcohol and Addictions (a nongovernmental organization), were also consulted.

A total of 42 countries and one territory (Hong Kong) were included in the comparative legal survey. The selection criteria were designed to include countries of varying social, cultural and economic characteristics, legislative systems, pattern of health services, economic development, and population size. Both countries in which drugs originate and those in which they are abused were included. Some countries where the legislation was concerned predominantly with the treatment of alcohol-dependent persons were included (e.g., Hungary, USSR) as well as some where the major emphasis was on the treatment of drug-dependent persons (e.g., Burma, Thailand). We have also included a few countries (e.g., Sweden, Switzerland) where the legislation contains provisions governing the treatment of both drug and alcohol dependence. In a few countries, new draft laws or provisions on treatment were being considered at the time of the survey; these are mentioned here, as are provisions in some countries that have special laws prohibiting or controlling the sale and use of narcotics or mental health laws as the sole legislation on the treatment of drug or alcohol dependence.

For countries with a federal structure, it was not practicable to include an analysis of the law in every state, province, or canton; it was therefore decided that the legislation of at least one state or its equivalent should be analysed.

The 51 jurisdictions included in the survey, by WHO Region, are as follows:

African Region: Kenya, Madagascar, Mauritius, Nigeria, Senegal, and Zambia.

Region of the Americas: Argentina, Brazil, Canada (Federal, British Columbia, Nova Scotia), Colombia, Mexico, Peru, Trinidad and Tobago, and the United States of America (Federal, Massachusetts, Wisconsin).

Eastern Mediterranean Region: Cyprus, Egypt, Iraq, Pakistan, Somalia, and Tunisia.

European Region: Finland, France, the Federal Republic of Germany (Federal, Bavaria, Hamburg), Hungary, Israel, Italy, Norway, Poland, Sweden, Switzerland (Federal, Geneva, St Gallen), the Union of Soviet Socialist Republics (Russian Soviet Federal Socialist Republic) and the United Kingdom (England and Wales).

South-East Asia Region: Bangladesh, Burma, India, Indonesia, and Thailand.

Western Pacific Region: Australia (Victoria), Hong Kong, Japan, Malaysia, Philippines, and Singapore.

A first draft report of the study was completed in the late summer of 1982 and was circulated for review and comment to experts on the treatment of drug and alcohol dependence and legislation and to selected national and international organizations, including the United Nations Fund for Drug Abuse Control, the United Nations Division of Narcotic Drugs, the International Narcotics Control Board, the International Council on Alcohol and Addictions, as well as to each of the six WHO regional offices.

The most important review of this first draft took place during a meeting of an Advisory Group held on 7–10 September 1982 at Harvard University, Cambridge, USA, and attended by 23 persons, including staff members from WHO headquarters and the Regional Office for the Americas. The meeting was also attended by representatives of relevant United Nations and nongovernmental agencies and WHO collaborating centres (see Annex 1 for list of participants).

After this meeting, a new draft was produced and circulated to the same experts as before. The data were reorganized and expanded and emphasis was placed on the objective evaluation and comparison of the texts of the various legislative provisions. The materials were brought together under three headings, as follows: (1) compulsory civil commitment; (2) diversion to treatment from the criminal justice system; and (3) provisions on compulsory reporting, central registries, and laboratory testing of addicts and suspected addicts, and community surveillance of addicted and formerly addicted persons. In addition, as recommended by the Advisory Group, a series of tables and lists was prepared in order to present the data in a simple, easily readable form.

After the revised draft had been circulated, it was presented for review to a second WHO Advisory Group meeting at Harvard University on 5–7 April 1983, attended by 14 persons, a number of whom had participated at the first meeting. The governmental and nongovernmental representation was largely the same. This smaller group, all experts in some aspect of treatment programmes or legislation in this field, or both, thoroughly reviewed the document, and endorsed the conclusions adopted at the first meeting.

1.4 Previous WHO studies

The present study brings up to date the WHO comparative survey of legislation of 1962 (2) and the 1977 WHO study entitled *The law and mental health: harmonizing objectives* (3) which did not specifically cover legislation on the treatment of drug and alcohol dependence.

1.4.1. *WHO Expert Committee on Mental Health: fourth report* (*1955*)

WHO has paid considerable attention in the past to national legislation on mental health, as well as drug and alcohol dependence. Thus the fourth report of the WHO Expert Committee on Mental Health, entitled *Legislation affecting psychiatric treatment*(*4*), emphasized that "the principles governing good psychiatric legislation arise out of the need both for adequate mental health services and for care of the patient and the protection of society". The report specifically mentioned the need for legislation that authorized compulsory treatment for alcoholics who were dangerous to themselves or others, but not for all patients suffering from alcohol dependence.

1.4.2 *Survey of legislation on treatment of drug addicts* (*1962*)

In 1962, WHO prepared and published a survey of existing legislation on the treatment of drug-dependent persons in a number of countries(*2*). This survey pointed out that, in some areas, individual clinical treatment was not feasible because of lack of facilities and professional manpower, and that the only alternative was to take more active measures directed primarily against sources of supply of narcotics. Even where official figures showed a low rate of drug addiction, many countries (e.g., Norway) nevertheless considered it to be a serious public health problem. It was noted in the survey that public attitudes varied in different sociocultural contexts, with the result that in some countries severe penalties for addiction were considered appropriate whereas in others a "habit" was considered "normal". Attitudes were found to be changing, however, leading towards the recognition that the drug addict was above all a sick person in need of suitable and effective treatment and rehabilitation. It was pointed out that drug addicts do not usually show marked criminal tendencies, but that the need to obtain supplies of narcotic drugs often leads them to commit breaches of the laws relating to traffic in such drugs. In the judicial systems studied, there was a tendency to resort to social aid instead of routinely imposing the prison sentences authorized by law for such offences. Subject to the consent of the addict and to certain specific conditions, therefore, addicts were not sent to prison but instead medical treatment (i.e., diversion from the criminal justice system) was ordered.

Prior to the 1962 study, much had been written about the nature of appropriate medical treatment. Some commentators were of the opinion that the only feasible solution to the problem of drug addiction was to order compulsory detention in closed high-security institutions. A WHO Study Group, investigating the subject of the medical and social treatment of drug addicts, considered that "traditional concepts of treating the first and second phases of addiction in closed institutions only should not necessarily be followed in all cases" (5) and that there should be legislative provision for treatment at home, at the physician's office, or in outpatient clinics in selected cases.

The 1962 study reported that the laws surveyed generally allowed for lengthy treatment, that the consensus of opinion among most of the commentators recommending commitment was that, in order to prevent relapses, the treatment must be of long duration (i.e., for two or three years), and that the period allotted for rehabilitation and psychotherapeutic care should also be of prolonged duration, followed by rigorous supervision in order to prevent possible relapses after discharge.

In the majority of countries surveyed in the 1962 report, legal provisions regarding treatment and hospitalization of drug addicts were included in legislation relating either to the treatment of mental patients or to traffic in narcotic drugs. Mental health legislation had been enacted in Brazil, Canada (province of Saskatchewan), the Federal Republic of Germany (in various *Länder*) and in Switzerland (the cantons of Neuchâtel and Vaud), while legislation on the control of drug traffic was found in the Dominican Republic, Egypt, Greece, Guatemala, the Islamic Republic of Iran, Italy, Morocco, Panama, the United Kingdom, Venezuela, and Viet Nam. A more unusual type of legislation was found in Australia (Western Australia), Finland, and Norway, where legal provisions relating to the treatment of alcoholics had been amended or adapted to include measures appropriate to the treatment of drug addicts.

The 1962 survey also called attention to special provisions on offences committed by drug addicts, whether against the narcotic drug laws or public law, which were laid down in the respective penal codes of many countries and, occasionally, even in special laws (e.g., the Belgian Social Aid Law). In Switzerland, provision was made for so-called security measures against offenders who were alcoholics or drug addicts. The same type of law also existed in the Federal Republic of Germany, where the courts could impose suspended sentences for terms of imprisonment not exceeding nine months. In such cases, the courts were also empowered to order addicts to undergo treatment for the duration of the probationary period.

Some countries included in the survey had no specific legal provisons on the subject, since the authorities considered that cases of abuse of narcotic drugs were so few in number that special legislation was unnecessary.

The majority of the legislative texts reviewed in the 1962 study had been enacted after 1945. Among the few earlier enactments were those of Brazil (1934), Switzerland (cantons of Neuchâtel, 1936 and Vaud, 1939) and Venezuela (1934).

The great majority of the legislative provisions considered did not contain any legal definition of a drug addict, but exceptions to this rule were found in the legislation of Canada (Saskatchewan) and the United States of America (District of Columbia). In Saskatchewan, the addict was defined as being "a person suffering from a disorder or disability of mind as evidenced by his being so given over to the use of alcohol or drugs that he is unable to control himself or is incapable of managing his affairs, or endangers himself or others". In the District of Columbia, a "drug user" was defined as "a person who habitually uses any habit-forming narcotic drugs so as to endanger the public morals, health, safety or welfare, or who is so far addicted to the use of such habit-forming narcotic drugs as to have lost the power of self-control with reference to his addiction". The 1962 survey emphasized that it was difficult for public health authorities to track down drug addicts or to keep up to date any register of such persons unless there was a system of notification. In many countries, however, notification was not compulsory and information was therefore not uniformly reliable. The 1962 survey included a review of laws governing standards and procedures for compulsory commitment for treatment. Provisions for such compulsory commitment were found in many countries, while in others, voluntary treatment was preferred.

1.4.3 *WHO Expert Committee on Mental Health: fourteenth report (1967)*

The fourteenth report of the WHO Expert Committee on Mental Health was published in 1967 (6) and brought together WHO policies and programmes for the prevention and treatment of dependence on alcohol and drugs. Similarities and differences in causation and treatment were carefully analysed. The report considered: (*a*) an approach to problems of dependence on alcohol and other drugs; (*b*) treatment services; (*c*) education and training; and (*d*) research. In conclusion, a number of recommendations were made, two of which are of special significance:

— Legislation on persons dependent on alcohol or other drugs should recognize that such persons are sick. Medical and public health experts should be involved in formulating such legislation.

— Adequate treatment and rehabilitation should, if necessary, be ensured by civil commitment of drug-dependent persons to the care of the medical authorities, who should direct and supervise such care, from initial diagnosis to rehabilitation.

The Committee also suggested that research should be carried out on a number of topics, one of which was a comparison of legislative and other measures for the control of drugs and the treatment of drug-dependent persons, including the enforcement of such measures, and a study of their possible effects on the extent and pattern of drug abuse.

1.4.4 *Study on the law and mental health* (*1977*)

A report on harmonizing objectives in law and mental health was published by WHO in 1977(*3*). This is concerned with ways in which law can be used to promote more effective and humane responses to mental disorders, and contains guidelines for use in assessing how existing legislation functions as well as alternative approaches to improving legislation. It was hoped that the report would stimulate legislative review at the national level and generate new approaches and creative drafting in future legislation.

Much of the report is concerned with evaluating national mental health legislation, its origins and development, and subsequent interest in changing the legislation. The various hospitalization procedures are reviewed and the trend towards voluntary care analysed. Attention is given to programme administration and the legal differentiation of mental disorders.

The report contains a summary of the legal provisions of 43 countries governing voluntary access to care, involuntary hospitalization, emergency hospitalization, and observational hospitalization. These procedures were compared against the background of information received in response to a questionnaire. Indicators were identified for use in examining the legislation. It was considered important to encourage the development of mental health legislation that is in harmony with the needs of mental health programme operations, policy, and objectives. Examples of legislation that accomplished this objective were sought.

Certain themes were identified and there appeared to be agreement on the following requirements:

1.   Mental patients should be handled as much like other medical patients as possible, thus removing the stigma associated with special treatment.

2.   Treatment should be provided on a voluntary basis if at all possible and involuntary measures used only as a last resort and in emergencies.

3.   It is important that all special legal "labelling" of the mentally retarded should be abolished; they should receive proper education and habilitation in the same manner as other citizens.

4.   Mental health programmes should be integrated into general health and social services, particularly at the point of delivery in hospitals and in the community.

Legislation on drug and alcohol dependence was not reviewed in the 1977 report except in the overall context of national mental health legislation. The present study is intended to complement and expand on this earlier work on the comparative analysis of mental health laws and should add an important dimension. We found parallel concerns for the problems of stigma associated with drug and alcohol dependence and for the integration of drug and alcohol treatment programmes into general health and social services.

The present study closely follows the procedural approach adopted in the mental health survey and is structured in a similar fashion. This uniformity of format, procedure, and analysis should facilitate comparative review as well as further and more detailed analysis of legislation on both mental health and on substance abuse.

1.4.5 *Study on sociocultural aspects of drug problems (1980)*

This study (7) involved 40 investigators from different countries, and covered many important aspects of the drug problem, including epidemiology, patterns of drug abuse, health care approaches, and treatment and prevention policies and strategies.

Different health care approaches to the management of drug dependence are presented, and it is emphasized that sociocultural considerations are important in selecting the one most likely to achieve the desired results; such considerations have a definite bearing on the difficulty a drug user may experience in giving up the habit.

A number of case studies are presented to illustrate how different countries have approached this problem. While it is possible to extract certain general principles from these experiences, there is no master strategy that will be applicable to all situations; the aim must be a flexible response that combines elements of the various strategies in accordance with local needs.

The practical conclusions of this wide-ranging study are brought together in a discussion of questions of policies and programme planning. The essential principles of such planning are described and an attempt is made to show how sociocultural awareness can be applied in practice when formulating policies and devising programmes, and to offer explicit, rational guidelines.

2. Treatment Programmes

2.1 Drug dependence

Throughout this book, we stress the importance of evaluating treatment programmes in terms of the objectives stated in the legislation. It is important to establish realistic and concrete objectives for treatment in addition to the overriding goal of reducing morbidity and mortality.

Treatment objectives can be set from the standpoint of the public health needs of a country or from the perspective of the individual in need of treatment. While these may be conflicting ideals, attempts should be made to reconcile the two approaches wherever possible. Legislation can play a key role in setting realistic, achievable, and measurable treatment goals, but the treatment process itself should, of course, be individualized and should address the specific needs of the patient.

Legislation must be dynamic and flexible and must be periodically updated. It should also facilitate treatment and not establish barriers by setting impossible goals. For example, countries with a major drug abuse problem but with limited facilities, personnel, and funds cannot eliminate the problem by treatment programmes alone. The most reasonable approach is therefore to set a series of intermediate objectives, which could include a reduction in consumption as a first step. Once this has been accomplished, a new series of goals could be set.

2.1.1 *Phases of treatment*

The therapeutic task varies considerably during the different phases of treatment. What follows here is presented not so much as a sequence through which all drug-dependent persons will pass as they recover, but rather as a touchstone whereby the subsequent findings can be more clearly understood.

Early phase. The detoxification process requires both a commitment by the dependent person to enter into a difficult struggle, and a willingness to seek and accept the support of others. Thus psychological and social factors, as well as the pharmacological aspects, are important for the person in treatment. Motivation for continued abstinence and acceptance of behavioural changes are the essence of this phase of treatment.

Several different approaches to detoxification from opiates are currently being used; these include methadone for opiate withdrawal (Australia, Thailand); tincture of opium and chlorpromazine (Burma); the major neuroleptic drugs, including antidepressants (Egypt); symptomatic treatment, including methadone on a voluntary outpatient basis (Hong Kong); gradual withdrawal using opium (India, Pakistan); prescription of morphine and pethidine (Indonesia); and "cold turkey" (i.e., sudden and complete withdrawal of narcotics) (Philippines, Singapore). The type of withdrawal method used depends both on overall country policies and available pharmaceuticals (see section 2.1.2). In some countries, it may not be possible for treatment to go beyond detoxification.

Entry into drug abuse treatment often involves a crisis of some sort, perhaps a family crisis, with threats of divorce or exclusion from the family. Financial crises occur as the person's productivity decreases and the cost of his drug abuse increases; this, in turn, may lead to acute drug withdrawal. Other medical crises include infection, trauma, malnutrition, depression, and psychosis. Theft or drug peddling can lead to arrest or imprisonment. Declining occupational or academic competence may result in unemployment or suspension from school. Loss of control over drug use can precipitate loss of self-esteem and an identity crisis. Frequently more than one of these crises co-exist.

The first therapeutic step is to meet the addict's acute needs. With adequate acute care, this early phase resolves within a period of between several hours and several weeks—usually within a few days. At this point, the drug-dependent person again feels comfortable and in control of his life. Unless the groundwork has already been laid for the next phase, most drug abusers leave treatment at this point, so that it is of critical importance to engage them in longer-term care before the acute stage is resolved. This is done in different ways by various practitioners and programmes. In some programmes, addicts are not admitted to treatment unless they commit themselves for some weeks or months. In other settings, the law makes follow-up treatment mandatory after discharge from a residential setting.

Failure to plan for, or to negotiate, rehabilitation during this early stage tends to waste precious treatment resources and to perpetuate addiction, the addict repeatedly returning for acute care of drug-related problems without resolving the drug dependence itself. This "revolving-door syndrome" is well known to clinicians who work in programmes where most addicts leave treatment after their crises have resolved.

Finally, an important aspect of this early phase is its role in attracting drug abusers to treatment. Programmes that are humanitarian, show respect for the individual patient, provide a range of services, and are attuned to the addict's culture are more likely to be sought. This function of attracting patients is not of such great importance for compulsory programmes, in which other methods, such as court orders or police arrests, bring addicts to treatment.

Intermediate phase. Immediately following the resolution of the acute crisis, patients often feel quite well for some hours, days, or weeks, but eventually their problems reappear. The objectives of the intermediate phase of treatment therefore have less to do with drug abuse *per se* than with adjustment of life-style.

One source of difficulty during recovery is the drug abuser's altered physiology and psychology. After a period of drug dependence, sleep cycles, weight, blood pressure and pulse may take several months or even as long as a year to return to baseline levels. Periods of depression and irritability frequently occur following abuse of drugs.

Numerous social problems may also arise. For example, during the period that a husband has been abusing drugs, his wife may have become the functional head of the household. While she may welcome certain aspects of his abstinence (such as his increased productivity or decreased spending on drugs) she may resent his attempts to take the leading role in the family or to resume a sexual relationship with her. At the same time, outside the family, he may be struggling to overcome his former social disgrace; this may mean giving up former drug-dependent friends while trying to regain the confidence and esteem of the community.

Fortunately, most drug abusers are able to resolve these personal, family and social problems, provided that they do not resume drug use for a year or two. It is during this critical period that it is necessary to bolster their resolve by means of, e.g., a peer group of recovering drug dependants, counsellors, friends or relatives in whom they can confide, or physicians who can provide support and symptomatic treatment.

Stabilization. After a few years, many former drug abusers no longer require supportive services, but others find that they still need some support, e.g., from a self-help group. Some may want to devote themselves to the care of other drug dependents. A few develop psychiatric problems, depression being the most common, and require psychiatric care.

By this time the recovering drug abuser can usually persist in abstinence from drugs. The goal of treatment in this phase is therefore not merely abstinence, but rather the return to a productive life that provides the rewards and enjoyments that he could formerly attain only with drugs.

2.1.2 Detoxification

This is only one aspect of the early phase of treatment but, because of its importance, is dealt with separately here. From the patients' standpoint, it is important in reducing the fear and anxiety that many of them experience before and during withdrawal. It is less important in reducing morbidity or mortality for most younger persons who are in reasonably good health, although the elderly and the debilitated do have an appreciable mortality if withdrawal is severe or prolonged. By itself, detoxification tends to have relatively little influence on the course of opiate dependence.

Similar principles are applied in the management of dependence on both opiates and non-opiates, with detoxification and pharmacological treatments playing a more prominent role in treatment programmes for patients dependent on opiates and sedative-hypnotics.

Two forms of opium maintenance are employed, namely opium tablets and opium tincture, the latter being used in Burma.

Methadone maintenance is commonly used in North America and some European countries. It is used as a means of attracting drug-dependent persons into treatment and is an especially attractive treatment choice in North American countries because of its low cost.

In some countries, narcotic antagonists are used, naltrexone being currently under investigation in the United States. Its advantages include the fact that adverse effects are uncommon, but it lacks appeal for the drug-dependent person, since it has no psychoactive effect.

A minority of drug-dependent persons experience major disabling depression during the early months following detoxification. Without treatment for such depression, a relapse into drug use often ensues, but if adequate treatment is provided, such patients may make good progress.

Pharmacological intervention for treatment of opiate abuse is only one approach. Such intervention is useful at times for some patients but should be part of a treatment programme that includes other approaches as well, such as psychosocial counselling and behavioural interventions.

It is important to emphasize that treatment is usually provided for other drugs of abuse besides the opiates. In some countries, opiates are not the primary problem and treatment and detoxification practices necessarily reflect this fact.

2.1.3 Social rehabilitation

The next major step in the continuum of treatment for the drug-dependent person involves not only rehabilitation in its classic sense of a return to a previous level of health and social functioning, but also, for some, social reintegration, since for them a return to a previous level of functioning means a return to conditions that may have contributed to their drug dependence. Rehabilitation often involves residence for long periods in a hospital, therapeutic community, halfway house, or day release centre.

Long-term residential care is not needed by all drug-dependent persons, but should be made available for those requiring such care. For many, outpatient rehabilitation is to be preferred. Some examples of the means used to provide appropriate care include social support centres (Burma); inpatient treatment centres and aftercare (Hong Kong); residential programmes (India); hospital and residential rehabilitation centres (Malaysia); on-the-job training (Pakistan); and residential rehabilitation centres (Singapore).

2.1.4 Aftercare

Aftercare involves regular visits by the drug-dependent person to an appropriate facility for a certain period of time, after either detoxification or rehabilitation. This aftercare phase can be particularly difficult for many patients since they are in the process of adjusting to being drug-free.

Some country examples of aftercare programmes include scheduled visits to residential social support centres (compulsory by law in Burma); voluntary aftercare (Hong Kong); individual counselling or psychotherapy, guidance by social workers (Indonesia); mandatory aftercare visits (Malaysia); social activities (Philippines); and aftercare by volunteers in conjunction with compulsory supervision (Singapore).

Aftercare programmes are less costly than residential care but give rise to a number of problems, one of the most important being that of keeping patients in such programmes, especially when different personnel are responsible for detoxification, rehabilitation, and aftercare.

2.1.5 Community outpatient programmes

Treatment programmes for drug dependence in many countries had their beginning in one of the three following inpatient settings: (a) specialized hospitals for drug dependence; (b) special drug-dependence units within psychiatric institutions; or (c) dependence units in general hospital settings.

In recent years, such programmes have been developed in outpatient services. There is an overlap between such services and aftercare, although the latter will have been preceded, e.g., by detoxification or rehabilitation, whereas outpatient programmes generally provide total care from admission to discharge, rely on early case-finding and intervention, and avoid the drawbacks of institutionalization.

The various types of outpatient programme include selfcare, vocational, occupational, and recreational training (Mexico); mobile health teams for detoxification and general health care (Pakistan); rural detoxification (Thailand); and adolescent outpatient care (Switzerland).

Outpatient care can be particularly appropriate for certain population groups, but is not suited to others, such as the severely disabled, who require special assessment and treatment in inpatient settings.

2.1.6 Traditional forms of treatment

Traditional practitioners throughout Asia have long used acupuncture for treating drug dependence, but its integration into the mainstream of science-based medicine began only a few decades ago in China. In electroacupuncture, as used to treat drug dependence, needles are inserted into both ears and a low-voltage (i.e., about 9 volts) current passed between them across the head. The procedure produces temporary relaxation and a feeling of well-being even in addicts undergoing moderately severe opiate withdrawal. It also relieves pain, agitation, anxiety, and insomnia in patients with a wide variety of ailments and is not specific to opiate or other drug withdrawal. Treatments (lasting about 20–40 minutes) are followed by a feeling of well-being that may last only minutes (in an acutely disturbed patient) or up to several hours.

Native healers and traditional medicine have a large following in some countries, examples including the detoxification of opiate-dependent persons by Buddhist monks (Burma); medical units in mosques (Egypt); and religious healing practices by native healers (Malaysia). These practices have distinct advantages, since they fit into the local culture and cost little.

2.1.7 Islam and the treatment of dependence

The influence of Islam on alcohol- or drug-dependent persons is of the highest significance for persons of the Muslim faith, many of whom live in the Eastern Mediterranean Region. The drugs commonly abused in the countries of that Region can be grouped into five categories: (a) opium and its derivatives; (b) cannabis; (c) khat; (d) alcohol; and (e) manufactured psychoactive chemicals. Muslim believers have been commanded to desist from alcohol, which means more than abstinence: the objective is to ensure strict prohibition of sale and distribution of alcoholic beverages. Islamic law clearly specifies that anything that constitutes a dependence-producing drug should not be used by a true Muslim, and Islamic scholars have defined a narcotic, based on the original Islamic concept of khamr (alcohol), as any substance that causes clouding of the mind and interferes with rational thinking.

Very few countries in the Eastern Mediterranean Region have developed integrated treatment programmes, but one interesting approach is the development of a treatment programme inside the Abu El Azayem Mosque in Cairo with the idea of exploring the potentialities of the available socioreligious resources within that setting. In 1977, prior to the establishment of the treatment programme, special efforts were made to prepare the public for it. The programme has evolved by integrating psychiatric and medical care into the religious institutions of the mosque. The experience of developing the treatment programme in the mosque has been fully described by Edwards & Arif(7).

2.2 Alcohol dependence

The increasing worldwide consumption of alcohol has stimulated endeavours to develop new ways of minimizing the harmful consequences of excessive or inappropriate drinking. The early definitions of alcoholism as a disease entity, which emphasized the treatment needs of alcoholics whose excessive drinking had given rise to dependence on alcohol, have proved to be of limited usefulness. There has been a shift towards recognizing and responding to a range of alcohol-related disabilities, including a syndrome of alcohol dependence(8). This new perspective also takes into account impairment of the physical, mental or social functioning of an individual, where alcohol is an identified cause but without the person necessarily being dependent. As a result, alcohol-related incidents of many kinds have become markers for evidence of drinking. This has stimulated an increased emphasis on recognition and intervention at an early stage in an endeavour to minimize harm.

The effects of alcohol include not only impairment of health, and social and economic effectiveness, but also damage to the family. In such circumstances it is clear that no single prescription will meet the needs of all those suffering from these disabilities. It is also evident that the form that alcohol problems take will depend on the prevailing culture and the patterns of alcohol consumption that predominate in it, its ways of defining and responding to problems, and the legal and policy framework. This was particularly apparent in the evidence derived from the WHO project on the community response to alcohol-related problems in three countries of widely differing socioeconomic characteristics (Mexico, Scotland, and Zambia)(9). Thus in any discussion of treatment trends it is first necessary to recognize the diversity of the problems concerned and the absence of any established therapeutic regime.

2.2.1 *Organization of treatment services*

Treatment approaches are in transition; new techniques are being tested, and old certainties, which often emphasized prolonged institutional and specialized care, are slowly being abandoned. Evaluation of treatment suggests that simple methods may prove as effective as more elaborate and costly ones(10). Such findings have given impetus to the search for simpler treatment strategies that can be applied by non-specialist personnel at an early stage. The trend towards management of alcohol problems by the primary health care worker has a number of advantages. Primary health care is more cost-effective and reduces the need for specialist workers, who will in any case never be available in sufficient numbers to deal with so common and widespread a problem. It is usually possible for such treatment to be offered at an early stage, the patient/client is not stigmatized or labelled by having to go to a specialized treatment centre, and treatment can be made more readily available to the population as a whole, particularly in areas where specialist services are not available. This shift in emphasis accords well with the primary health care approach advocated by the Declaration of Alma-Ata in 1978.

The recognition that effective help can be given without the need for institutional care or specialist clinics has been accompanied by the realization that treatment may be initiated in a wide variety of settings, for instance in general medical facilities, primary health care services, courts (e.g., programmes for the drunk driver), prisons, or at work. Treatment programmes for the employee whose work is suffering as a consequence of his or her drinking have proved most effective in a number of countries.

Accompanying the present trend towards the provision of treatment in community settings is an increase in the number of social workers, nurses, psychologists, counsellors and other non-medical or non-specialist persons dealing with alcohol problems. This diversity of professional inputs has further broadened the range of therapeutic techniques available. At an organizational level, it has underlined the need for intersectoral cooperation in the planning of services.

The conventional stereotype of the problem drinker has been, for many years and in many countries, the middle-aged male. While such people remain a very important group, this image alone is no longer adequate. In particular, with increased alcohol consumption among women, services require to recognize the special needs of the woman with alcohol-related problems. The younger problem drinker is also increasingly common and again requires special recognition of his or her needs.

2.2.2 Methods of treatment

Specific treatment approaches are characterized by their diversity and by increasing attempts to tailor the treatment to the requirements of the individual patient/client. The search for new treatment methods is partly based on four emerging research trends, as follows:

(a) current treatment research challenges rather than confirms conventional treatment approaches(10, 11);

(b) depending on criteria of outcome and other factors, the rule rather than the exception is that the patient receiving treatment will relapse;

(c) changes in drinking behaviour may be influenced far more by life events (such as finding a job, getting married) than by any treatment measures (12);

(d) the success of treatment often depends on the personality and socioeconomic characteristics of the person treated. Research consistently indicates that the characteristics of the patient rather than the specific type of treatment programme are the best predictors of outcome.

Given that factors such as social stability and personal characteristics are often more important to outcome than treatment approach, interest has increased in identifying ingredients common to all or most such approaches that are effective. These might include reinforcement of motivation for change, clarification of behavioural choices, enhancement of self-determination, and adaptive problem-solving. The establishment of treatment goals based on such factors is showing some promise as a treatment approach as compared with any specific method.

The realization that no one treatment approach is applicable to all cases and that an analysis of the individual pattern of drinking problems and psychosocioeconomic circumstances might be most revealing, has given rise to the "matching hypothesis", based on the following assumptions(13):

—different patients require different kinds of help;

—assessment of patients is extremely important;

—underlying and accompanying conditions must be identified and treated;

—there is a need for understanding of, and response to, the individual's readiness to change and to seek help from others;

—goals must be set and agreed upon, not imposed;

—the qualities of the therapist are important;

—self-determination, self-responsibility and self-monitoring are vital.

Trends in the development of specific treatment techniques can be tentatively identified in the light of the foregoing, as follows:

(a) *Psychosocial, psychological.* It is being increasingly realized that alcohol problems may be only one facet of a series of problems. Efforts have been made in recent years to put together individual programmes involving interventions that are psychosocial in orientation and attempt to deal with problems other than those directly caused by drinking. The assumption on which this approach is based is that excessive drinking is symptomatic of underlying disturbance so that psychological assistance is required in effecting the change in life-style that successful treatment demands. The approach involves:

—increasing emphasis on enhancing interpersonal skills;

—increasing emphasis on acquiring problem-solving skills and finding alternatives to drinking;

—increasing provision of therapy within group settings;

—increasing use of family therapy techniques;

—increasing use of social work, vocational guidance, and other activities that may have an impact on alcohol-related problems.

Behavioural approaches to the treatment of alcohol-related problems have received increasing attention in recent years, as have the possibilities of identifying treatment goals other than total abstinence, i.e., controlled drinking, or drinking only in certain appropriate circumstances. More research is needed to clarify the criteria for recommending controlled drinking rather than the more traditional and still more widely accepted goal of total abstinence (*14*). There is some evidence that degree of physical dependence on alcohol may prove to be one important criterion in allocating patients to one or other treatment goal.

(b) *Pharmacological/medical.* Tranquillizing drugs have an established place in the management of the symptoms that follow alcohol withdrawal in those who have become physically dependent. However, the danger that alcohol dependence may simply be replaced by dependence on tranquillizers is now well recognized. Long-term use of tranquillizers is therefore inappropriate.

Alcohol-sensitizing agents are used in some countries. Patients who take them regularly know that they will experience unpleasant effects if they drink. Their value depends to a large extent on the patients' motivation and willingness to cooperate. Offenders have sometimes been required to take such drugs, under the supervision of a nurse or probation officer, as part of the treatment imposed by a court order.

Aversive techniques, often employing emetic drugs, still have some adherents but have no clear advantages over other forms of therapy.

(c) *Self-help.* Self-help groups for alcohol problems are well established, Alcoholics Anonymous (AA) being the best known; there are currently AA groups in 92 countries. AA was founded more than 40 years ago and was one of the first self-help movements concerned with a specific disability. In recent years other groups based on somewhat different approaches to that adopted by AA have arisen and proved of lasting benefit, e.g., in Italy and Yugoslavia.

Self-help groups have undoubtedly been very successful with many people. Their success and their optimism about the outcome of help is probably due in large part to the fact that, in practice, they provide not only the therapy common to most treatment approaches, but also an intense supportive social network for the problem drinker—sometimes rarely achievable or affordable through professional services.

Individual self-help techniques have also come into prominence recently. Commonly, patients are encouraged by health workers or health educators to think about their drinking and to recognize potentially harmful patterns and levels. They are then given a variety of self-help manuals that contain information on alcohol and advice on techniques for acquiring less harmful drinking habits. Some of these manuals assume a continuing interaction with a health worker or a friend or family member, while others can be used in isolation (*15*).

2.3 Future trends

The trend towards finding appropriate simple interventions that can be delivered by primary health care workers seems likely to continue. Specialist services may increasingly be responsible for supporting and advising non-specialist agencies and for providing training in the skills and knowledge necessary to render the primary health care worker confident and effective. They will also continue to provide a source of research expertise and a testing ground for the development and refinement of new treatment techniques. Where specialist services exist they are likely to be responsible for helping to coordinate a network of services that meet the diverse needs of those with alcohol-related problems.

Some countries have shown particular interest in the biological aspects of alcohol misuse, but it is not yet clear how these are related to treatment. Current concern about alcohol-induced cognitive impairment and early brain shrinkage has given a new urgency to the need to detect brain damage at an early stage when recovery may be possible. It has also made clinicians more conscious of the need to assess cognitive damage before embarking on treatment approaches that require new material to be learned at a stage when the patient has not yet sufficiently recovered to be able to assimilate such new information. It is hoped that refinements in psychological testing and brain imaging techniques will lead to developments in this area.

Any discussion of treatment must necessarily focus on the individual but many of the approaches that may have the most potent influence in preventing alcohol-related problems require collective action at a community or national level. Such preventive approaches were stressed by the WHO Expert Committee on problems related to alcohol consumption (1) and included recommendations designed to limit the availability of alcohol and to reduce demand, by education and other means.

3. Comparative Survey of Legislation

3.1 General

The comparative survey of the legislation covered by this study showed that, in the various countries, provision is made for drug- and alcohol-dependence treatment programmes both separately and in combination, and that the corresponding legislation falls into a variety of categories (e.g., mental health legislation, public health laws, criminal laws, or specialized treatment laws). Some countries have not made any provision for such treatment programmes in any of the aforementioned categories of legislation; for example, legislation concerned specifically with the treatment of alcohol dependence does not exist in Thailand. Other countries have not enacted specific legislation on the treatment of drug dependence. Many countries have mental health legislation that also covers the treatment of dependent persons. The legal disposition of drug- or alcohol-dependent persons is often covered by the criminal law (e.g., under specified statutory offences) or mental health legislation (e.g., emergency or observational detention for mental illness involving danger to the patient himself or to others, or incapacity).

Many countries were found to have fully developed legislation in both the drug and alcohol fields, while others (e.g., Poland, Thailand) had such legislation in one area only. Some countries (e.g., Pakistan) were in the process of developing legislation.

In most countries, the legislation was part of a larger set of enactments including public health laws, criminal law, and mental health legislation.

No legislation governing the treatment of alcohol dependence was found in the countries of the Eastern Mediterranean and South-East Asia Regions.

Our overall review dealt with all legislative provisions on treatment whether in general health legislation, in mental health legislation, in separate legislation on drug or alcohol dependence expressly relating to treatment, or in criminal legislation.

The various WHO Regions will be considered in turn.

In the African Region, we surveyed the legislation of Kenya, Madagascar, Mauritius, Nigeria, Senegal, and Zambia. There is evidence that drug and alcohol problems are increasing in West Africa. Dependent persons who receive treatment in any form are usually self-referred voluntary patients. Provisions governing the treatment of drug- and alcohol-dependent persons frequently form part of the mental health legislation. In Nigeria, for example, there is no specific treatment programme for drug- and alcohol-dependent persons and compulsory civil commitment treatment programmes form part of the general mental health programme. In Kenya, although separate policies or legislation covering the treatment of drug and alcohol dependence do not exist, services are provided under mental health programmes. In Mauritius, provision is made for treatment under the penal provisions of the Psychotropic Substances Act of 1974. For those persons convicted of an offence under the Act, the court may (at its discretion and in addition to any other penalty imposed) order treatment, education, aftercare, rehabilitation, or social integration. Drug-dependent persons are admitted to a psychiatric hospital under the provisions of the Lunacy Ordinance of 1906 and can also be admitted to general hospital wards. In Senegal and Zambia, treatment provisions are contained, respectively, in: (*a*) compulsory treatment legislation, requiring detoxification in establishments under the jurisdiction of the Ministry of Public Health; and (*b*) dangerous drug regulations, permitting certain medical personnel to prescribe dependence-producing drugs for treatment purposes.

In the Region of the Americas, treatment provisions are contained in specific, general health and welfare, criminal, or mental health legislation, depending on the country concerned. We reviewed the legislation of the following countries: Argentina, Brazil, Canada, Colombia, Mexico, Peru, Trinidad and Tobago, and the United States of America. In Argentina, both criminal and civil legislation contain provisions governing the treatment of drug dependence, and provide for compulsory commitment. In Brazil, provisions on the treatment of drug dependence can be found in criminal legislation on the control of illicit traffic, while treatment provisions in Colombia, Mexico, Peru, and Trinidad and Tobago are found in civil laws, and again include compulsory commitment. In Canada (federal and provincial) and the United States of America (federal and state), provisions governing the treatment of drug and alcohol dependence are contained in both criminal and civil laws. In both countries, provision is made for compulsory civil commitment under both separate drug or alcohol legislation and mental health law. For example, in Massachusetts and Wisconsin, in the USA, treatment provisions are included in civil law providing for compulsory commitment for drug and alcohol dependence, and in criminal law providing for diversion to treatment. Voluntary programmes of admission for both drug and alcohol dependence were also found in the laws of both states. In Brazil, the legislation on the treatment of drug-dependent persons is specific and sets out the criteria for treatment and recuperation, which is on an inpatient basis initially. In Peru, a 1978 law was designed to combine the health services of the country so as to form a national health system. Under this legislation, drug dependence is a public health problem, and provision is made for the establishment of specialized treatment services and for compulsory treatment.

The Eastern Mediterranean Region provides an interesting variety of legislative approaches, reflecting the diversity of cultural, religious and legal systems. We reviewed the following countries in the Region: Cyprus, Egypt, Iraq, Pakistan, Somalia, and Tunisia.

The legislation of Cyprus (the Narcotic Drugs and Psychotropic Substances Law, 1977) empowers the Council of Ministers to make regulations requiring any medical practitioner to notify the authorities if he "attends" a person whom he considers or suspects to be "addicted to controlled drugs." The only specific provisions governing treatment in any legislation in Cyprus are those included in legislation implementing the 1961 Single Convention on Narcotic Drugs and the 1971 Convention on Psychotropic Substances.

Pakistan, a federal state with four provinces and two territories, is an Islamic country, 97% of the population being Muslims. The Islamic Religious Code forbids the use of alcoholic beverages by Muslims. The Prohibition (Enforcement of Haad) Order of February 1979 permits only non-Muslims to purchase (a specified amount of) alcohol. No specific legislative provisions on treatment are contained in the existing mental health legislation, but have been proposed. Criminal legislation proscribing drug addiction and alcoholism has been promulgated.

In Iraq, no general mental health law exists, although a draft law has been under consideration for some years. In 1981, a Regulation was adopted providing for the treatment of drug- and alcohol-dependent persons at particular health care establishments in the country dealing with drug and alcohol dependence.

In the Western Pacific Region, the review of the legislation revealed a diversity of approaches in the jurisdictions covered, namely Australia, Hong Kong, Japan, Malaysia, Philippines, and Singapore. In Hong Kong, the overall strategy for the control of drug abuse is based on the following main elements: (1) law enforcement; (2) treatment and rehabilitation; (3) prevention, education and publicity; and (4) international cooperation. The major emphasis is on law enforcement. Recent amendments to the law provide for: (*a*) prosecution for possessing even minute "unusable" quantities of drugs; and (*b*) protection of medical practitioners engaged by the Hong Kong police to search the body cavities of drug couriers; this protection was formerly limited to medical practitioners performing such searches for the Customs and Excise Service. There are three major treatment programmes in Hong Kong: a compulsory placement programme operated by the Prisons Department, an outpatient methadone programme provided by the Medical and Health Department, and a voluntary inpatient programme operated by the Society for the Aid and Rehabilitation of Drug Abusers (SARDA). The Hong Kong Narcotics Report of 1980 (*16*), prepared by the Government's Action Committee Against Narcotics, states that the Prison Department's programme is designed to cater for drug abusers who are convicted of either minor drug offences or minor non-drug offences and who are considered suitable by the courts for such a programme. The outpatient methadone programme (Medical and Health Department) is designed mainly for those who are motivated to give up heroin or opium use, but are not prepared to stay in a residential treatment centre for a relatively long period for reasons such as employment or family problems. The needs of drug abusers who wish to seek inpatient treatment and aftercare on a voluntary basis are met by the SARDA programme, which offers therapeutic community facilities at its two treatment centres. It was reported recently that efforts were being made by the Hong Kong Correction Service and the voluntary agencies to establish appropriate institutional linkages between voluntary and involuntary programmes.

In Australia, where health programmes are a matter for the individual states, treatment programmes are found in a variety of enactments. In Victoria, treatment programmes for drug and alcohol dependence include provision for both voluntary and involuntary admission. Other provisions governing treatment can be found in road traffic laws and the mental health legislation.

Japanese mental health legislation provides for the compulsory treatment of drug-dependent persons who abuse stimulants if the person concerned is found to be "dangerous to self or others due to his addiction". For narcotic dependence, compulsory treatment is provided under the Narcotic Control Law of 1953, as amended. The emphasis in Japan is on the criminal law, which relies on severe penalties, compulsory treatment and notification, urine testing and reporting. There are, however, also programmes for voluntary treatment. A brief account of the situation in Japan has been published by the Ministry of Health and Welfare(17).

In Malaysia, the Philippines, and Singapore, the main emphasis in the legislation is on strict law enforcement and compulsory treatment under the criminal code. Separate legislation on voluntary admission to hospital is, however, also found in the Philippines, while in Malaysia, provision is made for voluntary admission of drug-dependent persons to rehabilitation centres.

In the European Region, legislation varies considerably from country to country. We surveyed legislation in Finland, France, Federal Republic of Germany, Hungary, Israel, Italy, Norway, Poland, Sweden, Switzerland, the United Kingdom (England and Wales), and the Union of Soviet Socialist Republics (Russian Soviet Federal Socialist Republic). In many countries, legislation on treatment programmes is contained in the general health laws or in mental health provisions. In others (Finland, Hungary), legislative enactments are concerned almost exclusively with alcohol dependence. Thus in Hungary, the legislation provides for both voluntary outpatient treatment and compulsory treatment in institutions for such dependence. It was reported that abuse of organic solvents among young people is rising, but compulsory commitment of those involved is not possible under existing legislation.

In 1980, the European Public Health Committee of the Council of Europe published a report on the treatment of drug dependence(18) in which special attention was given to: (a) aims of treatment; (b) treatment and resocialization; (c) facilities; (d) staffing; and (e) evaluation of programmes in member countries. The Committee of Ministers of the Council of Europe subsequently formally adopted, and recommended to the governments concerned, certain measures concerning the treatment and resocialization of drug-dependent persons (Recommendation No. R(82)6, adopted on 16 March 1982) and the prevention of alcohol-related problems, especially among young people (Recommendation No. R(82)4, also adopted on 16 March 1982).

In the Federal Republic of Germany, treatment of alcohol- and drug-dependent persons is essentially voluntary and initiated by family doctors or by governmental (state or local) agencies or church groups offering assistance, advice, and help. Legislative provisions on drug- and alcohol-dependent persons are found in many different items of legislation. Health legislation is found at both the federal level and at that of the individual *Länder*. Both social insurance legislation and the criminal law contain relevant provisions. The Federal Law of 28 July 1981 (see p. 175) permits waiver or postponement of sentencing provided that the offender agrees to treatment.

In the South-East Asia Region, we reviewed the legislation of Bangladesh, Burma, India, Indonesia and Thailand. Neither Bangladesh nor India has enacted specific legislation governing the treatment of drug- or alcohol-dependent persons. However, it was reported that the proposed new Narcotic Drug Act in Bangladesh incorporates provisions for the treatment and rehabilitation of drug-dependent persons. There are no facilities specifically for drug-dependent persons in India; such people are treated in mental health facilities throughout the country.

No legislation on treatment for alcohol dependence was found in any of the five countries surveyed in this Region.

Legislation requiring compulsory treatment for drug dependence exists in Burma, Indonesia and Thailand. In Burma, the legislative grounds for compulsory treatment apply specifically to two classes of persons: (*a*) those addicted to narcotic and other dangerous drugs; and (*b*) "occasional users" of such drugs. In Indonesia, the legislation also specifies two classes of persons— under-age addicts and adults—while in Thailand, compulsory treatment is provided for any person addicted to a psychotropic substance.

Provision for the treatment of drug-dependent persons involved in the criminal justice system is made in the legislation of Burma, Indonesia and Thailand. In Burma, convicts who are addicts may be admitted to prison hospitals for treatment, while in Indonesia, treatment (medication and nursing) of narcotic addicts and the rehabilitation of former addicts is authorized (at the addict's own expense) in government-operated rehabilitation centres. An interesting provision of the 1979 Narcotics Law in Thailand (see p. 185) lays down that a person who has "consumed" certain narcotics and has applied for treatment in a medical establishment before being charged with a specified crime or arrested by the police and who has thereafter strictly complied with the regulations for treatment and has obtained a certificate of such compliance, is exempted from the penalties for the offences concerned.

Table 1 provides a summary of the types of legislation found; the legislation itself is summarized in Annex 2.

Table 1. Specific legislation on treatment of drug- and alcohol-dependent persons

Country or territory	Existing legislation			No legislation
	Drug-dependent persons	Alcohol-dependent persons	Both drug- and alcohol-dependent persons	
Argentina	x			
Australia (Victoria)			x	
Bangladesh				x
Brazil	x			
Burma	x			
Canada				x
British Columbia	x			
Nova Scotia	x			
Colombia	x			
Cyprus				x
Egypt	x			
Finland			x	
France	x			
Germany, Federal Republic of	x	x		
Bavaria				x
Hamburg				x
Hong Kong	x			
Hungary		x		
India				x
Indonesia	x			
Iraq			x	
Israel	x			
Italy	x			
Japan	x			
Kenya				x
Madagascar				x
Malaysia	x			

Table 1 (continued)

Country or territory	Existing legislation			No legislation
	Drug-dependent persons	Alcohol-dependent persons	Both drug- and alcohol-dependent persons	
Mauritius	x			
Mexico	x			
Nigeria				x
Norway		x		
Pakistan				x
Peru	x			
Philippines	x			
Poland		x		
Senegal	x			
Singapore	x			
Somalia	x			
Sweden	x	x		
Switzerland	x			
Geneva		x		
St Gallen		x		
Thailand	x			
Trinidad and Tobago		x		
Tunisia	x			
USSR (RSFSR)		x	x	
United Kingdom (England and Wales)		x		
United States	x			
Massachusetts	x	x		
Wisconsin		x		
Zambia	x			

In addition to providing information on the type of legislation in force, if any, in the various countries, the survey also pin-pointed certain serious problems relating to the legislation:

(1) In some countries, specific legislation has been enacted, but for various reasons has never been implemented.

(2) Some well drafted legislation authorizes excellent treatment programmes, but the resources needed in terms of qualified personnel and facilities have not been provided.

(3) Some legislation is too piecemeal or fragmented, and thus does not encourage a comprehensive, well-coordinated approach to treatment.

(4) In several countries, the legislation has clearly become outdated or obsolete, but there is no system for continuous monitoring, with a view to bringing it up to date.

(5) In several countries, there are no effective legal provisions for the treatment of drug- and alcohol-dependent persons, since the only legislation in the field is the general mental health code.

(6) Some legislation in the field does not provide for compulsory treatment or, alternatively, does not authorize voluntary treatment.

(7) Some legislation contains inadequate safeguards for the personal rights of the drug- or alcohol-dependent persons.

(8) Some legislation hinders rather than encourages certain aspects of treatment programmes.

Each of these problems is dealt with in this report, some in the context of the analysis of current legislative provisions, others as part of the chapter on guiding principles and alternative approaches.

We must admit, however, that our ability to cover all aspects of these issues was limited by the financial resources available for the study. We would suggest, therefore, that the problems identified should be the subject of future interdisciplinary research in this field.

3.2 Statutory definitions of drug and alcohol dependence

The issue of definitions transcends many aspects of the survey of national legislation. We are primarily concerned with what the law actually states in legislative language with regard to two terms: drug (or alcohol) dependence and treatment. There are several reasons why the legislation of a particular country might not include specific statutory definitions (or characterizations) of a drug- or alcohol-dependent person, the main reason appearing to be that many treatment provisions are found in mental health codes, where the emphasis is on definitions of mental illness and the grounds for civil commitment (e.g., "dangerous to self or others"). However, adequately drafted legislation will contain a section giving the precise definitions of the most important terms as they appear in the text of the legislation reviewed.

Specific statutory definitions of "drug dependence" or "alcohol dependence" (or an equivalent term) were found in the legislation of Burma, Canada, Colombia, Finland, Hong Kong, Indonesia, Israel, Japan, Malaysia, Mexico, Philippines, Singapore, Thailand, the Union of Soviet Socialist Republics, the United Kingdom, and the United States of America.

In some countries, a person's explicit behaviour was used as the test of drug or alcohol dependence. For example, Finnish law governing the treatment of persons making improper use of intoxicants applies to persons who are "given to insobriety or otherwise repeatedly making improper use of alcoholic substances or other intoxicants" and meet one of seven statutory tests ranging from "are manifestly violent, abuse their spouses or children . . ." to "are in need of social assistance".

In Poland, the legislation on the compulsory treatment of alcohol dependence does not define the term but lays down that "alcohol addicts whose behaviour causes disintegration of family life, demoralizes minors, threatens the security of the environment or systematically violates peace or public order" must undergo compulsory treatment.

Treatment provisions are often found in public health codes. This may reflect an emphasis on prevention or related approaches, so that a specific definition of a drug- or alcohol-dependent person is not a matter of high priority since the term is not of any great importance in such codes.

In other instances, only a general reference is made to drug or alcohol dependence in legislation or in implementing regulations, directives or resolutions. Thus Pakistan has no specific treatment legislation (although, as discussed elsewhere, there is a move to introduce such provisions) but is a party to the 1961 Single Convention on Narcotics. The Resolution of 8 March 1973 establishing the Pakistan Narcotics Control Board and requiring Pakistan to fulfil its obligations under the Convention therefore calls for the "rehabilitation of addicts". No definition of either the term "addict" or "rehabilitation" is provided in the Resolution.

Some examples of definitions of drug dependence (or of an equivalent term) found in the legislation are given below.

Country	*Definition*
Canada (Nova Scotia)	(Drug dependency is) "a state of psychological or physical reliance or both on one or more chemical substances that alter mood, perception, consciousness or behavior to the apparent detriment of the person or society or both as a result of the periodic or continuous use or administration of one or more chemical

Country	Definition
	substances and includes the use of nicotine or alcohol or both".
Colombia	(Drug dependence is) "the personal state brought about by periodic or continuous ingestion of drugs in any way".
Indonesia	(A drug-dependent person) "uses narcotics and is in a state of physical or mental dependence".
Iraq	(A drug-dependent person is) "a person who consumes drugs (including alcohol) to such an extent that he has reached a stage of manifest physical and mental disorder that interferes with his mental and physical health, or with the requirements of his economic life, or displays symptoms to a degree that necessitates medical treatment".
Malaysia	(A drug-dependent person) "through the use of any dangerous drug undergoes a psychic and sometimes physical state which is characterized by behavioural and other responses including the compulsion to take the drug on a continuous or periodic basis in order to experience its psychic effect and to avoid the discomfort of its absence".
Mexico	(A drug-dependent person) "other than for therapeutic purposes, voluntarily uses, or experiences the need to use, any narcotic or psychotropic substance".
Philippines	(Drug dependence is) "a state of psychic or physical dependence, or both, on a dangerous drug, arising in a person following administration or use of that drug on a periodic or continuous basis".

Country	Definition
Singapore	(A drug addict) "through the use of any controlled drug: (*a*) has developed a desire or need to continue to take such controlled drug; or (*b*) has developed a psychological or physical dependence upon the effect of such controlled drug".
Thailand	(A dependent person) "consumes, ingests, or applies by any means the psychotropic substance and shows the symptom of addiction to the psychotropic substance".
United Kingdom	(A person is to be regarded as being addicted to a drug) "if, and only if, he has as a result of repeated administration become so dependent upon the drug that he has an overpowering desire for the administration of it to be continued".

3.3 Statutory definitions of methods of treatment

In only a few countries (Burma, Colombia, Indonesia) is the term "treatment" or "rehabilitation" (or an equivalent term) specifically defined in the legislative texts. In some instances, the legislation contains terms such as "resocialization" and "reintegration" in connection with the aftercare of patients following medical treatment, but these are not specifically defined.

Some legislation, however, does specify the method or type of treatment to be administered, particularly in provisions for detoxification in drug or alcohol dependence. This treatment approach is frequently the only one specified.

If the treatment method is specified in the basic statutory enactment it will be more difficult to make changes quickly, so that flexibility is lost. On the other hand, if the legislature wishes to ensure that only a particular approach is to be adopted, it will find this procedure desirable.

The legislative method generally used to accomplish policy goals while retaining flexibility is to empower, e.g., the Ministry of Health, to make regulations (directives, notifications, etc.), under the basic law, specifying the treatment programmes to be employed. The procedural aspects of treatment programmes will then be found in such ministerial regulations, directives and orders, and these texts will contain many administrative (and legal) rules that govern the day-to-day operation of both programmes and facilities.

In most instances, the power to select the method of treatment is delegated to the head of the treating institution or to the local authorities responsible for supervising and directing the treatment programme. This is the case, for example, in Hungary, where the law provides for both voluntary and involuntary treatment. Ordinances have been promulgated to implement the legislation concerning the care and treatment of alcohol dependence and provide that the head of the "consultation service", the clinic near the person's place of residence or employment, has the power to decide the method of treatment to be used in an outpatient facility. The person concerned may also apply for inpatient care and, in such a case, the decision concerning treatment is made, after a medical examination, by the head of the department of alcohol detoxification of the hospital near the person's home.

3.4 Compulsory civil commitment

Compulsory civil commitment means the involuntary admission by judicial or administrative order, usually to an inpatient facility for treatment of drug or alcohol dependence, on the grounds stated in the civil law. Provision for compulsory civil commitment was found in the legislation of just over half the countries surveyed, those without such provisions tending to be the ones that had no legislation on hospitalization at all. Compulsory civil commitment provisions were found in the following five categories of legislation:

(a) general mental health legislation;

(b) mental health legislation specifically mentioning drug or alcohol dependence;

(c) special civil commitment legislation on drug dependence;

(d) special civil commitment legislation on alcohol dependence; and

(e) combined approaches.

The grounds for compulsory civil commitment varied widely, depending on several factors, including the type of legislation containing the provisions. For example, in mental health legislation, it is usually specified that, to be committed, a person must be a danger to himself or to others, or suffer from drug- or alcohol-induced psychosis or serious mental deterioration. In some jurisdictions, simple incapacitation due to alcohol abuse plus a need for medical attention are grounds for committal. In some special drug or alcohol legislation, the criterion for compulsory admission is solely that a person is dependent on drugs or alcohol (Canada (Nova Scotia), Indonesia, Japan, Malaysia, Mexico, Peru, Singapore, Thailand, and Tunisia). Dependence resulting in impairment to health as well as suitability for treatment are also among the criteria.

In many countries "dangerous behaviour" is specified in the mental health legislation as a ground for the commitment of the mentally ill. Frequently, drug or alcohol dependence is specifically mentioned as an associated or contributing factor in such dangerous behaviour or mental illness. This behaviour need not necessarily constitute an unlawful act or involve the person in any way in the criminal justice system.

Legislative provisions for the compulsory treatment of drug-dependent persons were found in many of the countries surveyed. Thus in Thailand, the Psychotropic Substances Law of 1975 (see p. 157) empowers the Secretary-General of the Narcotics Control Division to commit a dependent person for treatment or rehabilitation for a period of 180 days in a clinic or rehabilitation centre. The treatment may also be extended for a period of not more than 180 days. The Ministry of Public Health has the duty to provide suitable facilities for the treatment, education, training, aftercare, and rehabilitation of such persons so that they may be freed from their addiction and reintegrated into society. Under the same law, any person who refuses such treatment or rehabilitation may be fined or imprisoned.

In the Region of the Americas, numerous countries have made provision for compulsory treatment. Thus Peruvian legislation requires drug-dependent persons to undergo treatment either at home, in a private establishment, or in a State rehabilitation centre. The dependent person, his relatives, or the court itself may apply for such a person to undergo treatment, but he must first be examined by a medicolegal physician. Treatment is voluntary, except for recidivist addicts, for whom it is compulsory; they are treated in an official Centre for Drug Dependence by order of the court. In Colombia, Legislative Decree No. 1188 of 25 June 1974 (see p. 133) lays down that persons who, without having committed any offences under this Decree (e.g., traffic in drugs, etc.), are "suffering from the effects of consumption of drugs or substances which produce physical or psychic dependence", shall be compelled to undergo treatment. In Mexico, health professionals who treat cases of drug addiction are required, under the Regulations of 23 July 1976 concerning narcotic drugs and psychotropic substances (see p. 145), to notify the Ministry of Health and Welfare of the patient's condition and give their opinion on whether clinical intervention by the Ministry is needed. In appropriate cases, the Ministry may order the patient to be admitted to an institution for drug dependence, as designated under these Regulations.

Provisions for compulsory detoxification also exist in the African Region. Thus, in Tunisia, the Commission on Drug Dependence is authorized to compel any drug addict to undergo detoxification in a specialized treatment centre under the conditions established by order of the Secretary of State for Public Health. In Somalia, Law No. 46 of 3 March 1970 (see p. 151) provides that any person who, "by reason of serious mental deterioration caused by the habitual improper use of narcotic drugs, in any way endangers himself or others" may be required, at the request of the police or other interested party, to undergo detoxification treatment.

Provision for compulsory treatment after medical examination is also found in several countries of the South-East Asia Region. Under the Misuse of Drugs Act, 1973, of Singapore (see p. 149), if upon examination or observation it is determined that a person is a drug addict and is in need of treatment, the Director of the Central Narcotics Bureau may require that person to undergo treatment in an approved institution. In Malaysia, under the Dangerous Drugs Act, 1952 (see p. 144), if it appears necessary as a result of a medical examination, for a "certified" drug dependant to undergo treatment, he may be ordered by a magistrate to attend a rehabilitation centre for a period of six months.

Follow-up surveillance after compulsory hospitalization may be either compulsory or discretionary. Thus, in the European Region, under Swiss (federal) penal law, the cantons may order the hospitalization of drug-dependent persons for purposes of detoxification and treatment, followed by ambulatory treatment or surveillance after hospitalization. Legislation in the Russian Soviet Federal Socialist Republic, one of the constituent republics of the Union of Soviet Socialist Republics, requires chronic alcohol- and drug-dependent persons to undergo continuous observation and treatment at specialized follow-up centres. Such persons can be committed involuntarily for failure to accept voluntary treatment or for continued misuse of alcohol or use of narcotics after treatment. Under the Decree of 25 August 1972 (see p. 158), drug-dependent persons who are required to undergo treatment in therapeutic establishments, but who refuse to do so, are liable to commitment, on the decision of the *rayon* (municipal) people's court, to curative and labour rehabilitation preventoria for compulsory treatment for a period of between six months and two years. Reference should be made to this Decree for details of the commitment process, court proceedings, duration of detention, and administrative and enforcement provisions.

Table 2 lists countries providing for compulsory treatment of persons under: (*a*) mental health legislation; and (*b*) legislation specifically on drug dependence; and (*c*) legislation specifically on alcohol dependence. There is, of course, a certain degree of overlap, and reference should be made directly to the legislative texts for more detailed information.

Table 2. Compulsory civil commitment

Type of legislation	Countries
Mental health	Bangladesh, Federal Republic of Germany (Bavaria, Hamburg), Japan, Norway, Pakistan, Somalia, Trinidad and Tobago, United Kingdom (England and Wales), United States of America (Massachusetts, Wisconsin)
Drug dependence	Argentina, Burma, Canada (British Columbia, Nova Scotia), Colombia, Indonesia, Italy, Japan, Malaysia, Mexico, Peru, Singapore, Tunisia, Thailand, USSR (RSFSR), United States of America (Federal)
Alcohol dependence	Finland, Hungary, Norway, Sweden, Switzerland (Geneva, St Gallen), USSR (RSFSR), United Kingdom (England and Wales), United States of America (Massachusetts, Wisconsin)
Drug or alcohol dependence	Australia (Victoria), Colombia, Finland, Sweden

Under Swedish legislation on the detention of intoxicated persons, any person found in a public place in a state of intoxication, caused by alcoholic beverages or other intoxicants, may be detained by a policeman if his condition renders him unable to look after himself or he is otherwise dangerous to himself or others. The police are required to assist such persons in seeking medical and social aid and assistance. In Finland, Law No. 96 of 10 February 1961 (see p. 133) provides for the compulsory examination and treatment of persons making "improper use" of intoxicants, and contains lengthy and detailed provisions regarding the compulsory treatment of alcohol abusers. In Hungary, Ordinance-Law No. 10 of 1974 (see p. 138) provides for compulsory treatment of "alcoholics" in institutions. Generally, the decision to commit an alcoholic is taken by the regional court (or municipal or local court) on the grounds of "regular and abusive consumption of alcohol" and the endangering of his family, associates, or workplace. It is interesting to compare the provisions on the compulsory treatment of "alcoholics" in the Swiss cantons of Geneva and St Gallen. Both the law of 3 December 1971 in Geneva (see p. 155) and the Law of 18 June 1968 in St Gallen (see p. 156) contain provisions for voluntary admission as well as grounds for compulsory commitment. In Geneva, commitment is based on the mental health criterion that the alcoholic is a danger to himself or others, or that he acts in a way that is prejudicial to third parties or to the public order. In St Gallen, persons who are "difficult to cure" may be committed for a period of 1–3 years. If a person is considered to be a danger to the community, he is committed to a psychiatric clinic for as long as the danger persists. In Trinidad and Tobago, one of the objectives of the National Council on Alcoholism under its articles of incorporation is to "encourage the establishment of improved facilities for the treatment of alcoholism". Admission for treatment is compulsory under the mental health laws only for persons whose psychosis is the product of alcohol (or drugs). The National Council on Alcoholism is, however, attempting to persuade local magistrates to use their discretionary powers to commit alcoholics by court order. Voluntary admission is usual.

Legislative reliance on mental disability criteria for drug or alcohol dependence is exemplified by the Narcotic Control Law (No. 14 of 1953) of Japan (see p. 142), under which medical examinations and the compulsory treatment of "narcotic addicts" may be ordered. Stimulant abusers are liable to involuntary commitment under the Mental Health Law (No. 123 of 1 May 1950, as amended).

In the United Kingdom (England and Wales), the Mental Health Act of 1959 (which provides for compulsory admission to hospital for the treatment of mental disorder) was amended by Parliament in 1982. The amended Act now contains provisions to the effect that persons may be involuntarily admitted to a mental hospital only if their alcohol or drug dependence coexists or is associated with a mental disorder and then only if all other relevant conditions for admission are fulfilled. The amended section of the Act states that "Nothing in this section shall be construed as implying that a person may be dealt with under this Act as suffering from mental disorder by reason only of . . . dependence on alcohol or drugs".

Table 3 lists the grounds for compulsory civil commitment in 35 jurisdictions in 28 countries.

Table 3. Grounds for compulsory civil commitment

Country	Grounds for commitment
Argentina	Drug addicts who might impair their own health or that of others, or disturb the public peace
Australia Victoria	Alcoholic or drug-dependent person suitable for treatment
Bangladesh	Person who is psychotic as a result of drug use
Burma	(a) Addiction to narcotic and dangerous drugs; or (b) occasional use of narcotic and dangerous drugs
Canada British Columbia	Person in need of treatment for narcotic dependence
Nova Scotia	Person who is an addict
Colombia	Persons suffering from the effects of consuming drugs or substances that produce physical or psychic dependence
Finland	Grounds range from manifest violence to being in need of assistance, plus given to insobriety or otherwise repeatedly making improper use of alcoholic substances or other intoxicants
Germany, Federal Republic of Bavaria	Person who is mentally ill or suffering from psychiatric disturbance due to mental deficiency or addiction and presenting a substantial danger to public safety and order or a grave danger to his own life or health
Hamburg	Persons suffering from a psychosis, a mental disorder similar in effect to a psychosis, drug dependence, or mental retardation and disorder or disease constituting an imminent threat to public safety and order that cannot be averted by any other means, and whose behaviour constitutes a constant and unavoidable threat that they will commit suicide or seriously damage their health
Hungary	Alcoholic as a result of regular and abusive consumption of alcohol who endangers his family, the development of any of his under-age children or the safety of his associates, or who seriously and repeatedly disturbs the public order or professional activities at his workplace

Country	Grounds for commitment
Indonesia	Adult or under-age narcotic addicts
Iraq	Person who consumes "dependence-producing drugs" including alcohol to such an extent that he has reached a stage of manifest physical and mental disorder that interferes with his mental and physical health, or with the requirements of his economic life, or who displays symptoms to a degree that necessitates medical treatment
Italy	Use of narcotic drugs or psychotropic substances for personal, non-therapeutic purposes, plus need for medical treatment and assistance
Japan	
Narcotic Control Law	Narcotic addiction or suspicion of narcotic addiction
Mental Health Law	Diagnosis of stimulant addiction, plus liability to injure himself or others because of addiction
Malaysia	Any person reasonably suspected of being drug-dependent
Mexico	Drug-dependent person
Norway	
Mental Health Law	Person who abuses alcohol or other intoxicating or tranquillizing substance and is suffering from mental illness, if hospitalization will benefit patient, or is necessary for the public order or may prevent serious danger to the life or health of others
Law concerning temperance committees	Person who makes excessive use of liquors or other intoxicating or tranquillizing substances, is an obvious detriment to himself and his surroundings, and commits one or more of five acts listed in the statute
Peru	Drug addiction
Singapore	Suspicion of drug addiction; if after medical examination or urine tests, it appears that treatment, rehabilitation, or both are necessary
Somalia	Serious mental deterioration, caused by the habitual improper use of narcotic drugs, that in any way endangers self or others
Sweden	
Law of 1982 on care of alcoholics and drug abusers	Persistent abuse of alcohol or narcotic drugs by person urgently needing care in order to discontinue abuse, and who is seriously endangering his physical or mental health, or is liable to inflict serious harm on self or other persons; immediate custody permitted if there is presumption of grave deterioration

Table 3 (*continued*)

Country	Grounds for commitment
Sweden (*continued*)	
Law of 1976 concerning the detention of intoxicated persons	State of intoxication in a public place, unable to look after self or otherwise dangerous to self or others.
Switzerland	
Geneva	Abuses alcohol, jeopardizes his health or his own or his family's material or moral well-being; constitutes a danger to himself or to others, or acts in a way prejudicial to third parties or to the public order
St Gallen	Potential alcoholic who does not voluntarily accept advice and care, or if such measures fail to have a lasting effect
Thailand	Addiction to a psychotropic substance
Trinidad and Tobago	Mentally ill and in need of care and treatment in a psychiatric hospital
Tunisia	Drug dependence
USSR	
RSFSR	
Decree of 25 August 1972	Drug-dependent persons who evade treatment, continue to take narcotics after treatment, or infringe labour discipline, the public order, or the rules of socialist society, in spite of disciplinary measures or social or administrative actions
Decree of 1 March 1974	Chronic alcoholics who refuse to undergo voluntary treatment or continue to misuse alcohol after treatment, and who violate labour discipline, public order, or the rules of socialist community life despite administrative or community measures
United Kingdom	
England and Wales	Any person suffering from mental disorder, mental illness or severe subnormality, if adult, psychopathic disorder or subnormality, if under age 21, and when it is necessary in the interest of the patient's health or safety or for the protection of other persons that the person should be detained, but not solely by reason of dependence on alcohol or drugs
United States of America	
Federal	Certain persons addicted to narcotic drugs who are not charged with the commission of any offence
Massachusetts	
Alcoholism Treatment and Rehabilitation Law of 1971, as amended	Any person who is incapacitated (the condition of an intoxicated person who, by reason of the consumption of intoxicating liquors, is (1) unconscious; (2) in need of medical attention; (3) likely to suffer or cause physical harm or damage property; or (4) disorderly)

Country	Grounds for commitment
USA, Massachusetts (*continued*)	
Chapter 123 of the General Laws	Any person that a police officer, physician, spouse, blood relative or guardian reasonably believes to be an alcoholic, and there is a likelihood of serious harm as a result of his alcoholism
Wisconsin	
Alcoholism and Intoxication Treatment Act of 1978	An intoxicated person who has threatened, attempted, or inflicted physical harm on himself or on another or is likely to inflict such physical harm unless committed
Mental Health Act	Any person who is mentally ill, drug dependent, or developmentally disabled and is a proper subject for treatment and is dangerous

3.4.1 *Medical examinations*

Provisions governing medical examinations were found in 24 of the 27 countries with compulsory civil commitment legislation. In general, the legislation requires such examinations to be conducted by one or more medical practitioners, and only rarely is it specified that they must be psychiatrists. In some countries (e.g., Finland, Federal Republic of Germany (Hamburg), Italy, Somalia, Sweden, Switzerland (Geneva, St Gallen), the Soviet Union (RSFSR), the United States (Massachusetts)), medical practitioners are not mentioned and examinations may instead involve the police (administration of a breath test), medical and social welfare centres, or an expert appraisal of person's condition. In some items of legislation, the object of the examination is solely to determine whether the person is a "drug addict" since this may be the only ground for compulsory civil commitment.

In a few instances the examination is required to include other matters, such as the probability of repeated narcotic abuse if the person is not hospitalized (Japan), whether the person would benefit from treatment (United States, Massachusetts), and a statement of the reasons why hospitalization cannot be avoided (Federal Republic of Germany, Bavaria). On the whole, the legislation requires little more than a finding of drug or alcohol dependence, the examiner being given very much of a free hand in this connection.

Table 4 lists the medical requirements for compulsory civil commitment in 29 jurisdictions in 24 countries.

Table 4. Provisions governing medical requirements for compulsory civil commitment

Country	Requirements
Argentina	Certification by a medical officer
Australia Victoria	Two legally qualified medical practitioners must certify that person admitted to assessment centre is an alcoholic or drug-dependent person and medical officer of centre must agree
Burma	Medical officer in charge certifies drug addicts registration card for any addict who registers
Canada British Columbia	Medical and psychological examination of person by an evaluation panel of at least two medical practitioners and one other person from official list to determine need for treatment
Nova Scotia	Minister of Public Health is credibly informed person is addicted
Colombia	Entrance to establishment and termination of treatment require favourable medical statement
Finland	A person under surveillance must undergo medical examination
Germany, Federal Republic of Bavaria	Expert opinion of a medical practitioner of the health authority; explanations must be given why hospitalization cannot be avoided
Hamburg	Expert appraisal of person's condition
Hungary	Expert medical opinion by a medicolegal expert
Indonesia	Not stated
Italy	Competent medical and social welfare centre must give opinion
Japan Narcotic Control Law	Medical examiner of mental health diagnoses addiction and high probability of repeated abuse if not hospitalized
Mental Health Law	Medical examiner of mental health diagnoses mental disorder and agrees person is liable to injure self or others
Malaysia	Medical officer at a detention centre, after examination or observation, concludes that person can be certified to be drug dependent
Mexico	Not stated
Norway Mental Health Law	Doctor, following personal examination, must find it necessary that the patient be hospitalized or maintained in hospital or other place where responsible care can be provided

Country	Requirements
Norway (*continued*)	
Law concerning temperance committees	Where deemed necessary by a doctor; a doctor's certificate is required for compulsory committal to an inebriate sanatorium
Peru	Examination by a medicolegal physician taking into account: (*a*) nature and amount of substances that produced the dependency; and (*b*) history and clinical situation of the person
Singapore	Government medical officer or medical practitioner medically examines or observes person to determine whether treatment appears necessary
Somalia	Receipt of a medical report
Sweden	
Law of 1982 on care of alcoholics and drug abusers	Medical certificate from physician (which may not be contested) indicating abuser's current health status
Law of 1976 concerning the detention of intoxicated persons	Medical examination to determine need for social aid or assistance
Switzerland	
Geneva	Medical examination
St Gallen	Medical examination, possibly in a psychiatric or medical clinic
Thailand	Not stated
Trinidad and Tobago	Mental health examination
Tunisia	Not stated
USSR	
RSFSR	
Decree of 25 August 1972	Medical examination
Decree of 1 March 1974	Medical findings
United States of America	
Federal	Examining physicians conclude person is a narcotic addict and likely to be rehabilitated through treatment
Massachusetts	
Alcoholism Treatment and Rehabilitation Law of 1971, as amended	Police officer may request the person to submit to reasonable tests of coordination, coherency of speech and breath to determine if person is intoxicated
Chapter 123 of the General Laws	Court requests an examination by a qualified physician
Wisconsin	
Alcoholism and Intoxication Treatment Act of 1978	Court determination and finding that grounds for commitment are sustained by grounds in petition (need for emergency treatment)

Table 4 (*continued*)

Country	Requirements
USA, Wisconsin (*continued*) Mental Health Act	Personal examination by two licensed physicians specializing in psychiatry, or one licensed physician and one licensed psychologist, or two licensed physicians one of whom shall have specialized training in psychiatry, if available, or two physicians

3.4.2 *Length of stay and periodic review*

A review of the provisions governing length of stay reveals an extremely wide range of periods of treatment, from not more than eight hours to a term of up to 10 years. This variation appears to be related primarily to the purposes of treatment, which include: (*a*) short-term emergency assistance or treatment for alcohol dependence (e.g., Japan (stimulants), Sweden, United States of America (Massachusetts, Wisconsin)); and (*b*) medium-term periods of treatment, ranging from several days to six months, for drug or alcohol dependence. For drug and alcohol dependence associated with mental illness, the prescribed terms are generally longer, ranging from six months (Federal Republic of Germany (Bavaria)) to an indefinite term as long as the patient remains dangerous (Switzerland (St Gallen)). In some jurisdictions, relatively long terms of compulsory civil commitment are imposed, based solely on drug dependence and need for treatment.

Periodic review is conducted by a variety of bodies, including commissions or boards established by law specifically to review the status of committed persons (e.g., Canada (British Columbia), Malaysia, Switzerland (Geneva)). In other jurisdictions, periodic review is the responsibility of a government officer or the administrator of the hospital where the person is being treated (e.g., Japan). Table 5 lists the length of stay, frequency of periodic review and body or person responsible for conducting review (where stated) in 15 countries.

3.5 Diversion to treatment from the criminal justice system

At some stage in the criminal justice system, ranging from prearrest to postimprisonment parole, drug or alcohol dependence may become a factor in how this system deals with the dependent person. Thus, it is important to identify the ways in which various countries manage the drug- or alcohol-dependent offender.

The use of illicit dependence-producing drugs frequently makes the user liable to severe criminal penalties, including imprisonment or fine, depending on the substance involved.

Alcohol is also a dependence-producing drug, but in most countries of the world, its consumption does not constitute an illegal activity. The alcohol abuser nevertheless frequently becomes involved in the criminal justice system, since alcohol abuse can lead to behaviour that is dangerous to others, such as driving while under the influence of alcohol.

Some drug- and alcohol-dependent persons become involved in illegal activities for reasons that may be related to their dependence.

The legislation of many countries provides for the treatment of drug- or alcohol-dependent offenders. In many instances, this involves taking them out of the criminal justice system and placing them in a treatment setting, sometimes suspending punishment, or providing treatment while they are in confinement.

Of the 51 jurisdictions covered by the survey, 22 were found to divert persons for treatment at one or more of the following stages in the criminal justice process: (a) instead of arrest; (b) after arrest, pending trial; (c) after trial in lieu of imprisonment (e.g., sentence suspended or held in abeyance); and (d) correction with imprisonment (e.g., during confinement, or as a condition of parole).

One of the major policy questions facing legislators is whether diversion to treatment should be mandatory or merely made available for persons charged with certain serious offences, such as crimes of violence.

When diversion to treatment is mandatory prior to or instead of trial, this decision can be viewed as a decriminalization of the person's conduct.

Treatment pending or in lieu of trial (pre-trial diversion). This category includes diversion to treatment for drug- or alcohol-dependent persons involved in the criminal justice system up to but not including trial for a criminal offence.

Of the 22 jurisdictions containing diversion legislation, summarized in Annex 2, ten had provisions in this category, namely Egypt, France, Federal Republic of Germany, the Philippines, Sweden, Thailand, the United Kingdom (England and Wales) and the United States of America (federal, Massachusetts, and Wisconsin). There are several types of pre-trial diversion in the legislation, as described below.

Table 5. Length of stay and frequency of review in compulsory civil commitment

Country	Length of stay	Frequency of review and by whom conducted
Australia Victoria	Seven days (plus seven additional days, if ordered)	NS[a]
Canada British Columbia	Minimum three years in treatment programme; not more than six months in treatment centre and one year in treatment clinic	Board of review (not less than five members, at least one of whom must be a medical practitioner); may extend treatment for six-month or one-year period after hearing, upon application of the Province
Finland	One year commitment; two years if prior commitment in past three years; surveillance for 1–2 years	NS[a]
Germany, Federal Republic of Bavaria	Not longer than six months	Every six months
Hamburg	Not longer than one year	Extension beyond one year subject to review prior to end of one-year period
Hungary	Release when treatment no longer necessary; no longer than two years	NS[a]
Italy	Term of treatment necessary for social reintegration	Treatment centre must report to court at least every three months on treatment action
Japan Narcotic Control Law	Not more than 30 days	Administrator of hospital may submit request for further term to Narcotic Addiction Examination Committee
Mental Health Law	Not more than 48 hours	Administrator of mental hospital reports to Governor of Prefecture if he believes person not liable to injure self or others due to mental disorder even if not hospitalized

Malaysia	Six months	Board of visitors of rehabilitation centre may shorten the period of detention after four months; person in charge of centre may detain for further six months with consent of Board
Norway		
Mental Health Law	No more than three weeks	Subject to appeal to control commission
Law concerning temperance committees	No more than 90 days in one year for hospital treatment; no more than two years if committed in sanatorium	Subject to appeal to Supreme Court
Singapore	Six months, subject to early discharge or further six-month periods, but not more than a total of three years	Review committee, as often as practicable, considers whether person should be discharged, and may order early discharge or further detention; action subject to review by magistrate.
Sweden		
Law of 1982 on care of alcoholics and drug abusers	Not mandatory, two months, subject to extension order of two more months	NS[a]
Law of 1976 concerning the detention of intoxicated persons	Normally not more than eight hours	NS[a]
Switzerland		
Geneva	Six months or longer, but not exceeding one year; court may order maximum extension of one year	Commission for Surveillance of Alcoholics responsible for surveillance of persons committed to institutions for alcoholism
St Gallen	One year; difficult cases, 1–3 years; if person is dangerous, as long as danger persists	Commitment order may be suspended for a trial period of 1–2 years, during which person cared for in a welfare centre
Thailand	180 days, extension of not more than 180 days	Secretary-General of Office of Food and Drug Board may grant extension where necessary for treatment and rehabilitation

Table 5 (continued)

USSR **RSFSR** Decree of 25 August 1972 (drug dependence)	From one to ten years; for aversion treatment, period may be extended but not for more than one year; period may be reduced by up to one-half in event of successful treatment, but not for persons repeatedly committed	NS[a]
Decree of 1 March 1974 (alcohol dependence)	Same as above for drug dependence	NS[a]
United States of America Federal	Six months as inpatient; up to three years in community rehabilitation	After three months in confinement, upon petition of person, court inquires into health and general conditions of patient and need for continued confinement
Massachusetts Narcotic Addict Rehabilitation Act of 1966, as amended	Until no longer incapacitated, or 12 hours, whichever is shorter	NS[a]
Chapter 123 of the General Laws	Not to exceed 15 days	NS[a]
Wisconsin Alcoholism and Intoxication Treatment Act of 1978	Not longer than 48 hours (emergency)	NS[a]
Mental Health Act	First order of commitment not to exceed six months; all subsequent orders not to exceed one year	On patient's verified petition (except for minors under age 14), any involuntary patient may request a re-examination or request the court to modify or cancel the order of commitment

[a] Not stated.

The first relates to persons who are liable to arrest for commission of an offence, are taken into custody by law-enforcement personnel, but are in need of emergency treatment because of acute drug- or alcohol-induced incapacity. Typically, such situations involve the need for short-term (e.g., 24–48 hour) alcohol detoxification. The alcohol- or drug-dependent person is not arrested but taken, either at his own request or involuntarily, to a suitable treatment facility for a limited period and then either released or charged with an offence.

A second type of pre-trial diversion concerns persons making illicit use of narcotic or other drugs (not alcohol) or persons who are found in an intoxicated condition in violation of penal provisions, and who are put under surveillance and treatment. French legislation, for example, permits medical surveillance of narcotic-dependent persons, including outpatient treatment, in lieu of trial.

Finally, there are persons who have been arrested and thereafter are determined to be drug-dependent by medical examination, conducted either at the person's own request or by judicial authority. Where treatment is ordered after medical examination and successfully completed, prosecution may be waived. Such provisions are contained, for example, in the legislation of France, Federal Republic of Germany, the Philippines, Sweden, and the United States (Massachusetts).

Examples of provision for treatment *in lieu of* trial are found in the legislation of Egypt, France, Federal Republic of Germany, and the United States (federal, Massachusetts). In France, persons who have complied with prescribed medical treatment for narcotic dependence and have completed it are not liable to prosecution. In the Federal Republic of Germany, if an accused person is suspected of having committed a crime as a consequence of narcotic drug dependence and the penalty is imprisonment for a period not exceeding two years, the public prosecutor may refrain from prosecution if the accused proves that he has been undergoing treatment for at least three months and that rehabilitation is to be expected.

Examples of provision for treatment *pending* trial are found in the legislation of the Philippines and Sweden. In the Philippines, if a person is charged with an offence and found to be drug-dependent, the court may order treatment and, upon successful rehabilitation, he may be returned to the court for trial. If he is convicted, the court may then elect to reduce the period of confinement by taking the treatment period into account. In Sweden, in a criminal case in which the penalty can be imprisonment for misuse of narcotic drugs, the court may suspend the case until the person concerned has been treated. Such a decision by the court can be made only if: (*a*) at the hearing of the case, the accused has confessed to a certain act or convincing evidence has been produced that he has committed it; (*b*) the accused has declared that he is willing to undergo treatment; and (*c*) the result of the treatment can be deemed to have a bearing on the choice of penalty for the offence. A case that has been suspended must be reopened as soon as possible after one year following the court's decision. The case may be reopened less than one year following the court's decision for any of four reasons, one of which is that the accused has failed to follow the plan of treatment and his failure is of more than minor importance.

Voluntary application for treatment in designated facilities acts as a bar to criminal proceedings for certain drug-related offences in Egypt, the Philippines, and Thailand.

Treatment in lieu of imprisonment. Legislation in this category includes provision for suspension (or waiving) of execution of sentence *after conviction*, subject to successful completion of treatment. Of the 51 jurisdictions covered, such provisions were found in eight, namely the Federal Republic of Germany, Hong Kong, Indonesia, Malaysia, Senegal, Sweden, Switzerland (federal) and the United States of America (federal). In Switzerland (federal), the provisions apply when the offender is an alcohol-dependent person and the offence committed is related to this condition. In Indonesia and Senegal, treatment may be ordered for narcotic addicts instead of imprisonment. In Hong Kong, persons found guilty of an offence punishable by imprisonment who are addicted to any drug may be ordered to be detained in a treatment centre, in lieu of any other sentence. Under a recent (1981) legislative provision in the Federal Republic of Germany, time spent undergoing treatment can be credited against a prison sentence; when this credit amounts to two-thirds of the sentence, the court must suspend the remainder provided that the person concerned is placed on probation.

Treatment concurrent with sentence. Such treatment may be of several types, including: (i) treatment of convicted persons while serving prison terms; (ii) treatment prior to imprisonment, the period of which may be deducted from the prison term; or (iii) treatment as a condition of discharge from prison. Provisions imposing concurrent treatment were identified in ten jurisdictions.

The court may order treatment for drug dependence in addition to any penalty imposed for drug offences in: Argentina (for an indeterminate period that must be completed first and is then counted as time served under the sentence, which it may not exceed); Brazil (treatment in a clinic attached to the prison while serving the sentence); Burma ("addicts" may be admitted for medical treatment to prison hospitals); Hong Kong (a person may be transferred from prison to detention in an "addiction-treatment centre"); Israel (a detention order may be made for treatment for not more than three years, the treatment period being deducted at the discretion of the court from the prison term, which it may not exceed); Mauritius (treatment, education, aftercare, rehabilitation, or social reintegration may be imposed, in addition to any other penalty); Philippines (after rehabilitation, the person is returned to court for initiation or continuation of the prosecution of his case and, in case of conviction, all or part of the period spent undergoing treatment may be deducted from the sentence); Poland (a court may commit a person to treatment, before sentence is carried out, for a period of not less than six months or more than two years in the case of habitual use of alcohol or other intoxicant, and the court then reviews the sentence after discharge from the treatment institution in the light of the results of the treatment); Union of Soviet Socialist Republics (a person sentenced to imprisonment in a curative and labour rehabilitation preventorium or after commitment by a people's court for compulsory treatment for alcohol abuse is

Table 6. Diversion from the criminal justice system[a]

Type	Jurisdictions
Treatment pending or in lieu of trial	Egypt, France, Federal Republic of Germany,[b] Philippines, Sweden, Thailand, United Kingdom,[b] United States of America (Federal, Massachusetts,[c] Wisconsin[c])
Treatment in lieu of imprisonment	Federal Republic of Germany, Hong Kong, Indonesia, Malaysia, Senegal, Sweden, Switzerland (Federal),[b] United States of America (Federal)
Treatment concurrent with sentence	Argentina, Brazil, Burma, Hong Kong, Israel, Mauritus, Philippines, Poland,[b] Union of Soviet Socialist Republics (RSFSR),[b] United States of America (Massachusetts)[c]

[a] For drug dependence only unless otherwise indicated.
[b] Only for persons dependent on alcohol or other intoxicants.
[c] Separate legislation for drug dependants and alcohol dependants.

liable (after having served his sentence) to commitment to a preventorium for the period of treatment that has not been completed); United States of America (Massachusetts) (a drug-dependent person may be ordered to undergo treatment at a penal facility for all or part of his term of imprisonment; if the court does not order the defendant to be confined in such a facility, it may order that he be afforded treatment as a condition of probation).

Table 6 lists the jurisdictions in which diversion provisions are contained in the legislation. There are differences of detail in the various diversion provisions within each category so that reference should be made to the individual legal texts if precise information is required.

3.5.1 Medical examination

Of the 22 jurisdictions that have diversion systems, as reviewed in Annex 2, 15 provide for medical examinations. Such examinations usually involve at least one of three components: (a) examination by medical or other personnel for the purpose of determining whether the person is dependent on drugs (or, in some jurisdictions, chronically abuses alcohol); (b) an opinion or a report from either a physician or a corrections official concerning the health status of the person; and (c) an opinion as to the appropriate treatment programme for the person.

Medical personnel conducting the examination are required to have specialized training or be an expert (e.g., in psychiatry), in the following jurisdictions: Brazil, Israel, Switzerland, and the United States (Massachusetts). In France, Indonesia, Philippines, Senegal, and Sweden, either a physician or competent medical authority is designated. In Hong Kong, Thailand, and the Soviet Union, the Commissioner of Prisons or other appropriate official is responsible for making the requisite findings or reports.

Table 7 shows the type of medical examination required, by whom it is conducted, and the scope of the examination in the various jurisdictions.

3.5.2 Length of treatment and periodic review

The length of treatment is specified in the legislation of 11 of the 22 jurisdictions with legislation on diversion from the criminal justice process, and varies from a few months to an indefinite period. Provision for periodic review is also contained in the legislation of 9 of the 22 jurisdictions. The frequency of review varies as does the body conducting the review. In Hong Kong, Israel, the Philippines and the United States of America (Massachusetts), the review is conducted at specified intervals (e.g., quarterly progress reports are required in the United States). In France, a report is made at "regular" intervals, and in Brazil, after rehabilitation, the judge takes expert testimony and the opinion of the public prosecutor on whether to close criminal proceedings. In recent (1981) legislation in the Federal Republic of Germany, the burden is on the accused to prove that he has been undergoing treatment for his dependence and that his rehabilitation is to be expected in order for the suspension of prosecution to be prolonged. The various provisions are summarized in Table 8.

3.6 Compulsory reporting, central registries, laboratory testing, and community surveillance

Legislative provisions requiring the reporting, central registration, laboratory testing, and community surveillance of drug- or alcohol-dependent persons were found in half the jurisdictions surveyed, with a high concentration in the Eastern Mediterranean, Western Pacific and South-East Asia Regions.

Table 9 lists the jurisdictions with such legislation, but includes only those provisions relating to civil commitment or diversion to treatment from the criminal justice system. For some countries, such requirements are contained in more than one category of legislation. Under the heading of "testing", provisions are included covering both law enforcement (e.g., urine tests for use in screening) and medical examinations for use by courts in disposing of cases; this also applies to surveillance. The relevant legislative provisions are summarized in Annex 2.

3.6.1 *Compulsory reporting*

Provisions governing reporting were found in 21 of the 51 jurisdictions and generally require certain individuals to notify government officials of persons known or suspected to be drug-dependent. A few countries also have reporting requirements for alcohol dependence. The persons or organizations required to make such reports vary widely and include law-enforcement officials, public prosecutors, hospitals, clinics, parents, prison authorities, public authorities, and medical practitioners. Physicians and other medical personnel having first contact with

Table 7. Medical examinations for diversion to treatment from the criminal justice system

Jurisdiction	Type of medical examination and by whom conducted	Scope of examination
Brazil	Official expert evidence, or by medical practitioners appointed by judge	Person
France	Competent health authorities arrange for medical examination	Person; and investigation into family, professional, and social life
Germany, Federal Republic of	NS[a]	NS[a]
Hong Kong	Report of Commissioner of Prisons on the suitability of the person for cure and rehabilitation and on availability of places at "addiction treatment centre"; when persons are to be transferred to treatment from confinement, consideration is given to health, character, and previous conduct	Person
Israel	Opinion of psychiatrist that accused is addicted to dangerous drugs	Accused
Malaysia	Medical examination or observation by a medical officer at a detention centre; as a result of such medical examination or observation, the person can be certified to be drug-dependent	Person
Philippines	Examination by two physicians accredited by Dangerous Drug Board	Person
Senegal	By at least three physicians	Person; an investigation into person's family, professional, and social life must also be conducted

Sweden	Medical superintendent of treatment facility gives opinion on outcome of treatment	Person
Switzerland Federal	Judge orders expert appraisal of offender's physical and mental state and advisability of treatment	Person
Thailand	Competent official of treatment facility issues certificate of compliance with treatment programme	Person
Union of Soviet Socialist Republics	Medical findings indicate necessity of compulsory treatment for chronic alcohol abuse	Person
United Kingdom England and Wales	Constable's observation that person is drunk and incapable	Person
United States of America Federal	Two qualified physicians examine person to decide whether he is a "narcotic addict" and likely to be rehabilitated through treatment	Person
Massachusetts	Upon request by defendant, or by a psychiatrist (or if impracticable, a physician), who reports findings as to drug dependence of defendant	Person

[a] Not stated.

Table 8. Length of treatment and periodic review after diversion to treatment

Jurisdiction	Length of treatment	Frequency of review and by whom conducted	Initiator of review
Argentina	Indefinite, not to exceed length of sentence	NS[a]	NS[a]
Brazil	NS[a]	Not stated, but after rehabilitation, judge takes expert testimony on rehabilitation and opinion of prosecutor on decision whether to close the proceedings	NS[a]
France	NS[a]	Health authority follows progress of treatment and at regular intervals informs prosecutor of medical and social situation of person; alternatively physician responsible for treatment may propose that conditions of treatment be modified or person be transferred to other more appropriate facility	Health authority or physician responsible for treatment
Germany, Federal Republic of	At least three months	Accused must prove he has been undergoing treatment	Accused
Hong Kong	Not less than four months but not more than 12 months	Board of Review established for each addiction-treatment centre reviews progress of each person since admission and makes recommendations relating to release; interviews must be conducted: (a) during third month following admission;	Board of Review

Israel	Not more than three years or not more than prison term, whichever is the longer	(b) at least once every two months during four months following first interview and (c) thereafter at least once a month	Attorney-General or his representative
Malaysia	Six months subject to reduction or extension of period of detention at discretion of Board of Visitors of a rehabilitation centre	Every six months Attorney-General brings case before court, which may rescind order for detention	NS[a]
Philippines	NS[a]	Head of treatment centre, every four months; or, as court requires, a written progress report of treatment for those under compulsory confinement; at any time for voluntary patients	Head of treatment centre for persons under confinement; for voluntary patients, person or parents or guardian
Poland	Not fixed in advance but not less than six months or longer than two years	NS[a]	NS[a]
Sweden	Not more than one year	Criminal proceeding may be reopened (treatment discontinued for any of four reasons, including failure to follow treatment plan)	Court
Switzerland Federal	Up to two years	Suspended sentences may be executed: (a) if person is incurable; or (b) if requirements for conditional discharge are not met after two years	Court

Table 8 (*continued*)

Jurisdiction	Length of treatment	Frequency of review and by whom conducted	Initiator of review
United States of America			
Federal	Six months, plus up to three years of community rehabilitation	After three months' confinement, person may petition court, which must inquire into health and general conditions of patient and need for continuing confinement	Person
Massachusetts	Not more than 18 months or period of time equal to maximum sentence person could have received, whichever is shorter	Quarterly written reports on progress of treatment	Administrator of treatment facility
Wisconsin	Not more than 48 hours	NS[a]	NS[a]

[a] Not stated.

drug-dependent persons are most often specifically identified in the legislation and required to report to health or other authorities any drug- or alcohol-dependent persons that they encounter.

Of special interest are the criteria specified in the legislation for physicians to initiate the reporting process. This is important, because a reporting requirement puts the physician in the position of having to choose between protecting confidentiality and fulfilling the legislative requirements. Failure to report may make the physician liable to fines and/or imprisonment under the laws of many countries. Since a drug-dependent person will be aware that the physician is obliged to report him to the authorities, he may choose not to seek any medical care at all or turn to unqualified practitioners.

The agencies to be notified vary, but can be grouped into two broad categories: (a) administrative and law-enforcement agencies; and (b) ministries of health or social welfare. The agency prescribed will reflect the purpose of the legislation, which is designed predominantly for drug-control rather than treatment purposes. The content of the notification is clearly intended for use in individual record-keeping and for other administrative purposes.

Table 9. Compulsory notification, central registries, laboratory testing and community surveillance

Requirement	Jurisdictions
Compulsory notification	Burma, Colombia, Cyprus, Finland, France, Hong Kong, Indonesia, Italy, Japan, Malaysia, Mexico, Norway, Philippines, Senegal, Singapore, Somalia, Sweden, Switzerland (St Gallen), Tunisia, United Kingdom (England and Wales), Zambia
Central registries	Burma, Colombia, Hong Kong, Pakistan,[a] Union of Soviet Socialist Republics (RSFSR)
Laboratory testing	Hong Kong, Japan, Norway, Singapore, United States of America (Massachusetts)
Community surveillance	Finland, France, Hong Kong, Malaysia, Norway, Senegal, Sweden, Switzerland (federal), Union of Soviet Socialist Republics (RSFSR), United States of America (Massachusetts)

[a] Applies only to "opium addicts".

Table 10 lists the reporting requirements for the 21 jurisdictions in which the legislation contains provisions concerning reporting, the agency to be notified, and the content of the report.

3.6.2 Central registries

Registration of drug-dependent persons is required to serve different goals, as specified in the legislation. For example, under Burmese law, "drug addicts" are "requested" to register at medical treatment centres, where registration cards are issued to them by the medical officer in charge. For "occasional users" (defined as persons no longer needing to consume narcotics and dangerous drugs), separate detailed records (name, address, occupation, etc.) are kept. A register of "drug addicts" is kept by the Narcotics Drug Control Board, and contains complete personal particulars and circumstances of use and treatment.

Under the law of Hong Kong, a Central Registry of Drug Abuse is established for two purposes: (a) the collection, collation, and analysis of confidential information supplied by reporting agencies and of information on drug abuse and its treatment; and (b) the publication of statistical information on drug abuse and on various forms of treatment of such abuse. Colombian legislation is more specific and requires the Ministry of Public Health to keep a register of "drug addicts" containing all the data necessary for evaluating the trend of "this phenomenon" in the national territory. In the Soviet Union, the Commission to Combat Drunkenness may establish sections for the registration of persons misusing alcohol and suffering from "alcoholism".

3.6.3 Laboratory testing

This involves the clinical examination of a person's body fluids or breath to determine whether drugs or alcohol are present. Such testing may be conducted by law-enforcement, customs, or immigration officials in some countries, and failure to provide any necessary specimen may constitute a criminal offence. For example, under the Misuse of Drugs Act of 1972 in Singapore, any police officer not below the rank of sergeant may, if he reasonably suspects any person to have smoked or otherwise consumed a controlled drug, require that person to provide a specimen for a urine test; failure to do so constitutes an offence.

Similarly, in Hong Kong any officer of the Bureau of Narcotics, immigration officer, or police officer (not below the rank of sergeant) may, if he reasonably suspects any person to have committed an offence (generally possession of narcotics), require that person to provide a specimen of his urine for testing. If as a result of the test it appears to the Director of the General Narcotics Bureau that it is necessary for that person to undergo treatment or rehabilitation (or both), he may make a written order for that person to be admitted to an approved institution. In Japan, use of narcotics or stimulants by anyone is a criminal offence, and arrested persons are required to undergo urine tests. A Norwegian law of 1979 on prisons authorizes the director of a prison to order urine tests, breath tests, and such other examinations as can be performed without danger or significant discomfort, to be carried out in order to detect whether an inmate has consumed an intoxicating or psychotropic substance. In the United States (Massachusetts) any court may, in placing a defendant who is a drug-dependent person who would benefit by treatment, make it a condition of probation that the defendant receive treatment in a facility as an inpatient or outpatient. Periodic urinalysis to confirm the drug-free status of the probationer may be made a condition of probation.

3.6.4 Community surveillance

Provision for different forms of surveillance (supervision), including community surveillance, of persons at various stages of contact with treatment programmes is contained in the legislation of a number of jurisdictions. Community surveillance may be required either before or after the provision of treatment, and is frequently made a condition of probation or parole.

Community surveillance provisions were found in the legislation of ten of the 51 jurisdictions reviewed. In Finland, France, and Senegal, the legislation permits the authorities to order persons in need of treatment for drug dependence (France, Senegal) or alcohol dependence (Finland) to be placed under medical surveillance in lieu of mandatory detoxification. Such persons must usually be treated by a physician and report periodically to the health authorities. In the United States (Massachusetts) a court, and in Hong Kong the Commissioner of Narcotics, may impose on a person on probation certain reporting and testing requirements designed to ensure continuation of treatment or drug-free status. In the Soviet Union, the Commission to Combat Drunkenness is responsible for the surveillance of chronic alcohol-dependent persons in the community.

Table 10. Reporting requirements

Jurisdiction	Basis for notification and by whom made	Agency notified	Content of notification
Burma	Persons addicted to narcotics and dangerous drugs must apply for registration	Drug addicts registration and medical treatment supervision boards in various townships	Name of addict (for inclusion in register), or name, address and occupation (for inclusion in separate register for occasional users)
Colombia	Doctors treating patients who need drugs in quantities greater than therapeutic doses	Competent health authorities	Name, age, marital status, nationality, domicile, daily dose, how long drug used
Cyprus	Medical practitioner attending a person whom he considers or suspects to be addicted to controlled drugs	Prescribed authority	Such particulars about said person as may be prescribed
Finland[a]	Police, public prosecutor, prison authorities, military authorities when they find persons in intoxicated condition; medical practitioners are authorized to provide information	Social Welfare Board in person's commune	Fact of intoxicated condition, and all information concerning patient who meets legislative tests of dangerous or drunk driver
France	Public Prosecutor who has ordered a person to undergo detoxification or to submit to medical surveillance	Competent health authority	Fact that Prosecutor's order has been made
Hong Kong	Reporting agencies (hospitals, clinics, prison police, voluntary agencies providing services to drug abusers)	Central Registry of Drug Abuse, or a reporting agency	"Confidential information" defined in statute

Indonesia	Parents or guardian of under-age narcotic addict	An official of the Ministry of Health	Fact of addiction
Italy	Any physician attending or assisting a person using narcotic drugs or psychotropic substances	Centre established for care and rehabilitation of persons using narcotic drugs	Fact of use
	Police	Nearest centre and local magistrate	All cases of such use coming to their attention
Japan	Medical practitioners; narcotic control officers; public prosecutor; chief of correctional institution	Governor of Metropolis, Hokkaido or Prefecture	Name, domicile, age, sex, other matters (as applicable)
Malaysia	Registered medical practitioners of persons treated or rehabilitated by them who are drug dependants	Minister of Welfare Services	Identity of drug-dependent person
Mexico	Qualified medical personnel within eight days of observation of drug addiction in cases treated	Nearest office of Ministry of Health and Welfare	Identity of person, diagnosis, and opinion on need for treatment
Norway[a]	Police required to report to temperance committee all punishable cases of drunkenness	Temperance committee	Report of case
Philippines	Court at any stage of criminal proceedings finds person to be drug-dependent	Dangerous Drug Board	Copies of case record
Senegal	Any physician while carrying out diagnosis or treatment who becomes convinced person is illicitly using drugs	Chief Medical Officer of Region	Identity of person

Table 10 (*continued*)

Jurisdiction	Basis for notification and by whom made	Agency notified	Content of notification
Singapore	Medical practitioner who attends a person whom he considers or has reasonable grounds to suspect is a drug addict, within seven days of attendance	Director of Medical Services, and Director, Central Narcotics Bureau	Name, age, identity number, sex, address, drug used
Somalia	Medical practitioner who attends or examines a person suffering from chronic addiction produced by narcotic drugs, within 48 hours	Police and Central Narcotics Bureau	Report of case
	Police, regional directors and district medical officers must report all cases of drug addiction coming to their attention	Central Narcotics Bureau	Report of case
Sweden	Public authorities coming into regular contact with alcoholics and drug abusers, presumably in need of care; physicians are not required to report if person can be given satisfactory treatment by physician or other medical services	County administration	All particulars that may be relevant
Switzerland St Gallen	Every individual is entitled to report cases of alcoholism; official agencies must make reports	Welfare centre or guardianship authorities	Report of case

Tunisia	Physicians must report all cases of drug abuse detected in practice	National Bureau of Narcotics	Report of case
United Kingdom England and Wales	Doctor attending person suspected or considered to be addicted to controlled drugs	Prescribed authority	Such particulars as may be prescribed by regulations
Zambia	Any medical practitioner who prescribes dependence-producing drug for more than four months	Permanent Secretary administering the Dangerous Drug Act	Report of case

[a] Provisions apply to alcohol-dependent persons.

3.7 Recent legislation and legislation in course of development[1]

An important indicator of the status and effectiveness of legislation on the treatment of drug- and alcohol-dependent persons in any country is the interest in fundamental change in the field. During the two decades since the 1962 WHO survey (2), the legislation of many countries has been amended in response to both national initiatives and technological developments. More recently, there have been important changes, including a general reorganization of programmes, in several of the jurisdictions surveyed, some having already enacted new legislation while in others legislation is currently under development. This is true of Australia, Bangladesh, Canada, Federal Republic of Germany, Hong Kong, Israel, Pakistan, Poland, Sweden, Thailand, the United Kingdom, and the United States of America.

Significant new legislation providing for compulsory commitment of drug or alcohol dependants has been enacted in Sweden, and similar legislation has been introduced in two *Länder* (Bavaria and Hamburg) of the Federal Republic of Germany. In June 1980, the Swedish Parliament passed a new Social Services Law that replaced previous social welfare legislation (Temperance Law of 1954; Social Welfare Law of 1956; Child and Youth Welfare Law of 1960; Child Care Law of 1977). The Swedish Law came into force on 1 January 1982 and has been supplemented by special legislation on compulsory care of alcohol and drug abusers.

In the Federal Republic of Germany, the Federal Narcotics Law of July 1981 stipulates that offenders who have been sentenced to imprisonment for not more than two years may receive treatment prior to execution of sentence; alternatively, the public prosecutor may defer prosecution pending treatment. Compulsory hospital admission and treatment of addicted persons in the Federal Republic of Germany comes under the jurisdiction of the various *Länder*. The hospitalization laws of the ten *Länder* have very similar objectives but have been reformed over the past 30 years, particularly as regards strengthening of the rights of the detained person. Currently, Hesse has the oldest legislation, dating from 19 May 1952, and Bavaria the newest, dating from 20 April 1982 (see p. 136). Under the Bavarian law, compulsory hospitalization may be ordered for those who are mentally disordered as a result of "addiction" and are a danger to public safety or to their own lives.

---

[1] Some of the legislation discussed here is not included in Annex 2.

There have been significant developments in compulsory care for alcohol and drug dependants in Canada. The new Mental Health Act of Prince Edward Island (1981) permits police officers to enter private premises to remove a person considered by them to be suffering from mental disorder caused by the use of alcohol or other chemical substance; they may use such reasonable force as is necessary to take the person to a treatment centre. The British Columbia Heroin Treatment Act of 1979, which provided for compulsory civil commitment for narcotic dependence, was declared unconstitutional and beyond the power of the province by the Provincial Supreme Court, but on appeal to the Canadian Supreme Court this decision was reversed and the Act was held to be a valid exercise of provincial powers.

In the United States of America, significant national legislation, namely the Omnibus Budget Reconciliation Act, was enacted in 1981. The Act made fundamental changes in the role of the federal government in the provision of drug-abuse prevention and treatment services, and in the federal–state partnership for service provision. Eventually, as part of the governmental New Federalism initiative, federal block grant funding will cease, a period of transition funding will replace the previous grant programme and states will be expected to assume total fiscal and programme responsibility at some time between 1984 and 1988. If this overall programme is implemented, federal financial participation in community-based drug-abuse prevention and treatment services will end, further financial support then becoming the sole responsibility of the states.

Significant drug or alcohol treatment legislation was reported to be in various stages of review or development in four of the WHO Regions.

European Region. In Poland, a new act on "alcohol counteraction", which will significantly change the principles underlying the treatment of alcohol-dependent persons, was proposed in April 1982; this will include the development of voluntary treatment.

In the United Kingdom (England and Wales), the Mental Health Act of 1959, which is concerned with compulsory admission to hospital for treatment of mental disorder, was amended by Parliament in 1982 in such a way that alcohol- or drug-dependent persons may be compulsorily committed to hospital only if their alcohol or drug dependence coexists or is associated with a mental disorder. The new section of the Act states that "Nothing in this section shall be construed as implying that a person may be dealt with under the Act as suffering from mental disorder by reason only of . . . dependence on alcohol or drugs".

In Norway changes in the current treatment legislation are being considered in an effort to make it more relevant to current problems and new developments in the treatment of, and experience with different groups of drug- and alcohol-dependent persons. A major issue in the review is that of voluntary treatment as against compulsory commitment to institutions.

Eastern Mediterranean Region. There is a move to change the existing mental health legislation in Pakistan, to provide for the treatment of drug-dependent persons.

South-East Asia Region. In Bangladesh there is no legislation specifically dealing with the treatment of drug- or alcohol-dependent persons. A proposed Narcotic Drug Control Law is under consideration by the Government and does include provision for the treatment and rehabilitation of "drug addicts". In Thailand, the Office of the Narcotics Control Board and the Office of the Prime Minister, in cooperation with the Ministry of Public Health, are considering proposed changes in the Law on Narcotic Drugs of 1979, designed to give more power to the authorities concerned with the prevention, treatment, and control of drug-abuse problems.

Western Pacific Region. There are moves to change the legislation in Australia and Hong Kong. In South Australia, consideration is being given to redrafting the Alcohol and Drug Addicts Treatment Act in accordance with the recommendations of the South Australian Royal Commission into the Nonmedical Use of Drugs. Public drunkenness may be decriminalized and the State Department of Correctional Services is considering the development of bonds requiring community service as a way of dealing with alcohol- and drug-related offences. In Hong Kong, consideration is being given to revising the provisions on voluntary treatment, to eliminate the requirement that "drug addicts" remain as inpatients for at least six months. This change would bring the legislation into line with the existing informal practice of early release at the patient's request.

3.8 Federal legislative systems

Some of the countries surveyed have a federal system of government, so that both general and specialized health programmes are administered at the subnational (i.e., state, provincial, cantonal) level. One of the areas of interest in our study concerns the role of subnational governments in the delivery of treatment programmes for drug and alcohol dependence. This is particularly important in relation to the impact of international conventions on the enactment of national drug legislation and the implementation of obligations under the provisions, for example, of the 1961 Single Convention on Narcotic Drugs and the 1971 Convention on Psychotropic Substances. National governments enter into international agreements, yet treatment programmes are often implemented and services delivered at the subnational level.

Criminal law is usually the responsibility of the federal government (or shared with the subnational governments) and focuses on the control of illicit drug activities. In contrast, alcohol legislation usually originates at the subnational level and subnational treatment programmes predominate. In Canada, criminal law and drug-control legislation are primarily at the federal level. There are federal programmes for the control of illicit drug traffic and the regulation of the licit drug industry through enforcement of labelling restrictions and licensing of the dispensing of pharmaceuticals. Health services, however, and drug-dependence treatment programmes in particular, are the responsibility of the provinces.

In British Columbia, for example, the Heroin Treatment Act of July 1979 lays down that any persons found by an evaluation panel to be "in need of treatment for narcotic dependency" must be placed in a treatment programme lasting a minimum of three years. As already mentioned (see p. 79), this Act was declared unconstitutional, but that decision was later reversed.

The Canadian Parliament recently (December 1981) adopted a federal Constitution; this contains a Charter of Rights and Freedoms, applicable to all citizens of Canada, including "the right not to be subjected to any cruel and unusual treatment or punishment". It is thought that the new constitutional provisions may affect provincial legislation on compulsory commitment of, and treatment for alcohol- and drug-dependent persons.

In the United States of America, treatment programmes for "narcotic addicts" were introduced at the federal level in the 1930s, with the establishment of federal prison hospitals at Lexington, Kentucky, and Fort Worth, Texas. Although currently hardly ever used, the federal Narcotic Addicts Rehabilitation Act of 1966 (Public Law No. 89–793) provides for: (a) compulsory civil commitment in lieu of prosecution; (b) sentencing to commitment for treatment; and (c) civil commitment of persons not charged with criminal offences. This Act also established community-based aftercare programmes, and the federal government for the first time provided outpatient counselling and supportive rehabilitation services. In 1968 and 1970, amendments to the Community Mental Health Centres Act permitted funding for drug-treatment programme facilities. In 1972, the federal Drug Abuse Prevention and Treatment Act (Public Law No. 92–255) encouraged development of a single agency in each state to be responsible for drug-abuse prevention activities. During the ten-year period from 1972 to 1981, the federal government developed and provided financial and technical support to over 1400 community-based drug-abuse prevention and treatment agencies. Through this network of agencies, different types of services were developed, e.g., detoxification, methadone maintenance, counselling, and guidance, with a variety of settings, e.g., outpatient, day care, and residential. Recently, this community-based network of services became the responsibility of the states. Current federal legislation on the treatment of alcohol- and drug-dependent persons (Public Law No. 97–35) substantially reduces the federal role in service provision, but emphasizes federal responsibilities in areas where the states are unable to function as effectively or efficiently (e.g., research, new drug development, nationally focused epidemiology, prevention, and technology transfer). Under this new legislation, states are responsible for determining community needs and providing services. Under the block grant programme (see p. 79), the individual states are permitted to combine alcohol, drug-abuse, and mental-health services at the community level.

In the alcohol field, the most important earlier federal legislation was the Comprehensive Alcohol Abuse and Alcoholism Prevention, Treatment and Rehabilitation Act of 1970 (Public Law No. 91–616), as amended. This Act established the National Institute on Alcohol Abuse and Alcoholism and authorized financial aid programmes to the states to develop comprehensive alcohol programmes.

In Australia, each state is responsible for health services as well as for primary and secondary education, licensing laws, and law enforcement. Several states have enacted legislation empowering courts to order alcohol- or drug-dependent persons to enter treatment programmes. At the federal level, the Australian Royal Commission of Inquiry Into Drugs (1980)(*19*) reported that the nature and size of the problem of drug abuse in Australia was sufficient justification for a national policy to reduce drug abuse based upon concerted action between state and Commonwealth governments. The Commission's report recommended a continuing review of the efficacy of law enforcement, treatment and education in reducing drug abuse.

Brazil has adopted a centralized approach, based primarily on programmes administered at the federal level. Pursuant to a 1980 Decree, the National System for Prevention, Control, and Repression of Narcotic Substances was established, consisting of four organizations: a Federal Council on Narcotic Drugs (CONFEN), which is the main coordinating body; an organization for "sanitary surveillance" under the Ministry of Health; an enforcement group under the Federal Police Department; and the National Institute for Medical Assistance in the Department of Social Security. The 1980 Decree makes CONFEN responsible for determining national policy on narcotic drugs, and it is also charged with the duty of planning, coordinating, and supervising activities relating to traffic in, and use of narcotics. In fulfilling these responsibilities, the Council is reported to have issued directives concerning the treatment of drug dependants that give considerable freedom of action to physicians and health personnel in treatment programmes, particularly with regard to deciding whether drug-dependent persons should be hospitalized or cared for as outpatients.

3.9 International conventions and national legislation

The international conventions on drug control have had a somewhat mixed effect on the development and implementation of national legislation authorizing the treatment of drug-dependent persons. In countries where there was previously little legislation on treatment, they have stimulated the development of such legislation. In countries with well established laws and treatment programmes, however, they have had little overall impact.

The 1961 Single Convention on Narcotic Substances, as amended in 1972, and the 1971 Convention on Psychotropic Substances are the major international drug control treaties currently in force. As of January 1986, there were 114 parties to the 1961 Convention, and 81 parties to the 1971 Convention.

The 1961 Single Convention consolidated and simplified international agreements established since the International Opium Convention of 1912. It came into force in December 1964 and brought all narcotic substances under control. Thus it outlawed production, manufacture, trade and use of narcotic substances for nonmedical purposes, limited possession of all such substances to medical and scientific purposes and to persons authorized to possess them, extended the estimate system (of the 1931 Convention) to all narcotic substances, and stipulated that the system of import certificates and export authorizations had also to be applied to poppy straw, which is used as the raw material in the manufacture of morphine. The 1961 Convention also provided for the international control of all opium transactions by government agencies, by authorizing opium production only by licensed farmers in areas and on plots designated by these agencies.

Article 38 (as amended by the 1972 Protocol) of the 1961 Convention contains the following provisions relating to the treatment of drug-dependent persons:

—The Parties shall give special attention to and take all practicable measures for the prevention of abuse of drugs and for the early identification, treatment, education, aftercare, rehabilitation and social reintegration of the persons involved and shall co-ordinate their efforts to these ends.

—The Parties shall as far as possible promote the training of personnel in the treatment, after-care, rehabilitation and social reintegration of abusers of drugs.

—The Parties shall take all practicable measures to assist persons whose work so requires to gain an understanding of the problems of abuse of drugs and of its prevention, and shall also promote such understanding among the general public if there is a risk that abuse of drugs will become widespread.

An official commentary on the 1961 Convention (as amended by the 1972 Protocol) has been published(20) and contains a discussion of the approach to treatment envisioned by the terms of the Convention. In particular, it is recognized that the four stages of "treatment" referred to in the amended Article 38 quoted above cannot easily be separated in time or content. Of special importance is the comment that the terms "treatment", "aftercare", "rehabilitation" and "social reintegration", normally applied to different stages of treatment (in the broad sense) of abusers of narcotic drugs, were used in order to indicate that the Parties should take all "practicable measures", no matter to which discipline they may belong, that may be required for the successful treatment of abusers.

In August 1976 the 1971 Convention on Psychotropic Substances entered into force after having been opened for ratification in February 1971. Article 20 of the 1971 Convention deals with treatment, and states that:

—The Parties shall take all practicable measures for the prevention of abuse of psychotropic substances and for the early identification, treatment, education, after-care, rehabilitation, and social reintegration of the persons involved, and shall co-ordinate their efforts to these ends.

—The Parties shall as far as possible promote the training of personnel in the treatment, after-care, rehabilitation, and social reintegration of abusers of psychotropic substances.

—The Parties shall assist persons whose work so requires to gain an understanding of the problems of abuse of psychotropic substances and of its prevention, and shall also promote such understanding among the general public if there is a risk that abuse of such substances will become widespread.

The language of Article 20 of the 1971 Convention is very similar to that of Article 38 of the 1961 Single Convention (as amended), especially in the first two paragraphs. The meaning given to the term "practicable measures", as discussed earlier, is also applicable to Article 20. A useful commentary on the background and interpretation of the 1971 Convention has been published (21).

Article 36 of the 1961 Convention contains criminal law provisions, including diversion to treatment for persons who have committed punishable offences under the terms of the Convention. The relevant paragraphs of the Article are as follows:

(a) Subject to its constitutional limitations, each Party shall adopt such measures as will ensure that cultivation, production, manufacture, extraction, preparation, possession, offering, offering for sale, distribution, purchase, sale, delivery on any terms whatsoever, brokerage, dispatch, dispatch in transit, transport, importation and exportation of drugs contrary to the provisions of this Convention, and any other action which in the opinion of such Party may be contrary to the provisions of this Convention, shall be punishable offences when committed intentionally, and that serious offences shall be liable to adequate punishment particularly by imprisonment or other penalties of deprivation of liberty.

(b) Notwithstanding the preceding subparagraph, when abusers of drugs have committed such offences, the Parties may provide, either as an alternative to conviction or punishment or in addition to conviction or punishment, that such abusers shall undergo measures of treatment, education, after-care, rehabilitation, and social reintegration in conformity with paragraph 1 of article 38.

Article 22 of the 1971 Convention on Psychotropic Substances also contains criminal law provisions, including a subsection on diversion to treatment, as follows:

(a) Subject to its constitutional limitations, each Party shall treat as a punishable offence, when committed intentionally, any action contrary to a law or regulation adopted in pursuance of its obligations under this Convention, and shall ensure that serious offences shall be liable to adequate punishment, particularly by imprisonment or other penalty of deprivation of liberty.

(b) Notwithstanding the preceding subparagraph, when abusers of psychotropic substances have committed such offences, the Parties may provide, either as an alternative to conviction or punishment or in addition to punishment, that such abusers undergo measures of treatment, education, after-care, rehabilitation, and social reintegration in conformity with paragraph 1 of article 20.

The Addiction Research Foundation of Toronto has recently issued a report on the 1971 Convention (22). One of the 13 recommendations made in the report recognizes that national regulatory control measures are not the complete answer to the problem of psychotropic substance abuse and that development and application of social measures, including treatment, rehabilitation, and education at the national level, are needed to change the behaviour of drug-dependent persons. WHO has published guidelines on the implementation of the 1971 Convention, designed to facilitate and encourage the efforts of national governments to enact new legislation to give effect to their obligations under the Convention (23).

There is no analogous international convention on alcohol. Some attention has been given to the need to control its international marketing and to seek some reduction in demand. The WHO Regional Office for Europe, the Addiction Research Foundation of Toronto, and the Finnish Foundation for Alcohol Studies collaborated in the publication in 1975 of the report entitled *Alcohol control policies in public health perspective* (24). This report discusses international control of alcohol and concludes that the development of control policy would be aided by a knowledge of the quantities and types of alcohol consumed in the world and the ways in which they are supplied. It is also suggested that some form of international intervention is desirable in the spheres of both policy and information gathering.

3.10 Regional collaboration

Collaborative agreements among countries have been reached in various geographical regions to deal with the problems of drug and alcohol abuse and their control. This regional approach has developed essentially since the Second World War, and particularly in the last 20 years.

The various regional groupings are of widely different types, some being geographical and economic in character, such as the Pompidou Group of the Council of Europe and the South American Agreement, while others are not (e.g., the Colombo Plan). Some agreements are concerned primarily with drugs, while others focus on both alcohol and drug abuse. Some examples of regional organizations and their activities are described below.

Since 1973, the Drug Advisory Programme of the Colombo Plan Bureau has organized many activities designed to sensitize member governments to the need to formulate comprehensive programmes for the control of drugs.

The Association of South East Asian Nations (ASEAN) includes Indonesia, Malaysia, Philippines, Singapore, and Thailand. In June 1976, the foreign ministers of the ASEAN countries formally declared that, in the context of cooperation to combat the abuse of narcotic drugs, each member country would improve national legislation with the aim of intensifying the fight against the abuse of drugs and its consequences. Each country also undertook to exchange information and experience in nine areas, including treatment and rehabilitation.

The Sixth Meeting of the Conference of Ministers Responsible for Health of the Caribbean Community (July 1980) passed two resolutions designed to curb drug and alcohol abuse through coordinated country activities.

The South American Agreement on Narcotic Drugs and Psychotropic Substances came into force on 26 March 1977. As of 1 July 1980, it had been ratified by Argentina, Bolivia, Brazil, Ecuador, Paraguay, Peru, Uruguay, and Venezuela. The countries agreed to undertake specific measures to ensure information exchange and coordination of activities. The Agreement also calls for measures to be introduced to achieve close cooperation in the "treatment, rehabilitation, and social reintegration of drug addicts". Section 6 requires the legal regulations of the signatory countries to be harmonized in conformity with the First Additional Protocol. An important provision regarding criminal legislation is that, if a convicted person is "addicted", the court "shall always" order a course of treatment and re-education and may, in addition, depending on the circumstances of the case, consider the sentence as having been lifted. Alternatively, the court may order treatment to be undergone during or after a period of confinement. The South American Agreement specifies that the treatment programme to be carried out "shall consist primarily of appropriate detoxification measures, without prejudice to other types of therapy and whatever else is required for rehabilitation". Treatment is to be given in assistance centres, for an indefinite period, but may be terminated by judicial decision following a finding by experts that the person undergoing treatment has been rehabilitated, or that he is capable of attaining "an acceptable degree of rehabilitation". Regulations require that Parties ensure that every "addict" is confined in a "suitable establishment in case of danger to himself or to third parties". The Agreement also requires that "drug addiction" and habitual intoxication be treated as diseases and reported in confidence to local authorities. Drug-dependent persons may, after examination, be compulsorily confined in an institution for treatment for either a specific or indefinite period, but all such persons who have not been the subject of criminal proceedings must be treated as patients, in keeping with the national legislation of each country.

It is clear from the foregoing that regional collaboration can have a significant influence on national legislation.

3.11 Role of national advisory and coordinating bodies

Our survey indicated a general trend towards the establishment of national advisory and coordinating bodies on drug and alcohol dependence to provide guidance to governments at the national and subnational level. These bodies frequently take the form of drug or alcohol commissions, narcotic boards, or interministerial committees for drug or alcohol programmes.

Special commissions may sometimes be established and great attention is generally paid to their recommendations. More permanent boards may be established at the central government level and charged not only with policy formulation but also with coordination.

Such bodies have been established only since the Second World War. Early interministerial and national commissions in the field of alcohol abuse included the Swiss Federal Commission on Alcoholism (1945); the first State Commission on Alcoholism in the United States (Connecticut, 1947); and the Polish Interministerial Commission to Coordinate Efforts and Planning in the Field of Alcoholism (1957), established under the Minister of Labour and Social Services. The trend continued after the mid 1960s and expanded into the drug area, many national advisory and coordinating bodies being established in the 1970s. This trend suggests that governments find such coordinating bodies valuable in dealing with various alcohol and drug programmes. National bodies are generally of three types: (*a*) advisory; (*b*) coordinating; and (*c*) implementing. The first two are of special interest because of the link between policy development, programme planning, and legislative enactments. Some countries, however, have not established coordinating bodies, preferring informal consultation between different ministries.

Experience suggests that a comprehensive approach and the assignment of certain agencies specifically to coordinate policies and programmes for treatment can be most useful and effective. Effectiveness also depends on: (1) high-level governmental recognition (e.g., establishment of a presidential commission); (2) strong political support; (3) adequate funding to carry out the mission; (4) high-level and respected membership; (5) public awareness and support; and (6) prominent public visibility and priority within government.

The objectives of such bodies vary, but may include: regulation of the use and abuse of drugs, development of guidelines for the treatment of alcohol- and drug-dependent persons, and the implementation of international treaties on these subjects. This last objective is achieved by enacting legislation at national level, as required or recommended in the treaties.

In Pakistan, a Narcotics Control Board was established in 1973 under the Ministry of the Interior with a mandate to undertake drug-abuse control functions in the country. The Board includes members from both federal and provincial Ministries of the Interior, Health, Social Welfare, and Finance, the Central Board of Revenue, Excise and Taxation, the customs authorities and the police. Pursuant to the 1973 law setting up the Board, the National Health Coordinating Committee was established, composed largely of provincial and federal health coordinators, to advise the Board "in technical and institutional matters relating to the treatment and rehabilitation of drug dependent persons". Health matters are a provincial responsibility. Federal government policies on the treatment of drug dependants have been reported as being "in the process of formulation", but the only provision governing treatment is found in the 1973 law.

Other countries have established a number of statutory committees. For example, in Burma, one legislative enactment established 11 different committees for "mass combat by the whole nation in view of the danger of narcotic drugs as a national concern". In the United States of America, the function of the United States Interagency Committee on Federal Activities for Alcohol Abuse and Alcoholism (established in 1967 and abolished in 1983) was to coordinate efforts at the federal level in the fields of alcohol abuse and alcoholism. In Asia, many institutional mechanisms have been set up and have formulated comprehensive policies and launched effective programmes; they include the Dangerous Drug Board of the Philippines, the Office of the Narcotics Control Board in Thailand, the Office of the Narcotic Commission in Hong Kong and the National Committee in Malaysia. The various bodies have allocated available resources and manpower in such a way as to prevent overlap in function.

National commissions have often been established in response to a country's signature of one of the international conventions. In such situations, interministerial bodies have been set up, often subject to the authority of the Ministry of Public Health and with primary emphasis on the control of illicit traffic in drugs. To avoid interministerial conflict, however, and in view of the multifaceted nature of alcohol and drug problems, some bodies of this type are responsible directly to the chief executive of the central government.

It is clear that the Ministry or Department of Health is generally the focus for the establishment and implementation of treatment programmes for drug and alcohol dependence, but the Ministry of Social Welfare or a combined Health and Welfare Ministry may sometimes have this responsibility. For example, in Venezuela, the Ministry of Health and Social Welfare makes regulations on sanatoria for the social reintegration of psychiatric patients, including chronic alcohol abusers and other drug-dependent adults; in Finland, responsibility for the treatment of persons making improper use of intoxicants rests with the Ministry of Social Welfare.

Some countries have established special commissions, with various goals and functions. For example, in France a High Commission has been established, responsible for drawing up and organizing Government policy on the control of alcohol abuse and coordinating the activities of the various ministries in this area. This responsibility for coordinating interministerial activities highlights the difference from the terms of reference of some other coordinating bodies whose objective is only to share experience, to ensure cooperation so as to avoid overlap, and to plan cooperative activities.

Table 11 lists the advisory and coordinating bodies established within the past 20 years and known to be in existence at the time of publication of this study. Where possible, a brief description of the responsibilities of each body is included. For federal countries, some subnational bodies are also listed.

Table 11. Advisory and coordinating bodies

Country or jurisdiction	Title of body and responsibilities
Algeria	National Narcotics Commission
Argentina	CONATON: National Commission on Drug Dependence and Narcotics CO-TE-SAI: Consultative Technical Committee on Alcoholism
Australia Western Australia	Western Australian Alcohol and Drug Authority (1975): provides assessment, treatment, management, care and rehabilitation; makes recommendations on legislation to competent minister and attorney general
New South Wales	Drug and Alcohol Authority (1981): formulates programmes and other comprehensive studies to provide advice to minister
Bolivia	National Drug Council National Directorate for the Control of Dangerous Substances
Burma	Central Committee for the Prevention of Hazards due to Narcotics Committee for Narcotics Control (1976): overall policy and coordinating body for prevention, law enforcement, treatment, rehabilitation, and crop replacement
Canada Alberta	Alcoholism and Drug Abuse Commission (1972): operates hospitals for diagnosis, treatment, counselling, and rehabilitation
British Columbia	Alcohol and Drug Abuse Commission (1975): operates programmes for research, diagnosis and treatment; provides financial assistance to other organizations; submits annual report on progress and expenditures
New Brunswick	Interim Commission on Alcoholism (1974)
Quebec	Office for the Prevention and Treatment of Alcoholism and other Toxicomanias (OPTAT) (1971): carries out research, educates, informs, and treats along with advisory council, which submits recommendations
Chile	National Commission for the Control of Alcoholism and Alcohol Problems
Colombia	National Council on Narcotics (1978): formulates plans, policy, and programmes to be submitted to government for approval; coordinates programme upon approval; maintains contact with foreign governments and international agencies

Table 11 (*continued*)

Country or jurisdiction	Title of body and responsibilities
Denmark	Danish Government Commission on Alcohol and Narcotic Drugs
France	High Committee of Study and Information on Alcoholism Interministerial Committee for the Control of Alcoholism
Haiti	Sociomedical Commission under Ministry of Health
Hong Kong	Action Committee Against Narcotics, and Office of Commissioner of Narcotics: policy on, and coordination of, prevention and general information; international liaison
Hungary	Hungarian National Committee on Alcoholism (AEOB)
Iceland	State Council on Alcoholism
Indonesia	Presidential Committee for Implementation of Presidential Decree No. 6 (1971): international liaison
Madagascar	Central Bureau of Narcotics (1974): drafting items of legislation dealing with narcotics
Malaysia	Cabinet Committee on Narcotics: policy-making and coordinating body with drug-abuse research centre
Mexico	National Anti-Alcohol Council: interministerial, advisory, evaluative and coordinating body
Nepal	Narcotics Control Administration (1976): coordination, with assistance of customs, law-enforcement agencies, immigration authorities, health and welfare services
New Zealand	Alcoholic Liquor Advisory Council (1978): promotes, sponsors and encourages research, and makes recommendations to Minister of Justice with respect to control and regulation
Norway	The Central Council for Narcotic Problems
Pakistan	Narcotics Control Board: coordination, policy-making, law enforcement and international liaison
Philippines	Dangerous Drug Board (1972): coordinating, policy body whose duties include treatment, rehabilitation, education; also implements international treaties
Singapore	Central Narcotics Bureau: coordination of policy efforts, treatment, and international liaison
Spain	Interministerial Commission for the study of problems arising from the consumption of drugs Narcotics Control Service (1968): submits reports to General Directorate of Health on medical treatment, rehabilitation, and surveillance of "drug addicts"

Country or jurisdiction	Title of body and responsibilities
Sri Lanka	Narcotics Advisory Board
Sudan	Sudan National Narcotic Control Board
Sweden	Alcohol Affairs Committee: initiates alcohol policy measures
Switzerland	Federal Commission on Alcohol-Related Problems
Thailand	Narcotics Control Board: policy and coordinating body with divisions for law enforcement, treatment, rehabilitation, education, planning, crop replacement; also international liaison
Togo	National Commission on Narcotics and Psychotropic Substances
Trinidad and Tobago	National Council on Alcoholism (1977): stimulating public understanding of alcoholism
Union of Soviet Socialist Republics	Alcoholism Control Commission of the Ministry of Health of the Soviet Union
United Kingdom	The Standing Conference on Drug Abuse: represents voluntary agencies concerned with rehabilitation of drug abusers
United States of America	Office of Drug Abuse Policy (1977): makes recommendations to President on policy, objectives, and priorities National Advisory Council on Alcohol Abuse and Alcoholism (1970): advises, consults, and makes recommendations to Secretary of Department of Health and Human Services National Advisory Council on Drug Abuse (1972)
Yugoslavia	Commission on Narcotics and Psychotropic Substances

4. Basic Principles of Legislation on Drug and Alcohol Dependence

4.1 Introduction

With the aim of ensuring that the results of this international review are of the greatest possible practical value, we outline here some basic principles to be considered in improving legislation on drug and alcohol dependence. These principles are derived from the data gathered, an examination of the literature in the field, and discussions and correspondence with many people. They also reflect the views of the Advisory Group, whose members were drawn from the fields of law, medicine, and public health administration, and which met in Boston in September 1982 to consider the preliminary report. A number of alternative approaches are indicated, to permit administrators of drug and alcohol programmes, legislators, and others interested in legislative revision to apply the principles in a way that meets the needs of their own country and that is in line with the available resources.

We emphasize that reliable facts about the nature and extent of alcohol and drug problems are not available in many developing countries. The logic of legal control depends greatly on the national perception of the problem in the light of many other competing socioeconomic problems, and the national political milieu and sociocultural values are important factors in shaping and reshaping the formulation, enactment and impact of legal intervention.

Treatment programmes must be planned to meet the specific needs of each country. Legislation setting up these programmes, if not enacted and interpreted in accordance with the actual programme plans of the country, can disrupt services and create difficulties in programme implementation. It is our hope that the principles and alternative approaches presented here will prove useful in many areas of drug and alcohol programme planning and administration, and in mental health programmes in general, in both developing and industrialized countries. It is important to investigate fully the relevance of the legislation and actual treatment practices of other countries in order to determine how such approaches may be used to improve legislation and treatment in one's own country.

4.2 Basic statutory structure

The 1977 WHO report on harmonizing objectives in mental health law (3) was reviewed in Chapter 1. In the section of that report on guidelines in the mental health field, it was noted that a critical review of the mental health legislative programme of a country would be greatly aided by first constructing a model of what a complete statutory system should contain in order to function properly. Because of the close relationship between the above-mentioned report and the present study, we have adopted a similar approach here, and the same basic statutory structure will be assumed, as follows:

1. *Policy*	Establishment of broad public policy and objectives in the drug- and alcohol-dependence treatment programme.
2. *Authority*	Designation of proper authority for planning and carrying out the public policy and administering treatment programmes for drug and alcohol dependence (along with other health programmes of a public nature).
3. *Budget*	Outline of budgetary policy and provision of continuing fiscal support for publicly conducted treatment programmes for drug and alcohol dependence.
4. *Operations*	Provision of adequate structure for, and details about the operation of, treatment programmes for drug and alcohol dependence to enable administrators to follow and to implement them.

5. *Research, training and education*	Provision of central planning (and financing to the extent determined) for research on the treatment of drug and alcohol dependence and for the education and training of qualified personnel.
6. *Entry to services*	Provision for equitable, non-discriminatory entry to treatment programmes for drug and alcohol dependence and access to services.
7. *Protection of individuals*	Provision of protection by the law and through legal-judicial institutions (courts, tribunals, etc.) of the rights, welfare, property, and dignity of persons, especially those subject to compulsory reporting, registration, testing, surveillance, and confinement for treatment.
8. *Minimum standards for manpower and resources*	Establishment of the policy for minimum standards (in such detail as may be deemed necessary and desirable) for treatment programme manpower and resources, including regulation of professional competence and adequacy of treatment facilities.
9. *Regulation of treatment methods*	Establishment of the policy for regulating the methods and procedures used in the treatment programme, including clear statutory definitions of persons eligible for treatment, grounds, release, etc.
10. *Accountability and evaluation*	Provision of a complete and ongoing system of treatment programme accountability and evaluation.
11. *Delegation of regulatory powers*	Delegation of authority, within statutory limits, from the legislature to governmental agencies (such as public health authorities) to adopt administrative regulations, decrees, or other legal instruments, for further implementation of legislative policy, to apply technical detail to the programme, and to be able to adjust the content of the programme to changes in conditions in the field.

12. *Definition of*   Precise definition of major terms used in
      terms   the legislation.

The first two items deal with the establishment of policy and objectives in the treatment programme for drug- and alcohol-dependent persons and with the designation of the authority to carry it out. As a result of our survey, one of the major problems identified with regard to drug dependence is the difficulty in reconciling the policy objectives of law-enforcement agencies and those of treatment programmes.

This conflict is less marked in respect of alcohol dependence, especially in countries where the policy of decriminalizing public intoxication has been adopted.

The influence of international conventions on narcotics and psychotropic substances and the requirements for implementing their provisions add another dimension to the coordination of national policy on drugs.

We have already given examples of appropriate short- and long-term drug-treatment objectives identified by WHO in its report on drug problems in the sociocultural context (6). The two long-term objectives deserve most attention: to reduce the incidence and prevalence of drug dependence; and to develop mechanisms for the planning, evaluation, and modification of programme activities, in accordance with changing needs and continuing programme evaluation.

It would be realistic to limit the number of objectives in a country at any one time to those that reflect the most immediate and critical needs. Careful consideration should be given to defining and quantifying objectives that are attainable and realistic and perceived as such by policymakers and the public.

Items 3 and 4 (budget and operations) are essential to the execution of programmes. Often, despite the most enlightened policy intentions, financial and operational considerations are the determining factors in the decision-making and implementation phases.

Item 5 is a key factor in the long-range success of a treatment programme. Programme planning should be interrelated with support for research and the development of manpower. A major problem revealed in our survey is the fact that often it is difficult to train and place skilled professionals where they are needed most, e.g., in certain rural areas in countries where illicit drugs are cultivated and use is high, or in large conurbations where services are needed, but there are few incentives to attract needed personnel.

The importance of research and training in the fields of alcohol and drug dependence cannot be overemphasized. Research is an indispensable component in the evaluation of drug and alcohol programmes, and sufficient funds should be made available to support both basic and applied research. Legislatures frequently give low priority to requests for funds for research and training, and in times of budgetary difficulties such programmes are often the first to be cancelled. A strong case for their inclusion must therefore be made.

WHO has emphasized the need for drug and alcohol research programmes in many publications, especially in relation to prevention. Thus in *Drug problems in the sociocultural context* (6), evaluation and research are considered important features of drug-prevention programming. The important relationship between research and assessment and policy-making in respect of alcohol dependence was reviewed in 1979 (25). Government-sponsored organizations, such as the Addiction Research Foundation of Toronto, can play an increasingly important role in bringing to the attention of governments and legislatures the need for drug and alcohol research programmes and for the wide dissemination of research results.

Medical education on alcohol and drug dependence is greatly in need of improvement for several reasons. One is that physicians and other medical professionals are understandably hesitant to seek out positions in service delivery or research when they have not been properly trained. Formal training in medical school and thereafter in continuing programmes should therefore be encouraged. Legislatures can promote interest by providing leadership and funds.

Treatment-programme development must always take into account existing health and social services. Alcohol- and drug-treatment programmes within the general health service are likely to fail if physicians and other providers are not properly trained to detect and treat alcohol and drug dependence in their patients. An important model programme for education in this area was established in 1971 by the National Institute on Alcohol Abuse and Alcoholism of the United States of America, namely the Federal Career Teacher Program in Alcohol and Drug Abuse. This is designed to promote physician education and awareness regarding the medical aspects of substance abuse and to ensure optimal treatment.

Item 6 concerns entry to treatment services, where the focus is on:

(*a*) the type and quality of services provided; and

(*b*) substantive legal provisions and procedural practices for admission into the treatment system.

Item 7 deals with some of the basic safeguards necessary for the protection of the rights of individuals who are subject to compulsory treatment. Appropriate measures need to be taken to protect these rights during the period of treatment or confinement.

Items 8 and 9 (standards and regulations for manpower, resources and methods) are important components of the regulatory system in the treatment of drug and alcohol dependence. Both governmental bodies and private organizations may be responsible for setting standards.

Item 10 concerns accountability and evaluation, which are critical to the assessment of programme effectiveness. We found a lack of adequate evaluation criteria in the legislation surveyed and regard this as a major deficiency. Legislation cannot be responsibly reviewed and changed without proper systems of accountability and evaluation, which should be set out in the basic law or in implementing legislation.

Formal public accountability for treatment policies and programmes must be established at the various levels of policy development and implementation.

Ongoing accountability for treatment implementation is an essential component of overall planning and evaluation. The mechanism of accountability should be built into the planning phases of programme development at the time that legislative decisions are made and laws adopted.

The WHO report on drug problems in the sociocultural context (7) sets out the following useful guidelines for the development of short- and long-term objectives of national programmes in the drug-dependence field:

Ideally, programmes should begin with primary prevention, but, as in many countries when drug dependence is already a problem, intervention must begin with treatment and rehabilitation. For this, short-term objectives have to be established and facilities to achieve them set up in the health care system. The objectives should be clearly defined and attainable with existing resources; they should also be measurable so that progress towards achieving them may be evaluated. Common short-term objectives are as follows: to bring drug-dependent persons and experimental users into contact with treatment facilities; to persuade drug-dependent persons to accept treatment; to reduce the medical and psychological complications of drug abuse; to improve the social functioning of drug-dependent persons; to reduce criminal or unlawful behaviour associated with drug abuse; to establish aftercare services to prevent relapse; and to reduce illegitimate traffic in illicit drugs, by reducing demand. Two common long-term objectives are to reduce the incidence and prevalence of drug dependence and to develop mechanisms for planning, evaluation, and modification of programme activities, in accordance with changing needs and continuing programme evaluation.

The emphasis in this statement on clear definitions of objectives that can be realistically attained is important. Evaluation is meaningless unless goals are measurable. The need for such measurability for evaluation and other purposes is often overlooked, or avoided, at the time of programme planning and legislative enactment. For these and other reasons, it is sound policy for treatment programmes to develop effective working relationships with legislative assemblies, since they open up channels of communication and can result in greater understanding and cooperation on both sides.

Item 11, delegation of regulatory powers from the legislature (at the national or subnational level) to the ministries or departments of the executive branch, is an essential feature of an effective legal structure. Such delegation should be clearly defined and rules whereby the operations can be controlled by the administrative agencies mentioned should be laid down. Often, such rules will be embodied in specific items of legislation setting up particular programmes rather than in the enabling law creating the agency or ministry.

There are several distinct advantages in the use of regulations or similar legal instruments, such as circulars or notifications. In many countries, the enactment of laws may take years. In contrast, regulations can be adopted with less delay. Of course, such regulations must be consistent with the law under which they are made.

4.3 Working with legislatures

Treatment personnel communicate with legislatures in many ways, but usually in response to the initiatives that lawmakers take in developing legislation. In many developed countries, the legislative process at the national or subnational level may involve the establishment of public health committees or drug-abuse subcommittees within the legislature. Such committees often conduct public hearings in order to receive both expert and lay views regarding proposed legislation. This forum provides a valuable opportunity for the timely and constructive presentation of views and for participation in the creation of law. Testimony before such legislative committees often involves the presentation of formal reports by government agencies charged with implementing the legislation. Both the public and the legislature therefore have the opportunity to assess the effectiveness of programmes and to seek change where treatment programmes require a different emphasis or direction. Opportunities for proposing changes are provided by public hearings conducted by legislatures. As an example, in 1981, the Select Committee on Narcotics Abuse and Control of the United States Congress held hearings on:

(a) community action to combat drug abuse;

(b) sentencing practices and alternatives in narcotics cases;

(c) impact of federal budget cuts on local narcotic law enforcement;

(d) bail reform and narcotic offenders;

(e) community efforts in drug abuse prevention and intervention;

(f) drug abuse in the military;

(g) financial investigations of drug trafficking;

(h) federal drug strategy.

Although many countries will not have developed such specialized legislative committees or consider the range of subjects just mentioned, attempts should be made to create a central organization within the legislature where public, private, and governmental concerns can be aired.

4.4 Evaluation of legislation

Resistance to change can be very great. Often, alcohol- or drug-treatment professionals are forced to work with programmes based on legislative enactments that are out of date and inappropriate in the current circumstances. The need that the law was originally intended to meet may have been satisfied, sometimes with the result that the law is inappropriately used to serve purposes for which it was not designed.

Laws that are "on the books" but not applied should be repealed as they may impede the development of more modern enactments, and cause needless confusion and difficulties in programme coordination. Drug- and alcohol-treatment professionals and particularly programme administrators should take active steps to correct deficiencies in the legislation, especially when it is out of date and has an adverse effect on the programmes.

The law and the legislative process should be used to correct problems and create more effective and improved treatment programmes. Frequently, changes are imposed from outside the programmes. Professionals who may actually have desired a particular change for years, but have done nothing to bring it about through the legislative system, are then forced to accept other, perhaps unwanted, changes.

The legislature and its various committees can also perform the essential task of providing a forum for the discussion and review of competing points of view. Thus, the legitimate but often conflicting interests of law-enforcement and treatment groups can be reviewed in the light of the overriding need to coordinate efforts.

4.5 Review mechanisms

In order to be effective, drug- and alcohol-abuse legislation must not only be designed to create realistic programme objectives, but must reflect the general will and public attitudes. The law is, of course, influenced and shaped by many societal factors and should reflect moral standards and public mores. The legislature can and does define, protect, and uphold rights and standards by embodying them in law.

The approach to the evaluation of the law on the treatment of drug and alcohol dependence will vary from country to country, according to differences in the legislation. Some countries, e.g., Bangladesh, have no specific legislation on either type of treatment, and a review in such a country will therefore not have any legislative foundation to start from. This situation, however, offers the possibility of uniformity of approach to new legislative enactments.

In other countries where a complex series of laws on either drugs or alcohol already exists, a different approach is required. This calls initially for an inventory and analysis of existing laws, following which changes in the law may be found to be necessary.

All legal systems make provision for changing statute law through amendments, repeal and re-enactment. Changes can also be brought about through administrative measures and through interpretation of the law by the courts. It follows that a method for continuous evaluation of legislation is required, so that the need for change can be recognized. Such evaluation is of no direct value unless the results are presented in good time and in a useful form to legislative bodies for analysis and appropriate action.

4.5.1 *Statutory boards or commissions*

The review process must involve the bodies charged with coordinating national drug and alcohol programmes, e.g. narcotics boards or commissions. A major advantage of this approach is that members of such boards and commissions are usually drawn from government departments or other equivalent bodies.

These commissions often represent a wide range of interests, and their recommendations usually attract public attention and carry considerable weight. Their major disadvantage, particularly from the point of view of regular review, is that their mandate extends for a limited period. Accordingly, as reviewing bodies, they lack control over the information that they can consider.

A commission of the legislature (or similar body) may be best able to carry out an occasional broad review of treatment legislation, stimulating public awareness in the process. Legislatures are often induced to act on the recommendations and priorities set by the commission, which usually issues a final report containing up-to-date information and guidelines. It may be unrealistic, however, to expect such a body to carry out the detailed and specialized ongoing monitoring and review that is necessary in the drug and alcohol field.

In contrast to such a commission, a narcotics board is permanent and has permanent responsibilities, including the provision of periodic reports to the government. This approach has much to offer in the long term.

4.5.2 *Ministerial review*

In most countries, responsibility for the treatment of drug and alcohol dependence is vested in the ministry of health, and sometimes also in the ministry of social welfare or social security.

In a number of countries, services for the drug-abusing criminal offender are either wholly or partly the responsibility of the ministry of justice. The health and social welfare ministries should clearly be involved in the ongoing review of treatment legislation. The advantages of making periodic review the responsibility of the health or social welfare ministry are: (i) the ministry is responsible for both programme formulation and execution so that the review will be carried out in the context of overall programme goals; and (ii) the ministry is likely to be in the best position to obtain the information needed for the review.

However, some disadvantages are associated with assigning review and monitoring to the health ministry, the major one being that other government agencies (e.g., the police) are directly involved and often charged with conflicting responsibilities. Another problem is that, if the review is to be conducted by those responsible for programme implementation, it may be difficult to achieve objectivity in assessing services and the role of legislation. An internal review lacks not only credibility but also visibility, and public interest is unlikely to be stimulated. An independent evaluation mechanism is most likely to achieve maximum credibility.

4.5.3 Central government committee

Another type of review mechanism is the central government coordination committee, which may be interdepartmental, interministerial, or interagency, depending on how the government is organized. Coordination at the national level is a difficult task with any governmental structure and expectations should be realistic. Competing interests and differing objectives and methods of achieving results can cause "interagency rivalry" so that progress is impeded. Interministerial coordination can operate effectively only when the ministries concerned are willing to make it do so. The role of the chief executive of the central government is important in ensuring smooth and efficient operation.

4.5.4 National institutes of alcohol and drug abuse

Such institutes offer an alternative to the mechanisms previously considered. They can serve many functions, including: research (including basic and applied activities); prevention and education; treatment and rehabilitation; resource development; programme support and grants. In some countries an institute may serve more as a resource centre for other national agencies or departments or for subnational governmental units. This is the situation, for example, in the United States of America.

4.6 Development of legislation

4.6.1 *Coordination*

Each of the review mechanisms discussed has advantages and disadvantages. Any country reviewing its legislation will want to assess carefully the strengths of all of them so as to determine how the best features of each can be utilized. This may mean that separate review mechanisms, each with a different but complementary function are established or remain in being. The guiding principle should be to establish effective links between governmental agencies so as to create both harmony of purpose and the ability to accomplish the review.

A permanent interministerial coordinating committee might be a suitable arrangement in these circumstances. Its chairman and members would be jointly appointed by the executive branch of the government, on the recommendation of the ministers responsible for health care, social and welfare services, law enforcement and the judiciary. The secretariat would be provided jointly by the various ministries concerned. The committee would be involved directly in formulating the national policy and in the development of treatment programmes for alcohol and drug dependence. The overall objective of the committee would be to reconcile the various, and in many cases competing, objectives of the ministries. Harmony, consistent with national policy and legislation, would be the aim and a forum for frank discussion and evaluation of legislation and programmes would be provided. Access to the executive branch would be available, and well documented and timely recommendations could be presented to the legislature. Authority to implement changes under the direction of the chief executive of the country would increase the effectiveness of such recommendations.

4.6.2 *Assessment of existing legislation*

The first step in the ongoing assessment of legislation on the treatment of alcohol and drug dependence would be to identify the current objectives of such legislation. These would be revealed by making a careful inventory of the overall current objectives of the national programme. Attention should be given to those aspects of the national programme objectives to which revised legislation might best contribute. It is also very important to determine whether any new or revised legislation is really needed and if there are ways of delivering treatment to those who need it without such legislation. For instance, in some countries, traditional healers provide treatment services but do not operate under any formal legal system. In other countries, voluntary services or informal activities are conducted without reliance on formal legislation. In such circumstances, extensive legislative review would be unnecessary.

Old laws should be critically assessed in order to determine whether they are appropriate to the current situation. Laws borrowed or adopted from other countries in colonial times should also be closely scrutinized. Laws that are in conflict with each other as a result of the piecemeal development of legislation over a number of years must be closely examined. Areas of direct conflict or incompatibility should be identified.

Existing laws should be examined to determine whether they are likely to serve the future needs of treatment programmes, as they develop over the next few years. Such an inquiry may reveal that step-by-step development may be more effective and achievable than a "one-off" comprehensive legislative change.

The second component in the review process is the collection of data to assess the extent to which objectives are currently being attained. Such data are often difficult to obtain and may be incomplete or unreliable. It is important to find ways of securing the necessary information so as to create an adequate basis for evaluation. For the purposes of the review, resort to *ad hoc* measures of information gathering may be necessary. The establishment of modern, efficient, and comprehensive systems of data collection, storage, and analysis for the purposes of research and evaluation and for other legitimate needs, should be recommended.

The coordinating body will also need information on operational aspects of the legislation. As an aid in this process, we suggest that the operational review should include the following steps:

(1) Administrative measures to implement the existing legislation should be described by the relevant ministry. In some countries there have been considerable delays in implementing newly enacted legislation. The committee should examine the

reasons for any such delays and suggest ways in which they might be overcome.

(2) Information on changes in the organization and pattern of the general health services should be obtained. In many countries, radical shifts in health service policy are being considered.

(3) The review body should examine whether new methods of treatment or approaches to care mean that new, more ambitious objectives can be set or, alternatively, that former unrealistic or overambitious objectives should be modified. Information on technical advances and training methods should therefore be made available. It may be considered that simpler, more effective methods of treatment make it possible to widen the range of personnel actively involved.

(4) Information on the protection of patients' rights should be obtained.

(5) An assessment of "public attitudes" would be extremely useful. Clearly, there is no uniform set of such attitudes, but some indications of attitudinal shifts, areas of concern, levels of prejudice, fears, interests, etc., among the public may be obtained.

The review committee could pose a series of questions, similar to those contained in the WHO publication on the law and mental health (3), as follows:

— Has the law performed as well as expected? If not, what modifications would allow the original objectives to be achieved?

— Have there been changes in patterns of drug abuse that now require new methods of legal control and treatment programmes?

— Have changes in the health care and social welfare systems or newly available methods of diagnosis or management created a need for new legal provisions?

— Have there been changes in international agreements that call for the updating of national legislation?

— Is there public concern that would justify additional legal controls or checks?

— Are individual rights and interests adequately protected?

In answering these questions, value judgements must be made

and can be debated. The committee would, however, be expected to reach agreement and to formulate a series of recommendations concerning both legal and administrative provisions. In doing this, several practical issues would have to be considered. The committee should take into account the cost of administering legislation, particularly in terms of manpower resources. Realistic solutions should be sought, the most highly trained personnel being reserved as far as possible for the tasks that only they can perform.

Frequent statutory changes are unlikely to be feasible. Amendments to the basic law may be considered every few years, but comprehensive change (e.g., a completely new law) is rarely as frequent. In contrast, administrative provisions, as already pointed out, can be changed more readily (usually by a ministerial directive) and can lead to timely and substantial improvements in the operation of the law.

4.7 Criteria for legal provisions

The WHO report on harmonizing objectives in law and mental health (3) set out criteria for legal provisions in the mental health field with special reference to developing countries; similar criteria for legislation on treatment of drug and alcohol dependants are summarized below. Further analysis of these criteria should prove useful in efforts to harmonize approaches to the revision of legislation on both substance abuse and mental health.

Treatment laws cannot be assessed or drafted in isolation. As countries move towards integrated and more widely available services, the role of law will change.

A "basic statutory structure" consisting of a list of essential issues that should be addressed by the law and that can be applied to all countries is given in section 4.2 (p. 96). Some criteria by which legal provisions can be assessed are given below, and should be read in close conjunction with this "basic statutory structure".

(a) *"Negative" criteria (i.e., what the law should not do)*

— It should not impede desired change, e.g., by limiting the places where drug- or alcohol-dependent persons may receive treatment or limiting or restricting the ability of law-enforcement or judicial authorities to divert persons into treatment programmes.

—It should not require an undue level of resources or staff time in its operation. Alternatives to costly institutional care should be encouraged so as to create a range of services, including less costly ones with limited objectives.

—It should not impair helpful responses to the treatment of drug and alcohol abuse that already exist in the community. Legislation should encourage, not impede, traditional methods of treatment as well as volunteer and community organization programmes.

—It should not, in general, create a completely separate treatment service for drug and alcohol dependence. Legislation requiring separately administered programmes and services will make integration into general health and social services and coordination of programmes difficult.

—It should not create or reinforce negative attitudes towards the alcohol- or drug-dependent person. Legal provisions that contribute to stigmatizing such persons should be avoided. The terms "alcoholic" and "drug addict" should be avoided and replaced by, e.g., "alcohol dependant" or "drug dependant".

(*b*) *"Positive" criteria (i.e., what the law should do)*

—It should closely reflect the overall direction and approach of the national policy.

—It should exploit available manpower. Medical practitioners, other medical and social welfare personnel, as well as colleagues and acquaintances of drug- or alcohol-dependent persons, can assist in guiding them into appropriate treatment services. Academic and professional training for physicians and other health and social welfare personnel should include courses on drug and alcohol dependence in order to facilitate earlier diagnosis, treatment, and referral.

—It should require treatment for priority conditions to be available in all parts of the country where it is needed. Priority should be given to problems, especially of drug dependence, in urban areas and to uniform distribution of services throughout the country.

—It should stimulate intersectoral involvement. Coordination of law-enforcement, social welfare, health, and judicial programmes is necessary to serve the needs of alcohol- and drug-dependent persons. Competing interests and objectives should be identified and mutual collaboration promoted in legal provisions and administration mechanisms.

—It should protect civil rights of individuals, regardless of educational status, residence, etc. Legislation should ensure such protection at all stages of contact with law-enforcement and administrative agencies and the judicial authorities.

4.8 Entry into treatment

4.8.1 *Voluntary admission*

As already pointed out, governments have a legitimate interest in attempting to prevent dependence on certain substances, including alcohol. They also have a legitimate interest in establishing narrowly limited formal controls over drug- and alcohol-dependent persons in certain cases, e.g., when dependence has resulted in a drastic reduction in ability to function or in severely disruptive and dangerous behaviour.

The overall goal of the treatment of dependence is early re-socialization and reintegration into the community. Treatment goals must be realistic. Both the legal system and the treatment programme should facilitate the attainment of individual objectives. An individual's personal desire to be treated for alcohol and drug dependence is an extremely important indicator of likelihood of success in treatment. The legal provisions whereby a person is guided into the treatment system should be explicitly designed to maximize the free exercise of choice and discretion. Compulsion can sometimes be a positive element in the entry process, but cannot guarantee the success of the treatment programme. In order to maximize individual motivation for treatment, entry into and continuation of treatment for alcohol and drug dependence should be voluntary whenever possible within the context of the legal system, culture and socioeconomic development of the country.

Treatment services should be readily available, effective and attractive to both adults and minors. The need for a voluntary programme to be "attractive" to minors deserves special emphasis. For this purpose, treatment services for both drug and alcohol dependence should be provided on an absolutely confidential basis, without parental notification or consent being required. Failure to ensure voluntary access under legal provisions imposing strict confidentiality could effectively bar entry to young people.

Motivation for treatment is critical for the person contemplating voluntary admission. The conditions for both entry into and continuation of treatment should therefore be explicitly designed to encourage easy access to services. Requirements that persons stay in treatment for a prescribed period of time should be avoided. Although there may well be good reasons why a certain period is required for a particular treatment programme, a rigid time requirement may result in a decision not to seek voluntary admission. Since available facilities are likely to be inadequate, legislation should encourage or require initial treatment at outpatient centres, if they exist, since they are less costly to operate than inpatient units and have the added advantage of greater flexibility from the patient's point of view.

Alcohol- and drug-dependent persons frequently suffer relapses or may leave treatment against medical advice. Such persons should not be denied admission to voluntary care, since they will probably be more highly motivated, as a result of their experiences, in seeking such care.

The legislation should lay down the conditions governing participation in voluntary treatment programmes; for example, continuing failure to cooperate in the treatment prescribed could be considered appropriate grounds for terminating voluntary status.

4.8.2 *Compulsory civil commitment*

Compulsory confinement for treatment has been one legal response to deviant behaviour, including mental illness, and drug and alcohol dependence. When the purpose of such deprivation of liberty is treatment, however, such confinement necessarily involves a conflict with the legally protected values of individual liberty and freedom of decision.

Compulsory civil commitment of persons dependent on drugs or alcohol will continue to be considered in some countries as an appropriate method, under certain narrowly defined circumstances, for forcing persons to enter treatment. As mentioned in section 3.4 (see p. 45), some governments have enacted legislation designed, on the one hand, to protect their citizens from the damaging effects of certain dependence-producing substances and, on the other, to protect third parties from the dangerous behaviour that may result from the use of such substances. The legal basis of compulsory civil commitment on these grounds is the nation's interest in protecting the individual when, for example, he is unable to care for himself as a result of abuse of alcohol or drugs. Such commitment may be required for persons who are:

(a) in need of short-term emergency treatment because of their incapacity to function normally as a result of the use of drugs or alcohol; and

(b) severely mentally disabled as a result of the use of drugs or alcohol.

Such grounds for compulsory treatment were identified in many of the laws reviewed, whether in mental health codes or in specialized provisions on drug and alcohol abuse. The criterion of "dangerousness" is frequently and more appropriately embodied in mental health codes, either in conjunction with, or as an alternative to, other grounds. Such codes, where promulgated, can also provide alternatives to compulsory civil commitment. Drug- or alcohol-dependent persons who have been found to be mentally ill should be treated under the provisions of the legislation governing the commitment and treatment of the mentally ill.

Persons in need of short-term emergency commitment include incapacitated drug or alcohol dependants. Present legislative trends require the police to assist incapacitated alcohol abusers to enter the treatment system instead of arresting them. Similarly, a drug-dependent person may be incapacitated while under the influence of drugs and in need of medical care. He may also require emergency care as a result of acute withdrawal symptoms and be in need of detoxification. Treatment for such alcohol or drug emergencies should be for short periods only. The person should be immediately released from detention on the completion of medical treatment (detoxification).

In addition to such acute medical emergencies, compulsory civil commitment legislation might provide for the disposition of persons who are drug or alcohol dependants and, as a result, are severely mentally disabled. Many grounds for commitment relate to the severity or degree of impairment; words such as "serious" are frequently used in the legislation. For example, the criterion in Somalia is "serious mental deterioration caused by habitual improper use of narcotic drugs". Under the law of the Federal Rebublic of Germany, the criterion for committing a person suffering from "drug dependence" is behaviour that will "seriously damage their health".

Existing legislation in some countries makes periods of confinement mandatory, but compulsory civil commitment is justified only when an effective treatment programme, as well as adequate and humane facilities, are available.

The period of commitment should be limited, as already pointed out, and a person's involuntary status subject to periodic review. The legislation of Thailand embodies these principles in its provisions calling for "treatment or rehabilitation for a period of 180 days in a clinic or rehabilitation centre".

The person concerned should be afforded certain substantive and procedural legal rights during the commitment proceedings. In some countries these include the rights to timely judicial hearing; adequate and timely notice of the proceedings; counsel at an appropriate time; immunity from self-incrimination; confrontation and cross-examination of any witnesses; a standard of proof requiring substantial evidence to be produced by the State; effective and humane treatment; and meaningful and adequate review. The criteria for compulsory civil commitment of drug- or alcohol-dependent persons should be clearly stated in the legislation. Some provisions of this type can be found in the legislation summarized in Annex 2 (see p. 125).

One of the important tasks of an interministerial coordinating committee responsible for reviewing legislation on the treatment of drug and alcohol dependence will be to establish the substantive rights and procedural legal rules that should apply in the civil commitment process and associated treatment programme.

4.9 Diversion to treatment from the criminal justice system

Providing effective treatment services and making them available and attractive to the drug- and alcohol-dependent offender both serves the public and directly benefits the individual concerned. Such treatment should be made available at every stage of the criminal justice system from the point of initial contact of an individual with law-enforcement personnel (pre-arrest) to the post-institutional phase (conditions of parole). The length of any period of involuntary confinement for the purpose of treatment should not exceed that prescribed for the violation of the criminal law committed by the person being diverted to treatment. The various legislative approaches and specific provisions are summarized in Annex 2 (see p. 125).

When the alcohol- or drug-dependent person comes into initial contact with the police authorities because of behaviour that may make him liable to arrest, the possibility of treatment can be a very important positive factor in his rehabilitation. The confrontation with the police may create the kind of crisis that might motivate a person to undergo effective treatment. In an emergency, for example, when he is incapacitated and unable to function, the police should be both legally entitled and encouraged to refer a person directly to a treatment programme, in lieu of arrest, for a short period until the emergency passes.

At the pretrial (post-arrest) stage, similar considerations will apply. Government officials responsible for prosecution should have the option of recommending diversion to treatment prior to trial. Real possibilities of diversion must, of course, exist, i.e., humane facilities providing effective treatment programmes must be available to care for the drug- or alcohol-dependent offender. Courts may wish to exercise their judicial discretion to refer an accused person for treatment in lieu of prosecution, if this is authorized by law.

Many treatment provisions are found in legislation focused primarily on the control of dependence-producing drugs. This is true particularly in countries that have introduced legislation pursuant to the international conventions on the control of narcotic and psychotropic drugs, which are themselves not primarily concerned with treatment. Thus, national legislation drafted so as to reflect and provide for control mechanisms to implement the international conventions will give treatment provisions relatively little attention. The inclusion of treatment provisions in this way also has certain drawbacks:

(1) the treatment provisions are not given the weight that probably would be accorded to them if the legislation was primarily concerned with treatment;

(2) there may be temptations for legislatures not to develop other separate treatment laws, or separate treatment sections in either mental health or public health legislation; this may be the case especially where little use is made of treatment provisions by prosecuting or judicial authorities or when little public and professional interest exists in implementing them;

(3) treatment provisions included in control legislation may be used for a purpose (e.g., diversion to treatment) that is appropriate only under limited circumstances (this is probably the most serious drawback).

The advantage of including treatment provisions in drug control legislation is that it gives much-needed flexibility to courts in imposing alternatives to penal sanctions. As noted earlier, both international conventions contain specific reference to the treatment of drug offenders (see p. 83) and also call on countries that are Parties to these conventions to "carefully consider incorporation of such provisions in national legislation".

4.10 Confidentiality

One of the overriding principles in the patient's relationship with the medical profession is that all information about him should be strictly confidential. Legislation should therefore include specific provisions to protect information about the patient obtained during treatment or as a result of pretreatment activity. Such information includes:

(*a*) records kept by treatment personnel; and

(*b*) all information contained in the records, or gathered in the course of screening, testing, medical examination, surveillance and treatment.

The guiding principle should be that confidentiality of information will encourage voluntary entry into the treatment system. Since voluntary treatment is to be preferred, as it usually involves a higher level of motivation, policymakers should, wherever possible, seek to protect confidentiality.

In many countries where notification, reporting, registration, medical screening, or surveillance systems have been established, complete confidentiality may not be possible under existing law. Conflicts in these areas can be evaluated by interministerial review bodies and by legislative committees considering revised legislation. Discussion of these matters by medical and legal professionals and treatment personnel should be encouraged so as to identify conflicts more clearly and define alternatives.

4.11 Links with other health services

Health services can be integrated when the central authority for health affairs is concentrated in a single ministry or department. Administrative regulations (or ministerial directives), rather than the basic law itself, may be used to assign and coordinate authority as between the various ministries and departments and can perform a beneficial harmonizing function. This approach can facilitate the periodic reorganization of services or personnel without the need to return to the legislature.

The fourteenth report (1967) of the WHO Expert Committee on Mental Health (6) was concerned with services for the prevention and treatment of dependence on alcohol and other drugs. It was noted that, at the national level, governments had developed specific mechanisms for coordination purposes, e.g., intergovernmental committees to develop and coordinate comprehensive programmes concerned with alcohol dependence. At the community level, however, it was reported that a multiplicity of agencies were concerned in some way with the care, treatment and control of dependence on alcohol and drugs. At all levels of government, and between governmental and nongovernmental agencies at all levels, there was a need for examination of the extent to which interorganizational cooperation was necessary and feasible.

Our survey revealed a trend towards the establishment of advisory and coordinating bodies to provide programme guidance at national and subnational levels for drug- and alcohol-dependence programmes. Such bodies have been established in many cases as a consequence of the requirements of Article 17 of the 1961 Single Convention, which states that "Parties shall maintain a special administration for the purpose of applying the provisions of this Convention".

We have also suggested that consideration be given to the establishment of a coordinating group at the ministerial level to reconcile the competing interests of the various ministries concerned with the control and treatment of drug and alcohol dependence.

The WHO Expert Committee on Problems Related to Alcohol Consumption (1) recognized the extent of alcohol-related problems in many countries and recommended that governments should:

(a) review the nature and extent of these problems in their population, the resources already available for reducing their prevalence and impact, and the possible constraints to be met in establishing new policies;

(b) initiate the procedures necessary for the elaboration of a comprehensive national alcohol policy;

(c) establish coordinating mechanisms to implement preventive and management policies and programmes to ensure a continuing review of the situation; and

(d) implement these programmes within the framework of general health and national development, utilizing existing structures where feasible.

Integration of the services for the treatment of drug and alcohol dependence into the general public health services has been consistently recommended by WHO. The integrated approach is also an important component of WHO's long-term plan for health for all by the year 2000.

The Council of Europe has recommended the development and organization of comprehensive services and continuity of treatment for alcoholics (Resolution of October 1978). The Council's Committee of Ministers recognized that the main responsibility for the treatment of alcoholics may rest either with the health services or the social services, which should cooperate closely.

The Council of Europe has recently (March 1982) made the following recommendations, *inter alia*, to member governments:

1. aid and treatment for drug dependants should be integrated as far as possible into the general health and social care system;

2. where resources are provided for aid and treatment services for drug dependants, the problems of drug dependence should be seen in relation to health and social problems.

References

1. WHO Technical Report Series, No. 650, 1980 (*Problems related to alcohol consumption:* report of a WHO Expert Committee).
2. Treatment of drug addicts: a survey of existing legislation. *International digest of health legislation*, **13**: 4–46 (1962).
3. CURRAN, W. J. & HARDING, T. W. *The law and mental health: harmonizing objectives.* Geneva, World Health Organization, 1977.
4. WHO Technical Report Series, No. 98, 1955 (*Legislation affecting psychiatric treatment:* fourth report of the Expert Committee on Mental Health).
5. WHO Technical Report Series, No. 131, 1957 (*Treatment and care of drug addicts:* report of a Study Group).
6. WHO Technical Report Series, No. 363, 1967 (*Services for the prevention and treatment of dependence on alcohol and other drugs:* fourteenth report of the WHO Expert Committee on Mental Health).
7. EDWARDS, G. & ARIF, A., ed. *Drug problems in the sociocultural context: a basis for policies and programme planning.* Geneva, World Health Organization, 1980 (Public Health Paper, No. 73).
8. EDWARDS, G. ET AL. *Alcohol-related disabilities.* Geneva, World Health Organization, 1977 (Offset Publication, No. 32).
9. RITSON, E.B. *Community response to alcohol-related problems: review of an international project.* Geneva, World Health Organization, 1985 (Public Health Paper, No. 81).
10. ORFORD, J. & EDWARDS, G. *Alcoholism.* London, Oxford University Press, 1977.
11. POLICH, J.M. ET AL. *The course of alcoholism: four years after?* New York, Wiley, 1981.
12. VAILLANT, G.E. The doctor's dilemma. In: Edwards, G. & Grant, M., ed. *Alcoholism treatment in transition*, London, Croom Helm, 1980.
13. GLASER, F.B. Anybody got a match? Treatment research and the matching hypothesis. In: Edwards, G. & Grant, M., ed. *Alcoholism treatment in transition*, London, Croom Helm, 1980.
14. HEATHER, N. & ROBERTSON, I. *Controlled drinking.* London, Methner Publishers, 1981.

15. MILLER, W.R. *The addictive behaviours.* New York, Pergamon Press, 1980.
16. GOVERNMENT OF HONG KONG, THE ACTION COMMITTEE AGAINST NARCOTICS. *Hong Kong narcotics report 1980. A decade of achievement, 1971–80.* Hong Kong, 1981.
17. MINISTRY OF HEALTH AND WELFARE. *A brief account of drug abuse in Japan.* Tokyo, 1981.
18. COUNCIL OF EUROPE, EUROPEAN PUBLIC HEALTH COMMITTEE. *Final report on treatment of drug dependence.* Strasbourg, 1980.
19. AUSTRALIAN ROYAL COMMISSION OF INQUIRY INTO DRUGS, *Report.* Books A–F, Canberra, 1980.
20. UNITED NATIONS. *Commentary on the Single Convention on Narcotic Drugs, 1961.* New York, 1973.
21. UNITED NATIONS. *Commentary on the Convention on Psychotropic Substances.* New York, 1971.
22. ADDICTION RESEARCH FOUNDATION. *Report of the International Working Group on the Convention on Psychotropic Substances, 1971.* Toronto, 1980.
23. REXED, B. ET AL. *Guidelines for the control of narcotic and psychotropic substances: in the context of the international treaties.* Geneva, World Health Organization, 1984.
24. *Alcohol control policies in public health perspective.* Helsinki, Finnish Foundation for Alcohol Studies, 1975.
25. MOSER, J. *Prevention of alcohol-related problems: an international review of preventive measures, policies and programmes.* Toronto, Addiction Research Foundation, 1980.

List of Participants[1]

WHO Advisory Group Meetings on Legislation on Treatment of Drug- and Alcohol-Dependent Persons

Harvard University, Cambridge, MA, USA
7–10 September 1982
and 5–7 April 1983

Dr S.K. Chatterjee,[2,3] Senior Lecturer in International Law and the Laws of European Institutions, Faculty of Law, City of London Polytechnic, London, England

Dr M.R. Chaudhry,[2] Professor of Psychiatry, Department of Psychiatry, Mayo Hospital, Lahore, Pakistan

Dr H. Demone,[3] Dean, Rutgers University, New Brunswick, NJ, USA

Professor J.C. Ebie,[2] Provost, Aro Psychiatric Hospital, Aro, Abeokuta, Ogun State, Nigeria

Dr G.P. Harnois,[2,3] Director-General, Douglas Hospital, Montreal, Quebec, Canada

Mr D.C. Jayasuriya,[2,3] Attorney-at-law, Nawala, Sri Lanka

Professor J. Mendelson,[2] Harvard Medical School, Boston, MA, USA

Dr W.J. Muya,[2] Mathari Hospital, Nairobi, Kenya

Dr O. Schroeder,[2] Ministerial Counsellor, Federal Ministry of Youth, Family Affairs and Health, Bonn, Federal Republic of Germany

Representatives of the United Nations and other intergovernmental organizations

International Narcotics Control Board, Vienna, Austria:
Sir Edward Williams,[2] c/o Commonwealth Games Foundation, Brisbane, Queensland, Australia

United Nations Fund for Drug Abuse Control, Vienna, Austria:
Mr G. di Gennaro,[2] Director

United Nations Social Defence Research Institute, Rome, Italy:
Dr T. Asuni,[2] Director

Colombo Plan Bureau for Technical Cooperation, Colombo, Sri Lanka:
Mr P. Abarro,[2] Drug Adviser

Representatives of WHO collaborating centres

Addiction Research Foundation, Toronto, Canada:
Dr J. Blackwell [2]

National Institute on Drug Abuse, Rockville, MD, USA:
Dr D. Czechowicz,[2] Acting Director, Community Assistance Division

Dr J.P. Smith,[3] Assistant Director for International Activities

Representative of the International Council on Alcohol and Addictions

Mr A. Tongue,[2,3] Executive Director

Observers

Harvard School of Public Health, Boston, MA, USA:
Dr W.E. McAuliffe,[3] Associate Professor, Department of Behavioral Science

Mrs G.K. White,[3] Medicolegal Coordinator

National Institute on Alcohol Abuse and Alcoholism, Rockville, MD, USA:
Mr L. Towle,[2,3] Chief, International and Intergovernmental Affairs

WHO Secretariat

Dr A. Arif,[2,3] Senior Medical Officer in charge of Drug Dependence Programme, Division of Mental Health, WHO, Geneva, Switzerland (*Secretary*)

Mrs S. Connor,[3] Legal Counsel, WHO Regional Office for the Americas/Pan American Health Organization, Washington, DC, USA

Professor W.J. Curran,[2,3] Professor of Legal Medicine, Harvard Medical School, Boston, MA, USA (*Chairman*)

Mr S.S. Fluss,[2] Health Legislation, WHO, Geneva, Switzerland

Dr M. Katatsky,[2] Regional Adviser in Alcoholism and Drug Dependence, WHO Regional Office for the Americas/Pan American Sanitary Bureau, Washington, DC, USA

Dr W.K. Mariner,[2,3] Assistant Professor of Health Law, Harvard School of Public Health, Boston, MA, USA

Mr J. Ording,[2] Senior Scientist, Alcohol Programme, Division of Mental Health, WHO, Geneva, Switzerland

Mr W.L. Porter, Health Law Firm of Norris and Norris, Boston, MA, USA (*Temporary Adviser*)

---

[1] The following people were invited to one or both meetings, but were unable to attend: Dr O. Ayoush, Institute of Criminology, São Paulo, Brazil; Dr T.A. Baasher, Regional Adviser in Mental Health, WHO Regional Office for the Eastern Mediterranean, Alexandria, Egypt; Dr E.A. Babayan, Head of the Department of Evaluation of New Drugs and Medical Equipment, Ministry of Health, Moscow, USSR; Mr N. Boyer, Director, Health and Narcotics Programs, Department of State, Washington, DC, USA (invited as observer); Dr J.M.N. Chi'en, Society for the Aid and Rehabilitation of Drug Abusers, Hong Kong; Dr J. Cooper, Director, Medical and Professional Affairs Division, National Institute on Drug Abuse, Rockville, MD, USA; Dr R. de la Fuente, General Director, Mexican Institute of Psychiatry, Mexico City, Mexico; Dr R. Gonzalez, Regional Adviser in Mental Health, WHO Regional Office for the Americas/Pan American Sanitary Bureau, Washington, DC, USA; Dr J.D. Havard, Secretary, British Medical Association, London, England; Dr T. Mork, Director-General of Health Services, Oslo, Norway; Professor R. Pinto Ribeiro, Department of Psychiatry and Legal Medicine, Faculty of Medicine, Federal University of Rio Grande do Sul, Porto Alegre, Brazil; Dr Saleem Shah, Director, Center for Crime and Delinquency Studies, National Institute of Mental Health, Rockville, MD, USA.

[2] Attended the meeting in September 1982.

[3] Attended the meeting in April 1983.

Summary of Legislation

This Annex contains the results of the comparative survey of legislation, and covers legal provisions governing various forms of treatment. The material is divided into three categories, as follows: compulsory civil commitment (pp. 125–171); diversion from the criminal justice system (pp. 171–193); and compulsory reporting, registration, testing, and surveillance in the community (pp. 193–207). The countries and jurisdictions surveyed are listed alphabetically, information for each being presented in a standard format using a series of headings. In this way comparisons can readily be made between different countries and jurisdictions.

A2.1 COMPULSORY CIVIL COMMITMENT

Argentina

Legislation: Article 482 of Civil Code of Argentina.

1. *Grounds:* Persons who, as drug addicts, could impair their own health or that of others, or disturb the public peace.

2. *Application:* At the request of:

    (*a*) the undivorced spouse;

    (*b*) relatives of the addicted person;

    (*c*) any person in the community, when the demented person is violent or a disturbance to his neighbours.

3. *Decision-making authority:* At the request of any of the persons enumerated above, the judge may in a summary proceeding, direct the commitment, in an appropriate establishment, of a drug addict requiring assistance and must appoint a special defence counsel to ensure that the commitment continues for not longer than is absolutely necessary and even to avoid it, if the addict can be appropriately assisted by the persons required to provide maintenance.

4. *Medical examination:* Certification by a medical officer.

5. *Treatment programme:* Not stated.

6. *Length of stay:* Not stated.

7. *Appeal:* Not stated.

8. *Periodic review:* Not stated.

9. *Discharge procedure(s):* Not stated.

> Note: Law No. 20.332 of 1973 established, under the Ministry of Social Welfare, the National Re-education Centre to provide specialized care to adolescent and adult drug abusers of both sexes who voluntarily request care.

Australia (Victoria)

Legislation: Alcoholics and Drug Dependent Persons Act of 18 December 1968.

Note: This Act repealed the Inebriates Act of 1958 and provides for the treatment and rehabilitation of alcoholics and drug-dependent persons.

1. *Grounds:* An alcoholic or drug-dependent person suitable for treatment.

"Alcoholic" means a person who habitually uses intoxicating liquor to such an extent that he has lost the power of self-control with respect to the use of intoxicating liquor or to such an extent as to endanger the health, safety, or welfare of himself or other persons.

"Drug-dependent person" means a person who habitually uses drugs of addiction to such an extent that he has lost the power of self-control with respect to the use of drugs of addiction.

2. *Application:*

   (a) Upon complaint made to a judge of the Supreme Court or of the county court or to a stipendiary magistrate that a person is an alcoholic or a drug-dependent person and upon evidence (including at least one certificate from a legally qualified medical practitioner who has examined such person within 48 hours prior to such complaint) making it appear to the judge or magistrate that such person is an alcoholic or a drug-dependent person, the judge or magistrate may make an order directing that the person complained against be admitted to an assessment centre.

   (b) A complaint under (a) may be made only by:

   (i) the husband or wife of the person complained of or one of his parents;
   (ii) a partner in business;
   (iii) a brother, sister, son, or daughter of full age;
   (iv) a member of the police force of or above the rank of senior constable or for the time being in charge of a police station; or
   (v) a welfare officer.

3. *Decision-making authority:* Medical officer in charge of an assessment centre.

Where two legally qualified medical practitioners have certified in writing that any person admitted to an assessment centre is an alcoholic or a drug-dependent person and the medical officer in charge of the centre is of the same opinion, the medical officer in charge may, if he is satisfied that such person is suitable for treatment in a treatment centre, by order in writing commit him to a treatment centre for treatment.

"Medical officer in charge of an assessment centre" includes any medical officer engaged or employed at the centre who is authorized in writing by the medical officer in charge of the centre to make examinations for the purposes of the Act and to commit persons to treatment centres for treatment.

4. *Medical examination:* See paragraph 3 above.

5. *Treatment programme:* Subject to the supervision and control of the Minister of Health, the following services must be provided or the following institutions established and maintained for the care and treatment of persons who are or are likely to become alcoholics or drug-dependent persons and for their rehabilitation into the community:

   (*a*) research and preventive services;

   (*b*) day hospitals, outpatient, and community services;

   (*c*) reception and assessment centres for receiving, assessing, and classifying alcoholics and drug-dependent persons;

   (*d*) clinics and residential centres for the care of infirm alcoholics and drug-dependent persons;

   (*e*) clinics and residential centres for the rehabilitation of alcoholics and drug-dependent persons;

   (*f*) hostels for the accommodation for limited periods of rehabilitated alcoholics and drug-dependent persons;

   (*g*) detention centres for the detention, safe custody and treatment of persons convicted for offences in respect of which drunkenness or drug addiction is a necessary part or condition or contributed to the commission of the offence;

   (*h*) such other services as the Minister thinks fit.

"Treatment centre" means any clinic or residential centre for the care of infirm alcoholics and drug-dependent persons or any clinic or residential centre for the rehabilitation of alcoholics and drug-dependent persons but does not include a detention centre.

6. *Length of stay:* Seven days and, if the medical officer in charge of the assessment centre so directs, a further period of seven days.

7. *Appeal:* A person committed to a treatment centre for treatment as an alcoholic or drug-dependent person is entitled to appeal against the order for his commitment in all respects as if the order of the medical officer committing such person to a treatment centre were an order made by the judge or magistrate who directed such person to attend the assessment centre from which he was so committed and as if the judge or magistrate made the order in the course of some duly appointed sitting of the Supreme Court, the county court, or a court of petty sessions (as the case requires) in the place where the order was made.

8. *Periodic review:* Not stated.

9. *Discharge procedure(s):* The medical officer in charge of a treatment centre may order the discharge of any alcoholic or drug-dependent person detained therein or allowed to be absent therefrom upon trial leave or parole.

Bangladesh

Note: There is at present no legislation on either voluntary or compulsory treatment of drug-dependent persons, although persons who are psychotic as a result of drug use are compulsorily admitted under the Mental Health Act.

A new (draft) Narcotic Drug Act incorporates provisions for the treatment and rehabilitation of drug-dependent persons.

Burma

Legislation: Narcotics and Dangerous Drug Law, 1974, and Narcotics and Dangerous Drug Rules, 1974.

1. *Grounds:* These are as follows:

    (a) Addiction to narcotic and dangerous drugs;

    (b) Occasional use of narcotic and dangerous drugs.

    "Addict" means any person who has the desire to use narcotics and dangerous drugs and who is unable to refrain from taking such drugs and who suffers from withdrawal symptoms when he does not consume the same.

    "Occasional user" means any person who consumes narcotics and dangerous drugs occasionally and who, in spite of non-consumption of same, is free from withdrawal symptoms.

2. *Application:* Medical officer in charge of various clinics under the Government regulations for the registration of addicts.

3. *Decision-making authority:* Drug Addicts Registration and Medical Treatment Supervision Board acting pursuant to legislation requiring the Government to enforce strictly compulsory medical treatment for all persons addicted to drugs.

4. *Medical examination:* Not stated.

5. *Treatment programmes:*

    (a) *Addicts:* Medical officer in charge of clinic provides treatment in accordance with method of treatment prescribed in Government directives until addicts are cured. Treatment is to be given in specified medical centres and convicts may, if necessary, be admitted for treatment in prison hospitals.

    (b) *Occasional users:* Such users must be given medical treatment if necessary.

    The Ministry of Health issues guidelines on the provision of medical treatment. Medical treatment (not specifically defined) consists of "measures" to be taken by the Government so that addicts and occasional users will not be impaired, but instead rehabilitated, enabling them to perform their share of the duties of the State in their respective fields of choice. The legislation empowers the Government to take steps (after obtaining necessary assistance) for the rehabilitation in every way of such users of drugs, so as to enable them, on recovery after medical treatment, to resume their places in society as useful citizens.

6. *Length of stay:* Not stated.

7. *Appeal:* Not stated.

8. *Periodic review:* Not stated.

9. *Discharge procedure(s):* Not stated.

Canada (British Columbia)

Legislation: Heroin Treatment Act, 1979 (Chapter 166 of the Revised Statutes of British Columbia).

1. *Grounds:* In need of treatment for narcotic dependence.

   "Narcotic" is defined as heroin (diacetyl morphine) and other derivatives of opium, opium, methadone (6-dimethylamino-4,4-diphenyl-3-heptanone), any substance with morphine-like properties that is prescribed by regulation and anything that contains any of these substances.

   "Dependence" is defined, in relation to a narcotic, as a state of psychological or physical dependence, or both, on a narcotic following its use on a periodic or continuous basis.

2. *Application:* Director in charge of area coordinating centre applies to court for an order declaring that the person is in need of treatment for narcotic dependence.

   Note: The following provisions govern attendance at area coordinating centres:

   (*a*) Where a peace officer believes on reasonable grounds that a person is dependent on a narcotic, he may give the person a written notice specifying a date and time, not less than 24 hours or more than 48 hours from the time of the giving of the notice, at which the person is required to attend and submit to examination at the area coordinating centre specified in the notice.

   (*b*) The director of the area coordinating centre specified in a notice under (*a*) has an absolute discretion, at the request of a person to whom the notice was given, or on his own initiative, to give the person a written notice requiring the person to attend and submit to examination at the area coordinating centre at a specified later date or time.

   (*c*) Where a person does not comply with a notice given to him under (*a*) or (*b*), the [coordinating control] commission may apply *ex parte* to a judge for a warrant authorizing a peace officer to take the person into custody and to take him to an area coordinating centre, and the judge may, if it appears to him that the notice was given to the person in accordance with (*a*) or (*b*) and that the person has not complied with the notice, issue the warrant.

   (*d*) In an application under (*c*):

       (i) a certificate signed by the peace officer or by a director of an area coordinating centre that he gave the written notice to the person is proof, in the absence of evidence to the contrary, that he gave the written notice to the person; and

(ii) a certificate signed by the director of an area coordinating centre that the person named in the notice has not attended at the area coordinating centre is proof, in the absence of evidence to the contrary, that the person has not complied with the notice.

(e) A certificate given under (d) is evidence of the statements contained in the certificate without proof of the signature of the official character of the person appearing to have signed the certificate.

The following provisions apply to the detention of patients:

(a) Where the Act authorizes or requires that a patient be detained, a peace officer may, without a warrant, take him to a treatment centre for detention.

(b) A director may, in writing, consent to the absence of a detained patient from a treatment centre, where the absence is necessary for medical reasons.

(c) The director may require as a condition of his consent under (b) that the patient be accompanied by an escort, and the escort must direct and supervise the patient during the patient's absence from the treatment centre.

3. *Decision-making authority:* Supreme Court.

4. *Medical examination:* An evaluation panel must be set up, as follows:

(a) The Lieutenant Governor in Council must compile for each area coordinating centre a list of persons consisting of medical practitioners, psychologists registered under the Psychologists Act and other persons eligible to sit on an evaluation panel, and the Lieutenant Governor in Council must designate one person on the list to act as chairman and one as vice-chairman of the panel.

(b) An evaluation panel must be formed at the call of the chairman or vice-chairman from the list referred to in (a) and must have a membership of at least two medical practitioners and one other member, and may, but need not, include the chairman or vice-chairman designated under (a).

The provisions governing the medical examination itself are as follows:

(a) Where a person attends at an area coordinating centre for examination, an evaluation panel for the area coordinating centre must at once conduct a medical and psychological examination of him and may detain him for a period of 72 hours, or a lesser time as the director in charge of the area coordinating centre orders.

(b) Within 60 hours after a person is admitted to an area coordinating centre for examination, the evaluation panel must report in writing to the director in charge of the area coordinating centre as to whether the person is or is not in need of treatment for narcotic dependence and where, in its opinion, treatment is needed, make recommendations to the director respecting the treatment.

(c) In an examination of a person it is not necessary for all the members of the evaluation panel to personally examine him, nor is it necessary for those members who examine him to be present at the same time, and in forming their opinion and making their report and recommendations under this section they may rely on analyses and tests carried out at the direction of a member of the evaluation panel by an employee of the commission or another person.

(d) The director in charge of an area coordinating centre must at once on its receipt give a person examined a copy of the report and of any recommendations made by the evaluation panel.

(e) Where a person examined consents in writing to treatment, the director in charge of an area coordinating centre may commit him to treatment at once without an application to the court.

(*f*) Where the members sitting as the evaluation panel have unanimously reported that a person examined is in need of treatment and the person is not committed under (*e*), the director in charge of the area coordinating centre must apply to the court for an order declaring that the person is in need of treatment for narcotic dependence.

(*g*) Notice stating the time and place of the application must be served personally on the person who is the subject of the application.

(*h*) Where on hearing an application under these provisions the court is satisfied that the person is in need of treatment for narcotic dependence, it must commit him for treatment.

5. *Treatment programme:*

   (*a*) A director must develop programmes for the treatment of patients, and the programmes may be designed for the treatment of patients generally, or for the treatment of an individual patient.

   (*b*) A treatment programme for a patient must last for three consecutive years and may include some or all of the following:

      (i) where a director directs, detention in a treatment centre for a period not exceeding six consecutive months;
      (ii) attendance at a treatment clinic at times and over periods, not exceeding one year in total, as a director requires;
      (iii) supervision and direction of a kind and of a duration a director requires.

   (*c*) Detention is limited to a total of six months.

   (*d*) The director for the time being in charge of a patient's treatment programme may change the treatment, but he may not shorten or rescind a requirement for detention or change a direction of the board of review (see paragraph 8).

6. *Length of stay:* See paragraph 5 above.

7. *Appeal:* An appeal may be made to the Court of Appeal against an order of the Supreme Court.

8. *Periodic review:*

   (*a*) The Lieutenant Governor in Council must appoint a board of review of not less than five members of whom at least one must be a medical practitioner and must appoint one of the members as chairman.

   (*b*) A member is appointed for a term of three years.

   (*c*) A quorum of the board is one medical practitioner and two other members.

   The Board may, on the application of the director, and after hearing the director and the patient, direct that the duration of a patient's treatment under section 5 be extended beyond the six months referred to therein as needed for the care of the patient.

9. *Discharge procedure(s):* See paragraph 5 above.

Canada (Nova Scotia)

Legislation: Narcotic Drugs Act of 1967 (Chapter 205 of the Revised Statutes of Nova Scotia).

Note: This law is reported not to be in current use.

1. *Grounds:* Person who is an "addict".

"Addict" means any person addicted to the improper use of cocaine, opium, or their derivatives, or any other narcotic drug which for the time being is included in the schedule to the Opium and Narcotic Drug Act (Canada).

2. *Application:* The Minister of Public Health or other person charged with the administration of laws relating to public health in the Province.

Where the Minister is credibly informed that an addict is resident within the Province of Nova Scotia, he may give notice in writing to such addict requiring him to consult a legally qualified medical practitioner and submit himself for treatment, within such time as the Minister may prescribe, and to continue such treatment until cured.

Should the addict fail to submit himself to such treatment within the time prescribed by the Minister, or to continue the treatment until cured, or should the treatment fail to effect a cure, the Minister may report the circumstances to any justice, whereupon the justice may cause such inquiries to be made as he may think fit.

3. *Decision-making authority:* Any justice. If in his judgement it appears desirable in the public interest that the addict be committed to an institution for treatment, he may make such order as he may see fit for the detention and treatment of such person in any hospital, jail, or place of detention in the Province.

"Justice" means a justice of the peace and includes two or more justices, if two or more justices act or have jurisdiction, and also a police magistrate, a stipendiary magistrate or any person having the power or authority of two or more justices of the peace.

4. *Medical examination:* See paragraph 2 above.

5. *Treatment programme:* Every hospital, jail or place of detention designated by regulations of the Governor in Council is required to make effective provision for the examination, treatment, and detention of such addicts as may be committed to such institution by any justice.

6. *Length of stay:* Not stated.

7. *Appeal:* Not stated.

8. *Periodic review:* Not stated.

9. *Discharge procedure(s):* Not stated.

Colombia

Legislation: Legislative Decree No. 1188 of 25 June 1974 promulgating the National Statute on Narcotic Drugs.

1. *Grounds:* Persons who, without having committed any of the offences described in the Decree, are suffering from the effects of consuming drugs or substances that produce physical or psychic dependence.

   "Physical dependence" means a state of adaptation to a drug or substance that creates an organic need for it.

   "Psychic dependence" means the compulsive, habitual use of a drug or substance.

2. *Application:* Such persons must be sent to establishments listed in Articles 4 and 5 of Decree No. 1136 of 1970 (i.e., clinics, rest homes or hospitals).

3. *Decision-making authority:* In accordance with Articles 4 and 5 of Decree No. 1136 of 1970 (admission to an establishment is subject to medical assessment).

4. *Medical examination:* See paragraph 3 above.

5. *Treatment programme:* The main object of health and social measures for the treatment and rehabilitation of drug addicts is to enable the individual to become a useful member of the community again. The Ministry of Public Health must include among its programmes the provision of services for the prevention of drug addiction and the treatment and rehabilitation of addicts. Treatment must be furnished in a public establishment, except when the patient or his family request that it be given in a private facility, at his own expense.

6. *Length of stay:* Not stated.

7. *Appeal:* A person may petition the Departmental Governor for a review of his case; the Governor's decision must be rendered within 30 days.

8. *Periodic review:* Not stated.

9. *Discharge procedure(s):* Termination of treatment must be preceded by a favourable medical opinion.

Finland

Legislation: Law No. 96 of 10 February 1961 on the treatment of persons making improper use of intoxicants.

1. *Grounds:* This Law applies to persons given to insobriety or otherwise repeatedly making improper use of alcoholic substances or other intoxicants, if such persons:

   (a) are manifestly violent, abuse their spouses or children or are otherwise a danger to themselves or to the health or personal safety of others;

   (b) have been convicted during the preceding 12-month period of having driven a motor or other vehicle while in a state induced by drunkenness or while under the influence of intoxicants;

(c) cause a flagrant disturbance or scandal in their dwellings or elsewhere;

(d) have on three or more occasions during the past 12-month period rendered themselves liable to the enforcement of the measures prescribed in the penal code for a variety of criminal offences;

(e) neglect the maintenance and care of any person whom they, pursuant to law, a court order or an agreement, are bound to support, or repeatedly neglect the work upon which they depend for their livelihood;

(f) become a charge on their relatives or on other persons close to them;

(g) are in need of social assistance.

Note: If it has not been possible by means of surveillance to cause a person needing treatment [as referred to in 1 (a)] to abstain from the improper use of intoxicants, such person shall be ordered to be committed to a treatment institution.

A person [as referred to in 1 (a)] who is in need of treatment and who is dangerous, must be ordered to be committed to a treatment institution even without previous surveillance if there is no assurance of his obtaining treatment by other means. Any person other than one needing treatment [as referred to in 1 (a)] may also be ordered to be committed to a treatment institution if it is obvious that he cannot otherwise be caused to abstain from the improper use of intoxicants.

If a person needing treatment [as referred to in 1 (a)] has become so dangerous that, even before the initiation of any action (under this Law) necessary security measures have to be urgently applied in respect of that person, the police authorities are entitled to take such measures.

If the need for treatment in an institution is particularly urgent on other grounds, the person needing treatment may, where the chairman of the Social Welfare Board or the competent department thereof so agrees, even before any decision has been taken by the Provincial Government or the Ministry of Social Welfare, be sent for a period not exceeding one month to a treatment institution, hospital, or other corresponding establishment.

Under this Law, "intoxicants" includes, apart from alcoholic substances, such medicaments or other substances as are capable of inducing in persons using them a state of intoxication or a state comparable thereto.

2. *Application:* The social welfare board is responsible for the general administration, in the commune, of treatment as referred to in this Law.

The social welfare board must, in particular, make applications for persons needing treatment to be ordered to be committed to a treatment institution and take steps for the implementation of decisions adopted on the basis of such applications.

An application for a commitment order to a treatment institution may be made to the Provincial Government not only by the social welfare board, but also by the chief of police within whose jurisdiction the person needing treatment is resident, or is staying, or has been found in an intoxicated condition.

3. *Decision-making authority:* Provincial Government.

4. *Medical examination:* Not stated, except that a person subject to surveillance must, where necessary, undergo medical examination and treatment.

5. *Treatment programme:* The treatment measures contemplated under this Law and applied as necessary and appropriate in each individual case, are:

(*a*) advice and guidance;

(*b*) surveillance; and

(*c*) treatment at an institution or other centre.

The purpose of such treatment measures is to assist persons needing treatment to abstain from the improper use of intoxicants and to avoid the dangers involved thereby both to themselves and to others. The treatment measures contemplated under this Law may not be applied if they are inappropriate on account of an acute or chronic mental, or physical disorder or defect on the part of a person making improper use of intoxicants.

In the application of treatment, both open and institutional, special attention should be paid as far as possible to:

(*a*) treatment measures based on the fact that the person concerned has sought such treatment of his own free will;

(*b*) the reasons why treatment is needed, individual considerations, and advice to and support of members of such person's family;

(*c*) awakening and encouraging a sense of confidence and responsibility, as well as a personal effort and a positive attitude on the part of the person undergoing treatment; and

(*d*) application of medicinal methods of treatment, and cooperation with the medical authorities.

Where advice and guidance are regarded as being necessary and appropriate, the person needing treatment must, as far as possible:

(*a*) be assisted towards an understanding of the dangers involved in the improper use of intoxicants;

(*b*) be brought into contact with suitable companions and leisure pursuits;

(*c*) be assisted in finding living accommodation and employment;

(*d*) be assigned to outpatient or other special treatment, to treatment in a hospital, or to treatment at an institution or other suitable centre; and

(*e*) in some other convenient and appropriate way be assisted to abstain from the improper use of intoxicants.

If the measures referred to above have not been or obviously are not suitable for affording adequate assistance, the person needing treatment must be placed under surveillance, which must continue for a period of one year. If such surveillance during that time has not been shown to afford adequate assistance, such period may be extended by not more than one year.

Surveillance may be suspended before the stipulated time limit, provided that it is likely that the person needing treatment, if he is prematurely released from surveillance, will not make improper use of intoxicants. A person needing treatment and placed under surveillance must: (i) where necessary undergo medical examination and treatment; (ii) at certain times, or otherwise, whenever summoned, report to the social welfare officer or to the authority or supervisor designated by the social welfare board, to supply the information necessary for purposes of surveillance; and (iii) observe the instructions given him with regard to his place of residence or domicile.

6. *Length of stay:* Any person committed to a treatment institution must be detained there for one year. If he has undergone treatment at such an institution under an earlier official commitment order during the three years preceding issuance of the new commitment order, he must be detained in such institution for two years.

7. *Appeal:* Not stated.

8. *Periodic review:* Not stated.

9. *Discharge procedure(s):* A person committed by order to a treatment institution may be conditionally discharged from the institution before the expiry of the period prescribed in paragraph 6 above if it is likely that, after being discharged from the institution, he will not make improper use of intoxicants, or if the circumstances otherwise so justify.

A person committed by order to a treatment institution must be subject to surveillance as prescribed in paragraph 5 above for one year after his final or conditional discharge therefrom. Surveillance may cease before the appointed date, if appropriate.

Any person conditionally discharged from a treatment institution may be sent back to such institution during the period of surveillance, if he makes improper use of intoxicants. In such cases, he must be detained in the institution for not longer than the period remaining to be served at the time of his conditional discharge therefrom.

Federal Republic of Germany (Bavaria)

Legislation: Law on the hospitalization of the mentally ill and their care (Hospitalization Law) of 20 April 1982.

1. *Grounds:* Those who are mentally ill or suffer from psychiatric disturbance due to mental deficiency or addiction and therefore present a substantial danger to public safety and order may, against or without their consent, be hospitalized in a psychiatric hospital or other suitable institution. Such hospitalization is also admissible, in particular, if a person poses a grave danger to his own life or health. Hospitalization may be ordered only if the danger cannot be averted by less drastic measures.

2. *Application:* Competent administrative authority of the district.

3. *Decision-making authority:* Local authority.

4. *Medical examination:* The expert opinion of a medical practitioner of the health authority is required, and the practitioner must also explain why hospitalization cannot be avoided through other remedies (detention as *ultima ratio*).

5. *Treatment programme:* Treatment is given in a psychiatric hospital or other suitable institution, such as institutions for alcohol-dependent or other addicted persons, which may be entirely unlike a psychiatric hospital in their structure. Hospitals are obliged to admit the person to be detained if they dispose of the necessary facilities for keeping him in safe custody. The person detained is entitled to be treated as a patient and to receive the "necessary curative treatment".

6. *Length of stay:* When a person is detained under the Law, the court order stipulates a fixed period that must not exceed six months.

7. *Appeal:* There is a "right of immediate appeal" against the court decision.

8. *Periodic review:* Every six months.

9. *Discharge procedure(s):* Sections 32–35.

Federal Republic of Germany (Hamburg)

Legislation: Law of 22 September 1977 on assistance and protective measures in connection with mental diseases.

1. *Grounds:* Persons suffering from a psychosis, a mental disorder similar in effect to a psychosis, drug dependence, or mental retardation may be committed only if, and only for such time as, their behaviour towards themselves or others as a result of their disorder or disease constitutes an imminent threat to public safety and order that cannot be averted by any other means, or if their behaviour constitutes a constant and unavoidable threat that they will commit suicide or seriously damage their health. Unwillingness to undergo treatment does not itself constitute grounds for commitment.

2. *Application:* Competent administrative authority of the district.

3. *Decision-making authority:* Local court.

4. *Medical examination:* Expert appraisal of person's condition.

5. *Treatment programme:* Assistance to mental patients should consist of personal medical and psychosocial counselling and care adapted to the patient's condition and designed to enable him to live in the community in a manner compatible with human dignity. Such assistance is also to include support of persons dwelling with mental patients, by means of counselling and instruction as to appropriate methods of care. Assistance must take the form of prophylactic and follow-up care.

Prophylactic care must ensure that, where a disorder or incipient mental disease is detected, the patient receives medical treatment in good time, that the treatment is accompanied by suitable social welfare assistance, and that, where possible, the patient is not removed from his normal living environment.

Treatment that involves surgery or that seriously endangers the patient's life or health or that entails a major or long-term change in the patient's personality may be carried out only with the patient's consent (or, in certain cases, that of his legal representative), and only if the treatment is commensurate with the anticipated results. Consent to treatment that would modify fundamental aspects of the patient's personality is not permitted.

6. *Length of stay:* Not exceeding one year.

7. *Appeal:* Not stated.

8. *Periodic review:* Any decision to extend the period by more than one year must be made by a review procedure instituted before the end of the one-year period.

9. *Discharge procedure(s):* Section 41.

Hungary

Legislation: Ordinance-Law No. 10 of 1974 on the compulsory treatment of alcoholics in institutions.

1. *Grounds:* Any alcoholic who, as a result of his behaviour caused by regular and abusive consumption of alcohol, endangers his family, the development of any of his children who have not attained the age of majority, or the safety of his associates, or who seriously and repeatedly disturbs the public order or professional activities at his workplace, may be immediately ordered to undergo treatment in an occupational therapy centre (referred to hereafter as "institutional treatment"):

   (a) if he does not submit voluntarily to alcoholic detoxification treatment and it may be assumed that treatment carried out in a clinic or in a service for alcoholic detoxification will be ineffective; or

   (b) if it may be assumed, on the basis of observations made during an earlier course of treatment that has been completed or intentionally interrupted less than two years previously, that treatment carried out in a clinic or in a service for alcoholic detoxification will be ineffective.

2. *Application:* Public prosecutor, but any state agency or social agency (institution, establishment, undertaking, etc.) attached to a health agency, any cooperative, or the person concerned may request that the necessary proceedings be instituted.

3. *Decision-making authority:* The regional court (or the municipal court or court of an urban ward) decides on the imposition of institutional treatment on the basis of a petition submitted by the public prosecutor, on the proposal of the specialized administrative agency responsible for health matters to the executive committee of the council.

4. *Medical examination:* The regional court decides on the petition following a special procedure and with the cooperation of people's assessors, as follows:

   (a) the health agency must procure and attach to its proposition all the evidence (expert medical opinions, documents relating to prior treatment and other hospital records, etc., documents dealing with the upkeep of the family or children of the person concerned, the results of an on-the-spot inquiry, etc.) necessary for the examination of the petition;

   (b) an expert medical opinion must be obtained before a proposal for institutional treatment can be submitted. This opinion must be drawn up by a medicolegal expert, who may be specially designated for the purpose. The person for whom the procedure has been initiated must be required to undergo an examination by the expert;

   (c) the health agency must communicate the results of the proceedings in writing to the public prosecutor, the person for whom the procedure has been initiated, and the person who initiated the procedure.

5. *Treatment programme:* On the basis of a medical report, the director of the institution

must determine the nature of the treatment that the institutionalized person must undergo and the nature of the work for which he is fitted.

Work carried out within the institution must be remunerated in accordance with the special provisions in force.

The institutionalized person must submit to the treatment and perform the work to which he is assigned. Coercive measures may be used in dispensing the treatment.

During institutional treatment, the occupational status of the institutionalized person, or his rights and obligations arising from his status as a member of a cooperative, must be suspended; however, the period spent in the institution must be taken into account in calculating the period of time devoted to the person's occupation or membership of a cooperative.

Institutional treatment may be repeated on several occasions. A single course of treatment may not, however, be extended over a period of more than two years.

The following may not be ordered to undergo institutional treatment:

(*a*) persons under 18 years of age;

(*b*) persons requiring hospital treatment or who are suffering from another disease that is incompatible with the application of occupational therapy treatment or on account of which it may be assumed that the latter treatment will prove ineffective.

6. *Length of stay:* See paragraph 9.

7. *Appeal:* The institutionalized person and the public prosecutor may appeal against the decision of the regional court. The appeal must be heard on an extraordinary basis. The decision ordering institutional treatment is enforceable irrespective of the appeal proceedings.

8. *Periodic review:* See paragraph 9.

9. *Discharge procedure(s):* The need of the person for inpatient treatment must be determined, and the person committed to the institution must be discharged where:

(*a*) the continuation of the treatment is not necessary;

(*b*) circumstances arise that are incompatible with the continuation of the treatment or it may be assumed that the continuation of the treatment will prove ineffective;

(*c*) a period of two years has elapsed since the commencement of the treatment.

The regional court decides as to the termination of institutional treatment on the basis of medical findings.

Indonesia

Legislation: Law No. 9 of 1976 on narcotics.

1. *Grounds:* There are two categories of narcotic addicts, as follows:

(*a*) under-age narcotic addicts;

(*b*) adult narcotic addicts.

"Narcotic addict" is someone who utilizes narcotics and is in a state of dependence on narcotics, physically as well as mentally, resulting from the use or abuse of narcotics.

"Rehabilitation" is an endeavour to make a narcotic addict recover so that he regains his physical and mental health in order to readapt to his living environment and improve his dexterity, knowledge, and skill.

2. *Application:* Parents or guardians are obliged to report an under-age addict to an official assigned by the Minister of Health and are obliged to bring him to a hospital or to the nearest physician to receive necessary medication and nursing.

Adult narcotic addicts are obliged to report themselves to an official assigned by the Minister of Health.

The establishment, organization, and function of rehabilitation institutions and branches are determined by the President. Involvement of private and government community agencies is sought.

3. *Decision-making authority:* Minister of Health.

4. *Medical examination:* Not stated.

5. *Treatment programme:* Medication and nursing of narcotic addicts and rehabilitation of ex-addicts is to be carried out in rehabilitation institutions.

6. *Length of stay:* Not stated.

7. *Appeal:* Not stated.

8. *Periodic review:* Not stated.

9. *Discharge procedure(s):* Not stated.

Iraq

Legislation: Regulation No. 1 of 8 January 1981 on the Medical Centre for the Treatment of Alcohol and Drug Dependence, Ibn Rushd Hospital.

Note: Iraq has no law on commitment for treatment on mental health grounds, but a draft law has been under consideration for some years and is described in detail in the 1977 WHO study (5). The Regulation of 1981 deals with the specialized centre at the Ibn Rushd Hospital for Psychiatric Medicine, but it also indicates that the provisions are applicable to all other health-care facilities providing treatment for alcohol and drug dependence.

1. *Grounds:* The Regulation applies to any "drug-dependent person" and covers alcohol and other substance abuse quite broadly. A drug-dependent person is one who consumes drugs or alcohol to such an extent that he has reached a stage of manifest physical and mental disorder that interferes with his mental and physical health or

with the requirements of his economic life, or displays symptoms to a degree that necessitates medical treatment.

2. *Application:* Patients may be admitted either involuntarily or informally at the request of the patient.

3. *Decision-making authority:* Not clearly stated.

4. *Medical examination:* Involuntarily admitted patients are subject to examination by the medical committee of the centre or hospital.

5. *Treatment programme:* The patient is treated by a team consisting of a consultant psychiatrist, a resident physician at the centre, a clinical psychologist, a social worker, a rehabilitation therapist, and a nurse. Treatment includes both individual and group therapy. The patient must follow instructions regarding rehabilitation or be transferred to a locked ward.

6. *Length of stay:* Between 30 and 90 days.

7. *Appeal:* Not stated.

8. *Periodic review:* Not stated.

9. *Discharge procedure:* The consultant psychiatrist may discharge the patient at any time. Appointments for subsequent check-ups are arranged at the centre's outpatient department.

Italy

Legislation: Law No. 685 of 22 December 1975 on control of narcotic drugs and psychotropic substances, prevention and cure of dependence on such drugs or substances and rehabilitation of persons dependent on them.

1. *Grounds:* Person using narcotic drugs or psychotropic substances for personal, non-therapeutic purposes who has been reported by a medical practitioner (or police authorities), but who has not voluntarily undergone therapeutic and rehabilitative treatment or has interrupted treatment before having completed it.

2. *Application:* Any medical and social assistance centre or police authority may notify the local magistrate who, after hearing the person concerned and obtaining relevant information, if he considers the situation an emergency (or upon any notification from parents or other relatives of the person), must notify the judicial authorities.

3. *Decision-making authority:* Whenever the judicial authorities perceive the need for medical treatment and assistance, they must in every case, after the person concerned and the competent medical and social welfare centre have been heard, make an order for the admission of the person concerned to a hospital, other than a psychiatric hospital, if this is absolutely necessary, or for appropriate outpatient or home treatment. In every case, the judicial authorities must place the person to be assisted in the charge of the treatment centre, which must take the necessary action and report thereon at least every three months to the said authorities.

Except in the case of a minor, where competence lies with the juvenile court of the locality where the minor resides, a specialized division of the civil court having its seat at the headquarters of the court of appeal district in which the person to be assisted resides is the appropriate judicial body.

4. *Medical examination:* The competent medical and social welfare centre must give its opinion.

5. *Treatment programme:* The person concerned must be placed in the charge of the centre for the presumed duration of the treatment and assistance necessary for his social reintegration. If, when medical treatment as an outpatient has been ordered, the person concerned interrupts the treatment and refuses to resume it, the judicial authorities may order his admission to a suitable hospital, other than a psychiatric hospital.

6. *Length of stay:* See paragraph 5 above.

7. *Appeal:* An appeal against the order may be made within 30 days of its communication. A decision on the appeal must be taken, in the order of their respective competences, by the juvenile division of the court of appeal or a specialized division of the civil court of appeal consisting of a judge of the Court of Cassation.

8. *Periodic review:* The measures indicated above may be modified at any time. They must be revoked as soon as it is possible to assume that the person concerned is no longer in need of care and assistance. Treatment centres must report at least every three months to the judicial authorities on action taken in the course of treatment.

9. *Discharge procedure(s):* See paragraph 8 above.

Japan

Legislation: Narcotic Control Law (Law No. 14 of 17 March 1953), as amended.

1. *Grounds:* Narcotic addiction or suspicion of narcotic addiction.

"Narcotic addict" means a person who is in a state of narcotic addiction.

"Narcotic addiction" means chronic intoxication with narcotic drugs, cannabis, or opium.

Note: Compulsory hospital admission for stimulant addiction (e.g., to amphetamines, ephedrine) was ordered under the Mental Health Law (Law No. 123 of 1 May 1950, as amended). Under this Law, the term "mentally disordered persons" includes persons who are psychotic as a result of intoxication.

2. *Application:* The governor of the Metropolis, Hokkaido or Prefecture may, in cases where he considers it necessary with respect to a narcotic addict or a person who is suspected to be a narcotic addict, order a "medical examiner of mental health" to examine such person.

3. *Decision-making authority:* The governor of the Metropolis, Hokkaido or Prefecture may, when he finds, as a result of the medical examination, that the medical examinee is a narcotic addict and, if not hospitalized, is particularly liable to use repeatedly a narcotic drug, cannabis or opium owing to his narcotic addiction, hospitalize such examinee in the hospital designated by Ministry of Health and Welfare Ordinance, where he must undergo the necessary medical treatment.

4. *Medical examination:* In order to conduct the medical examination, a medical examiner may enter the place of residence of the examinee. The medical examiner, in the conduct of the medical examination, must be careful not to hurt the honour of the medical examinee and afford such examinee an opportunity of expressing his opinion on the question of his addiction.

5. *Treatment programme:* The necessary medical treatment must be provided.

6. *Length of stay:* If the person is a narcotic addict, the medical examiner of mental health provisionally determines the period of hospitalization, which must not exceed 30 days, pending the governor's decision to hospitalize. The administrator of a hospital for treatment of narcotic addicts must, if he finds it necessary to continue hospitalization for longer than the period determined by the medical examiner of mental health, report the reason therefor and the period of further hospitalization necessary to the Narcotic Addiction Examination Committee, and request the Committee to examine whether the reason and the period are adequate or not.

7. *Appeal:* Not stated.

8. *Periodic review:* The Narcotic Addiction Examination Committee must, if it has been so requested, examine questions concerning further hospitalization and report its decisions thereon to the governor of the Metropolis, Hokkaido or Prefecture as expeditiously as possible. In this case, the Narcotic Addiction Examination Committee must, when it considers it appropriate to discharge the hospitalized addict in question prior to the expiration of the period determined by the medical examiner of mental health, report the date when the hospitalized addict is to be discharged to the governor of the Metropolis, Hokkaido or Prefecture.

The Narcotic Addiction Examination Committee must, if it makes an examination under the preceding paragraph, hear the opinions of the hospitalized addict in question and the medical practitioner in charge of the treatment of the hospitalized addict.

9. *Discharge procedure(s):* The governor of the Metropolis, Hokkaido or Prefecture must, in accordance with the decision of the Narcotic Addict Examination Committee, discharge the hospitalized addict in question, or decide the period of hospitalization of the hospitalized addict and notify the period to the administrator of the hospital for the treatment of narcotic addiction. The period of hospitalization under these provisions must not exceed three months from the day on which the hospitalization of the hospitalized addict began. The period of hospitalization may not exceed six months in all.

Malaysia

Legislation: The Dangerous Drugs Act (No. 234 of 1952) (revised 1980).

1. *Grounds:* Any person reasonably suspected of being drug-dependent.

   "Drug-dependant" means a person who through the use of any dangerous drug undergoes a psychic and sometimes physical state which is characterized by behavioural and other responses including the compulsion to take the drug on a continuous or periodic basis in order to experience its psychic effect and to avoid the discomfort of its absence.

2. *Application:* Any social welfare officer or any police officer not below the rank of sergeant or an officer in charge of a police station may take into his custody any person whom he reasonably suspects to be a drug dependant and must within 24 hours produce such person before a magistrate.

3. *Decision-making authority:* If the magistrate has reasonable cause to believe that the person so brought before him is a drug dependant, he may order such person to be remanded and be medically examined or observed by a medical officer at a detention centre.

4. *Medical examination:* As a result of such medical examination or observation, such person can be certified to be a drug dependant.

5. *Treatment programme:* The magistrate has two options:

   (a) if it appears necessary for such person to undergo treatment and rehabilitation at a rehabilitation centre, he may order such person to attend a rehabilitation centre for a period of six months; or

   (b) if it appears unnecessary for such person to undergo treatment and rehabilitation at a rehabilitation centre, he may order such person to be supervised by a social welfare officer for a period of two years.

6. *Length of stay:* The period of detention in a rehabilitation centre is six months, with the provisos that:

   (a) the Board of Visitors of a rehabilitation centre may, in its absolute discretion, shorten the period of detention for reasons that appear to it to be sufficient, if such person has already completed a period of four months in a rehabilitation centre; and

   (b) no such person must be released from a rehabilitation centre during the first four months of the period of detention without the consent of the Minister of Welfare Services in writing.

   Note: Where any person below the age of 21 years is found guilty of an offence against the Dangerous Drug Act, the Court may, with or without recording a conviction:

   (i) release the offender on probation to be supervised by a social welfare officer for a period of two years; or

   (ii) require him to undergo treatment and rehabilitation at a rehabilitation centre for a period of six months.

7. *Appeal:* Not stated.

8. *Periodic review:* See paragraph 6. If the person in charge of a rehabilitation centre is satisfied that a resident, whose period of detention therein is about to expire, needs

further treatment and rehabilitation he may, if the Board of Visitors of the rehabilitation centre consents, detain him for a further period not exceeding six months.

9. *Discharge procedure(s):* After discharge from the rehabilitation centre the person must be under the "aftercare" of a social welfare officer (or delegate) for two years.

The Board of Visitors of a rehabilitation centre may, if it is satisfied that a person against whom an aftercare order is in force has failed to comply with any requirement of the order, recall such person to the rehabilitation centre; if he fails to return, such person may be arrested by a police officer, returned to the rehabilitation centre, and detained for a further period not exceeding six months.

Mexico

Legislation: Regulations of 23 July 1976 concerning narcotic drugs and psychotropic substances.

1. *Grounds:* Drug-dependent person.

"Drug-dependent person" means any person who, other than for therapeutic purposes, habitually uses, or experiences the need to use, any narcotic or psychotropic substance.

2. *Application:* Qualified medical personnel who treat cases of drug addiction must report such cases to the nearest office of the Ministry of Health and Welfare within eight days of the date on which the case comes to their attention, enclosing their diagnosis and opinion on the need for intervention by the Ministry.

3. *Decision-making authority:* When so required, the Ministry of Health and Welfare may order the patient to be admitted to any of the institutions referred to in the Regulations.

4. *Medical examination:* Not stated.

5. *Treatment programme:* The Ministry of Health and Welfare must issue and publicize a national directory of institutions providing treatment services for drug addicts. The Ministry will proceed to locate known addicts and provide them with medical care.

For the purpose of controlling drug addiction, it is the responsibility of the Ministry of Health and Welfare:

(*a*) to issue general standards for treatment;

(*b*) to provide medical care for invalid drug addicts in accordance with the law;

(*c*) to act in an advisory capacity in treatment of this nature, when so requested;

(*d*) to create, promote, and augment the establishments or services providing medical care in this area.

Qualified medical personnel who treat drug addicts must observe the general standards for treatment issued by the Ministry of Health and Welfare.

6. *Length of stay:* Not stated.

7. *Appeal:* Not stated.

8. *Periodic review:* Not stated.

9. *Discharge procedure(s):* Not stated.

Norway

Legislation: Two separate laws are in force, namely the Mental Health Law of 1961, as amended, and the Law of 1932 concerning temperance committees, as amended.

A. *Mental Health Law of 1961.*

Note: Persons who abuse intoxicating or tranquillizing substances other than alcohol—when the circumstances mentioned hereafter are present—may be committed to sanatoria for a period of up to two years.

1. *Grounds:* A person suffering from mental illness may be admitted to hospital without his own consent if his nearest relatives or the public authorities have so requested and if the medical superintendent is of the opinion that hospitalization: (*a*) will be beneficial to the patient; (*b*) is necessary for public order; or (*c*) may prevent serious danger to the life or health of others.

Note: No one can be admitted under the above provisions if the nearest relatives oppose such admission, unless the medical superintendent decides that, because of the patient's mental condition, admission is necessary for the patient's own protection, that the possibility of cure or essential improvement would otherwise be lost, or that the patient constitutes a serious danger to himself or others.

Mental illness is not defined in the Law.

2. *Application:* Nearest relatives or the public authorities.

3. *Decision-making authority:* The medical superintendent. Evidence likely to be of importance in the decision can be taken and recorded. If a person is to be hospitalized without his consent, the patient or any other person acting on his behalf must be given the opportunity of making a statement before the decision is made.

4. *Medical examination:* The doctor, following personal examination, must find it necessary that the patient—at the request of his nearest relatives or the public authority—be hospitalized or kept in hospital or any other place where responsible care can be provided, but not for more than three weeks without the patient's expressed consent.

The doctor must make it clear to the patient that he may appeal against the decision to the Control Commission (see below). The appeal has no delaying effect unless the doctor decides to the contrary.

5. *Treatment programme:* Not stated.

6. *Length of stay:* No more than three weeks.

7. *Appeal:* See paragraph 4 above. The patient, his nearest relatives or the authorities—whichever requested hospitalization—may appeal to the Control Commission (composed of one judge, one doctor, and two other members) against the decision of the medical superintendent. This also applies if the medical superintendent has refused to admit or to keep the patient. The appeal should not have any delaying effect, provided that the Control Commission does not decide otherwise.

If a person is admitted to or kept in hospital under these provisions, the medical superintendent must immediately inform the Control Commission. If the patient has been admitted to or kept in hospital at the request of the authorities, the medical superintendent must also inform the nearest relatives. The patient and the nearest relatives must always be informed of the right of appeal to the Control Commission with regard to admission and discharge as well as complaints relating to treatment.

8. *Periodic review:* See paragraph 7 above.

9. *Discharge procedure(s):* Application for discharge may be made by the patient himself or, if he is incapable of so doing, by his nearest relatives. When discharge has been requested, the patient may not be kept in hospital unless the medical superintendent considers that, if discharged, he would constitute a danger to himself, or that the possibility of cure or essential improvement would be lost, or that the patient, because of his mental condition, might then suffer or that he would constitute a significant danger to the life or health of others.

B. *Law of 1932 concerning temperance committees.*

1. *Grounds:* Person residing or living in the municipality who by reason of excessive use of liquors or other intoxicating or tranquillizing substances is an obvious danger to himself and his surroundings. The temperance committee must without delay investigate such cases. The committee may also on its own initiative take action against such persons and make investigations.

2. *Application:* The following are entitled to make a request to the temperance committee for commitment:

   (*a*) the person concerned or his spouse, relatives in the direct line, brothers and sisters or in-laws of equal relationship, and—if applicable—guardian or public trustee; the relationship between foster parents and adopted children and their relatives in the direct line of descent is considered as the equivalent of consanguinity;

   (*b*) a person or doctor, provided the request is made with the consent of the person concerned or with that of any relative mentioned under (*a*);

   (*c*) assistance societies and protection and parole societies or the police.

Under regulations later adopted by the Ministry of Health, the police are required to report to the committee concerned all punishable cases of drunkenness.

3. *Decision-making authority:* There are two procedures:

   (*a*) The temperance committee can—where a doctor deems it necessary—compel the person concerned to submit to examination or a course of treatment in a hospital selected by the temperance committee, for a period not exceeding 30 days. After consultation with the doctor in charge of the hospital, the committee can order extension of the stay in hospital by up to 30 days at a time, provided the total period of hospitalization ordered by the committee does not exceed 90 days in the course of one year.

(b) If the person does not obey the orders given by the committee, or if it should otherwise be found necessary, the committee may decide to commit him, whether he consents thereto or not, to an inebriate sanatorium for a maximum period of two years if, as a result of excessive use of intoxicating liquors or narcotics; he:

(i) ill-treats his spouse or his children or exposes his children to moral debasement or neglect;

(ii) neglects his duty to support his family according to the laws in force;

(iii) exposes himself to serious physical or mental harm, exposes himself or other persons to danger, or repeatedly molests his surroundings;

(iv) becomes a burden on the Public Welfare Board or on his family;

(v) squanders or dissipates his possessions to such an extent that he himself or his family are likely to fall into need.

Note: When the temperance committee finds that a case should be dealt with under this provision, the committee forwards the decision and other documents of the case to the judge and requests him to preside over the proceedings. The person against whom proceedings are taken must be summoned for examination. If he fails to appear without reason the committee may have him detained by the police.

4. *Medical examination:* See paragraph 3(a) and (b) above. When decisions are made providing for compulsory committal to an inebriate sanatorium, a doctor's certificate should be made available. If the medical certificate leaves any doubt as to whether the person concerned is insane, the committee may decide that he be made to undergo a psychiatric examination.

5. *Treatment programme:* Not stated.

6. *Length of stay:* Not exceeding 90 days in one year for treatment in hospital; maximum of two years if committed to a sanatorium.

7. *Appeal:* Appeals against decisions (providing for action under paragraph 3 above) may be made to the Supreme Court by the person against whom the decision is made. With the consent of the Judicial Committee on Appeals, the case may be brought before the Supreme Court. Such consent should not be given unless it is considered likely that the decision will be changed. The time limit for appeals is two weeks.

When it has been decided to commit a person to an inebriate sanatorium and there is reason to fear that he may do serious injury to himself or others, the committee may have him taken into custody irrespective of the appeal. The committee may request the public prosecutor to order the arrest of the person.

Decisions otherwise made by the temperance committee or its chairman may be taken to the Judicial Committee on Appeals of the Supreme Court by the person against whom they are made.

8. *Periodic review:* Not specified.

9. *Discharge procedure(s):* A person who has been committed to an inebriate sanatorium under this Law may be discharged on probation before the expiry of the period for which he was committed if there are grounds for assuming that he will lead a sober and orderly life.

Pakistan

Note: There is no specific legislation on either voluntary or compulsory treatment of drug-dependent persons but a proposed amendment to the Mental Health Code recommends treatment for such persons.

Peru

Legislation: Decree-Law No. 22095 of 21 Feburary 1978.

1. *Grounds:* Drug addiction (not defined).

2. *Application:* By the drug-dependent person, his relatives, or "judicial authority".

3. *Decision-making authority:* Judge, at the request of the Ministry of Public Health or any interested person.

4. *Medical examination:* The condition of the drug addict is determined only after an examination by a medicolegal physician at the request of the competent judge. This examination takes into account: (*a*) the nature and amount of substances that produced the dependence; and (*b*) the history and clinical situation of the person.

5. *Treatment programme:* There are two components:

   (*a*) medical detoxification; and

   (*b*) biopsychosocial rehabilitation.

   In order to carry out this treatment, "specialized treatment services" must be established.

6. *Length of stay:* Not stated.

7. *Appeal:* Not stated.

8. *Periodic review:* Not stated.

9. *Discharge procedure(s):* Not stated.

Singapore

Legislation: The Misuse of Drugs Act of 16 March 1973 (No. 5 of 1973, as amended) to provide for the control of dangerous or otherwise harmful drugs and for the purposes connected therewith.

1. *Grounds:* Persons who are suspected by the Director of the Central Narcotics Bureau

of being a drug addict and after medical examination or urine tests it appears necessary for the person to undergo treatment or rehabilitation or both.

"Drug addict" means a person who through use of any controlled drug:

(a) has developed a desire or need to continue to take such controlled drug; or

(b) has developed a psychological or physical dependence upon the effect of such controlled drug.

2. *Application:* The Director of the Central Narcotics Bureau may require any person whom he reasonably suspects to be a drug addict to be medically examined or observed by a Government medical officer or a medical practitioner.

3. *Decision-making authority:* The Director of the Central Narcotics Bureau.

4. *Medical examination:* Required if treatment appears necessary. If, as a result of such examination or observation or as a result of a urine test, it appears to the Director of the Central Narcotics Bureau that it is necessary for any person to undergo treatment or rehabilitation or both at an approved institution, the Director may make an order in writing requiring that person to be admitted for such purpose to an approved institution.

5. *Treatment programme:* Except as otherwise provided, every inmate must, upon completion of his medical examination, undergo a period of detoxification during which no medication is given unless, in the opinion of a medical officer, it is necesssary to save the inmate's life. The period of detoxification must not exceed seven days.

No inmate who is above the age of 55 years must be made to undergo detoxification.

No inmate who is certified by a medical officer to be medically unfit to undergo detoxification may be made to do so until such time as a medical officer finds him fit enough for it.

The Minister of Home Affairs may for special reasons exempt any inmate from undergoing detoxification.

An approved institution may admit any drug addict for voluntary treatment.

6. *Length of stay:* Six months unless discharged earlier by the Director of the Central Narcotic Bureau or the Review Committee of an approved institution. If the latter is of the opinion that an inmate whose period of detention in the institution concerned is about to expire requires further treatment or rehabilitation or both, the Committee may by order in writing direct that the inmate be detained in the institution for a further period or periods not exceeding six months at any one time.

No person in respect of whom an order has been made may be detained in an approved institution or institutions for a period of more than three years after his admission to any approved institution pursuant to such order.

7. *Appeal:* Where a complaint is made on oath to a magistrate that any person is improperly detained in an approved institution by reason of any misconduct or breach of duty on the part of any officer in the discharge of his functions pursuant to the Act or any regulations made thereunder, the magistrate may either inquire into the complaint himself or direct a police officer to make an inquiry for the purpose of ascertaining the truth or falsehood of the complaint and report to him the result of the inquiry.

Every inquiry so made is to be conducted in private, but the procedure for conducting any inquiry must be such as the magistrate considers appropriate in the circumstances of the case.

A magistrate or a police officer conducting any such inquiry has all the powers conferred on him by the Criminal Procedure Code in relation to the attendance and examination of witnesses, the taking of evidence and the production of documents.

If, after considering the result of any such inquiry, the magistrate is satisfied that any person who is detained in an approved institution ought not to be so detained he may make an order for the discharge of that person from the approved institution and that person must be discharged accordingly. Any order or decision of the Magistrate so made is final.

No evidence taken for the purpose of any such inquiry is admissible in any civil or criminal proceedings where the person who gave such evidence is charged with giving or fabricating false evidence.

8. *Periodic review:* The Minister must appoint for any approved institution or institutions a Review Committee (see paragraph 6 above).

The Review Committee of an approved institution must keep the case of every inmate under review and, as often as practicable, consider whether he should be discharged.

The Director of the Central Narcotics Bureau or the Review Committee of an approved institution may at any time by order in writing:

(*a*) discharge any inmate;

(*b*) transfer any inmate from one approved institution to another approved institution.

9. *Discharge procedure(s):* See paragraphs 6 and 8 above.

Somalia

Legislation: Law No. 46 of 3 March 1970 concerning the production of, trade in, and use of narcotic drugs.

1. *Grounds:* Serious mental deterioration caused by the habitual improper use of narcotic drugs, if the person concerned in any way endangers himself or others.

2. *Application:* Police authorities or other interested party.

3. *Decision-making authority:* Not stated.

4. *Medical examination:* Upon receipt of medical report.

5. *Treatment programme:* Not stated.

6. *Length of stay:* Not stated.

7. *Appeal:* Not stated.

8. *Periodic review:* Not stated.

9. *Discharge procedure(s):* Not stated.

Sweden

Legislation: Two separate laws are in force.

A. *Law of 1 January 1982 on care of alcoholics and drug abusers.*

1. *Grounds:* If any person, owing to the persistent abuse of alcohol or narcotic drugs, urgently needs care in order to discontinue the abuse, and such care cannot be provided under the Social Services Law of 1980 or any other enactment, he may be provided with care under the above Law with or without his consent, if one of the following situations also exists:

   (*a*) the individual concerned is seriously endangering his physical or mental health through the abuse; or

   (*b*) he is liable to inflict serious harm on himself or on some person near to him through the abuse.

   A police authority may take an alcoholic or drug abuser into custody immediately if:

   (i) he can probably be given care pursuant to this Law; and

   (ii) it is impossible to wait for a court order for care to be made since there will presumably be a grave deterioration in his health status unless he receives immediate care, or because there is an imminent risk, due to his condition, of his inflicting serious harm on himself or on some person near to him.

   After the county administration has applied for care pursuant to the Law, the court may also make an order for the alcoholic or drug abuser to be taken into custody immediately.

2. *Application:* The county administration must investigate whether there is cause for a person to be provided with care pursuant to the Law. If such cause is thought to exist, the county administration must apply for care.

   The application must include an account of the abuser's circumstances and of measures taken previously. It must also indicate the care that the county administration considers necessary, where that care should commence and to which home admission is possible.

3. *Decision-making authority:* Orders concerning the provision of care pursuant to this Law are made by a county court.

   The care order made by the court must be executed by the social welfare committee.

   If care has not commenced within two weeks after the day on which the court order acquired force of law, the order lapses.

4. *Medical examination:* A medical certificate indicating the abuser's current health status

must be produced during the proceedings. In the absence of any special impediment, the county administration must append such a certificate to its application.

If the question has arisen whether a person should be provided with care under this Law, the county administration must order a medical examination and appoint a physician for this purpose. If the county administration's application for a care order does not include a medical certificate, the court itself may arrange for a medical examination to be carried out. Orders requiring a medical examination may not be contested.

5. *Treatment programme:* The function of the social services, as laid down in Section 1 of the Social Services Law of 1980, is to guide all care designed to help individuals to discontinue the abuse of alcohol or narcotic drugs. Care must be based on respect for the self-determination and privacy of the individual, and must as far as possible be planned and conducted in partnership with the individual.

Under Section 11 of the Law of 1 January 1982, care pursuant to this Law is to be provided through homes run by county councils or municipalities and which, in keeping with the plan indicated in Section 23 of the Social Services Act of 1980, are specially intended for the provision of care under this Law. Every such home must have a governing body.

Care must commence in hospital if this is judged appropriate with regard to the care otherwise planned and if the preconditions for hospital care are satisfied. Should any person during the care period require medical care that cannot be provided by the home, care must be continued in hospital.

A person taken into custody, as provided for in Section 8 of the Law, must without delay be provided with care in a home referred to in Section 11, or, in the cases referred to above, in hospital. It is the responsibility of the social welfare committee to arrange such care after the police authority has reported that a person has been taken into custody.

Decisions concerning admission to and discharge from homes referred to in Section 11 of the Law are to be made by the governing body or the person in charge of care at the home concerned.

6. *Length of stay:* Under Section 7 of the Law, care pursuant to it must terminate as soon as its purpose has been achieved and not more than two months after its commencement, unless an extension order has previously been made, as provided for in Section 16. Care is terminated by a discharge order, as laid down in Section 13.

Section 15 of the Law lays down that a person receiving care pursuant to it should be given the opportunity, as soon as possible with regard to the care that has been planned, of leaving the home to which he has been admitted pursuant to Section 13 in order to receive another form of care or to live in his own home on a trial basis.

Section 16 of the Law prescribes that the care period may be extended by up to two months if the inmate needs further care on account of his health status or if there are other special reasons for an extension.

Extension orders are made by the governing body of the home concerned. The power to make such orders may not be delegated.

Immediate custody orders take effect at once. Administrative appeals against judicial custody orders can be made at any time.

Transfer orders pursuant to Section 13, subsection 2, may be made with immediate effect if this is necessary for reasons connected with care. Other orders by the governing body or any other person responsible for care at a home referred to in Section 11 take effect immediately.

The court may rule that an order made by the court is to take effect immediately.

7. *Appeal:* Not stated.

8. *Periodic review:* Not stated.

9. *Discharge procedure(s):* Not stated.

Note: Under Section 31, if a person for whom care has been provided pursuant to the Law is suspected of a criminal offence not punishable by more than one year's imprisonment, and if the offence was committed before care began or during the care period and is a matter for public prosecution, the prosecutor must consider whether it is appropriate for proceedings to be taken. The governing body of the home where the suspect is being cared for or, if the care has been concluded, the county administration, must be consulted in this matter unless such consultation is unnecessary.

B. *Law No. 511 of 10 June 1976 concerning the detention of intoxicated persons.*

Note: This Law repeals an Ordinance of 1841 on drunkenness.

1. *Grounds:* Any person found in an indoor or outdoor public place, in a state of intoxication caused by alcoholic beverages or other intoxicants, may be detained by a policeman if his condition renders him unable to look after himself or otherwise dangerous to himself or to others.

2. *Application:* Detention by police.

3. *Decision-making authority:* Police.

4. *Medical examination:* If his condition so requires, the person must undergo a medical examination as soon as possible and, if necessary, be hospitalized.

5. *Treatment programme:* If it is found that the person is in need of social aid or assistance, the police are required to provide him with advice and information, and, where convenient, to consult other social welfare bodies responsible for meeting such needs. Alcoholic drinks or other intoxicants found on persons detained under this Law are normally to be confiscated, this requirement being likewise applicable to syringes or cannulas that may be used for injecting substances into the body.

6. *Length of stay:* The person may not normally be detained for longer than eight hours.

7. *Appeal:* Not stated.

8. *Periodic review:* Not stated.

9. *Discharge procedure(s):* See paragraph 6 above.

Switzerland (Geneva)

Legislation: Law of 3 December 1971 on the treatment and commitment of alcoholics.

Note: This Law repeals the Law of 18 June 1927 on the same subject.

1. *Grounds:* Any person who, as a result of abuse of alcohol, jeopardizes his health or his own or his family's material or moral well-being, constitutes a danger to himself or to others, or acts in a way which is prejudicial to third parties or to the public order.

2. *Application:* The spouse, parents, children, or siblings of an alcoholic, or any judicial or administrative authority, is entitled to seek the intervention of the Guardianship Court. The Guardianship Court is entrusted with the implementation of this Law and must assign one of its members to conduct inquiries and take preventive measures.

3. *Decision-making authority:* The Guardianship Court, which orders one of the following measures to be taken:

   (*a*) an expert medical appraisal, the results of which are to be communicated to the person concerned, who may seek a second opinion;

   (*b*) outpatient or inpatient medical treatment;

   (*c*) commitment to an institution.

   The Court may, where necessary, call on the assistance of the police in order to compel the alcoholic to appear before it.

4. *Medical examination:* The Guardianship Court may, depending on the results of the inquiry, invite the person concerned to undergo a medical examination, and attempt to persuade him to undergo medical treatment on a voluntary basis and to take all measures deemed adequate. If the preventive measures prove to be of no avail, or if the case is sufficiently urgent or serious, the Guardianship Court grants a hearing (or rehearing) to the person, if this is feasible, and extends the inquiry as required.

5. *Treatment programme:* Medical treatment.

6. *Length of stay:* The normal duration of commitment is six months and may not exceed one year, although the Court may order a maximum extension of one year if it deems this necessary in the light of a medical opinion and a report from the director of the institution. The period of commitment may be fixed at two years if the person concerned has undergone two complete or partial periods of compulsory commitment within the five years preceding the opening of the proceedings.

7. *Appeal:* The person concerned may appeal to a panel of three judges belonging to the Court of Justice within ten days following receipt of the notification of commitment.

8. *Periodic review:* The Court may at any time cancel or suspend a measure that it has ordered, or substitute a different measure, and is empowered to order a stay of execution of a commitment order, on condition that the person concerned abstains from all consumption of alcohol. The stay of execution is rescinded if the conditions upon which it is contingent are not complied with.

9. *Discharge procedure(s):* A probation committee may be established with responsibility for the surveillance of persons who are discharged from a treatment establishment. The probation period may not exceed two years.

A special commission, known as the Commission for Surveillance of Convicted Alcoholics, is responsible for the surveillance of persons committed to institutions for alcoholics or to hospitals by decision of a penal court. The Commission is authorized:

(a) to order a person's discharge as soon as he is regarded as cured;

(b) to order conditional discharge and to place the person on probation;

(c) to order, where necessary, the person's readmission to the institution or hospital. The provisions concerning surveillance cited above are applicable in such cases, and the probation period may be extended to three years.

Switzerland (St Gallen)

Legislation: Law of 18 June 1968 on the prevention and control of alcohol abuse.

1. *Grounds:* The potential alcoholic does not voluntarily accept advice, and care or such measures fail to have a lasting effect.

2. *Application:* The welfare centre reports the case to the guardianship authority, which summons the potential alcoholic and admonishes and counsels him. If the admonition and counsel fail to achieve the desired results, the guardianship authority may order certain measures to be taken (e.g., prohibiton of alcohol consumption by the person concerned). If the person fails to comply with the measures ordered, he is required to undergo a medical examination, possibly in a psychiatric or medical clinic.

3. *Decision-making authority:* Guardianship authority, upon the approval of the competent department.

4. *Medical examination:* Possibly in a psychiatric or medical clinic.

5. *Treatment programme:* Treatment in a psychiatric clinic or a sanatorium for inebriates for a period of one year. Cases which are difficult to cure may be committed to an appropriate establishment for a period of 1–3 years. If the person is a danger to the community, he is committed to a psychiatric clinic for as long as the danger persists.

6. *Length of stay:* See paragraph 5 above. The execution of the commitment order may be suspended for a trial period of 1–2 years, during which period the person is cared for at a welfare centre. If this proves unsuccessful, the commitment order is implemented. Should the person fail to obey the medical orders or the internal rules of the establishment, he may be transferred to another appropriate establishment.

7. *Appeal:* Appeals against measures ordered by the guardianship authority may be lodged with the *Regierungsrat* (agency in charge of guardianship matters).

8. *Periodic review:* See paragraph 6 above.

9. *Discharge procedure(s):* After completion of the prescribed period of commitment, the person is conditionally discharged for a probationary period of 1–3 years. Should the person revert to his previous habits (relapse) during this period, he must again be committed to an institution for a period of 1–3 years, depending on the results of a medical examination. Satisfactory completion of the probationary period results in final discharge.

Thailand

Legislation: Psychotropic Substances Law of 1975.

Note: Thailand has no legislation on the treatment of alcohol-dependent persons.

1. *Grounds:* Addiction to a psychotropic substance, defined as "a psychotropic substance which is natural or derived from nature, or synthetic".

   An "addict to a psychotropic substance" means a person who consumes, ingests, or applies by any means the psychotropic substance and shows the symptoms of addiction to the psychotropic substance that may be detected by a method of medical science.

2. *Application:* The Secretary-General of the Narcotics Control Board (or delegate).

3. *Decision-making authority:* The Secretary-General of the Narcotics Control Board, upon the recommendation or advice of the Psychotropic Substances Board. Any person dependent on a psychotropic substance who refuses to accept treatment or rehabilitation is liable to imprisonment and fine, after which the person is to be committed for treatment or rehabilitation in accordance with the original order.

4. *Medical examination:* Not stated.

5. *Treatment programme:* Commitment is for treatment or rehabilitation and restoration of ability (not specifically defined). The Ministry of Public Health has the duty to provide appropriate treatment, education, training, aftercare, or rehabilitation and restoration of ability for committed persons so that they may be socially reintegrated and free from addiction to the psychotropic substance.

6. *Length of stay:* 180 days.

7. *Appeal:* Not stated.

8. *Periodic review:* In cases where it is necessary for treatment or rehabilitation and restoration of ability, the Secretary-General (or delegate) may grant an extension of not more than 180 days.

9. *Discharge procedure(s):* Not stated.

Trinidad and Tobago

Legislation: Act No. 30 of 1975 (An Act to provide for the admission, care and treatment of persons who are mentally ill).

Note: Persons who are drug- or alcohol-dependent are dealt with under the mental health legislation.

Tunisia

Legislation: Law No. 69–54 of 26 July 1969 prescribing regulations concerning poisons.

1. *Grounds:* Drug dependence detected by:

   (*a*) physicians in their practice; or

   (*b*) public health authorities in prescribing drugs subject to abuse.

2. *Application:* The Commission on Drug Dependence receives information and documents submitted by public health authorities or physicians suspecting drug dependence.

3. *Decision-making authority:* Commission on Drug Dependence, composed of three physicians nominated by the Secretary of State for Public Health.

4. *Medical examination:* Not stated.

5. *Treatment programme:* Detoxification in a specialized establishment, under the conditions laid down by order of the Secretary of State for Public Health.

6. *Length of stay:* Not stated.

7. *Appeal:* Not stated.

8. *Periodic review:* Not stated.

9. *Discharge procedure(s):* Not stated.

Union of Soviet Socialist Republics
(Russian Soviet Federal Socialist Republic)

Note: Under the laws of the Presidium of the Russian Soviet Federal Socialist Republic, chronic alcoholics and drug-dependent persons are required to undergo continous observation and treatment at specialized follow-up centres. Chronic alcoholics and drug-dependent persons who refuse voluntary treatment or continue to misuse alcohol or to use narcotics after treatment, and who violate labour discipline, the public order, or the rules of socialist community life, are committed to curative and labour rehabilitation preventoria for compulsory treatment.

Legislation: Two decrees are in force.

A. *Decree of 25 August 1972 on the compulsory treatment and labour rehabilitation of drug-dependent persons who evade treatment or continue to take narcotics after initial treatment.*

1. *Grounds:* Drug-dependent persons who evade treatment or continue to take narcotics after treatment, or who infringe labour discipline, the public order, or the rules of socialist society, in spite of disciplinary measures taken in their regard or social or administrative actions.

2. *Application:* Petition by public organizations, workers' collectives or state agencies.

3. *Decision-making authority:* The hearing must be held in an open court session to which the person to whom the petition relates is summoned to appear. Where necessary, representatives of the public organizations, workers' collectives or State agencies that submitted the petition shall attend.

The preparation and submission of documents to be examined in court are undertaken by the agencies responsible for internal affairs.

If the person to whom a petition for compulsory treatment and labour rehabilitation relates does not come for medical examination or appear in court, he is liable to arrest by the agencies responsible for internal affairs.

The court's decision must be executed by the agencies responsible for internal affairs not later than ten days after the date on which the decision is pronounced.

The following are not to be committed to preventoria:

(*a*) persons suffering from chronic mental diseases, certain classes of disabled persons, pregnant women and nursing mothers, and persons suffering from certain serious diseases contraindicating their stay in a preventorium;

(*b*) males above 60 years of age and females above 55 years of age, as well as persons below 18 years of age. In exceptional cases, drug-dependent minors who have reached the age of 16 may be committed to preventoria.

4. *Medical examination:* Clinical examination.

5. *Treatment programme:* Drug-dependent persons are required to undergo "a complete course of special treatment in curative and prophylactic establishments of the Ministry of Health of the RSFSR at their place of domicile."

6. *Length of stay:* 1–10 years. If treatment is evaded, the period of detention may be extended for a period not exceeding one year by the *rayon* (or municipal) court competent for the place where the preventorium is located.

If curative and labour rehabilitation treatment is successful, the period of detention may, on the basis of medical findings, be reduced by not more than one-half by the *rayon* (or municipal) court competent for the place where the preventorium is located. The period of detention must not be reduced in respect of persons who have been repeatedly committed to curative and labour rehabilitation preventoria.

7. *Appeal:* The court's decisions on initial commitment, extension of commitment due to evasion of treatment, and reduction of the commitment period because of successful treatment, are final and not subject to appeal.

8. *Periodic review:* See paragraph 7 above.

9. *Discharge procedure(s):* Persons detained in the preventorium may, by the court's decision, be discharged early if their further stay in the establishment is contraindicated by a serious disease.

B. *Decree of 1 March 1974 on the compulsory treatment and occupational rehabilitation of chronic alcoholics.*

1. *Grounds:* Chronic alcoholics who refuse to undergo voluntary treatment or continue to misuse alcohol after treatment, and who violate labour discipline, the public order,

or the rules of socialist community life despite administrative or community measures adopted in their regard, are liable to commitment to curative and labour rehabilitation preventoria for compulsory treatment and labour rehabilitation.

2. *Application:* As for drug-dependent persons, except that "social organizations" may make application.

3. *Decision-making authority:* As for drug-dependent persons.

4. *Medical examination:* Medical findings.

5. *Treatment programme:* Chronic alcoholics must undergo a complete course of special treatment in therapeutic and prophylactic institutions of the Ministry of Health of the RSFSR at their place of residence.

6. *Length of stay:* As for drug-dependent persons.

7. *Appeal:* As for drug-dependent persons.

8. *Periodic review:* As for drug-dependent persons.

9. *Discharge procedure(s):* As for drug-dependent persons.

Note: Any person who has been sentenced to imprisonment for an offence committed in a curative and labour rehabilitation preventorium, or committed prior to admission thereto but after commitment by a people's court for compulsory treatment for chronic alcoholism, is subject (after having served his term of imprisonment) to commitment to a preventorium for the period of treatment that has not been completed, where medical findings indicate the necessity of such treatment.

United Kingdom (England and Wales)

Note: The Mental Health Act of 1959 governs the reception, care, and treatment of mentally disordered patients and provides both for compulsory admission to hospital and for guardianship. Drug- or alcohol-dependent persons may be compulsorily admitted to hospital, but it is laid down in a section of the Act amended in 1982 that "Nothing in this section shall be construed as implying that a person may be dealt with under the Act as suffering from mental disorder by reason only of . . . dependence on alcohol or drugs".

United States of America (Federal)

Legislation: Narcotic Addict Rehabilitation Act of 1966, as amended (Public Law No. 89–793).

Note: Section 3401 (Declaration of policy) states that it is the policy of the Congress that certain persons charged with or convicted of violating Federal criminal laws, who are determined to be addicted to narcotic drugs, and likely to be rehabilitated through treatment, should, in lieu of prosecution or sentencing, be civilly committed for confinement and treatment designed to effect their restoration to health, and return to society as useful members.

It is the further policy of the Congress that certain persons addicted to narcotic drugs who are not charged with the commission of any offence should be afforded the opportunity, through civil commitment, for treatment, in order that they may be rehabilitated and returned to society as useful members and in order that society may be protected more effectively from crime and delinquency which result from narcotic addiction.

1. *Grounds:* Persons addicted to narcotic drugs, but subchapter II (Civil commitment of persons not charged with any criminal offence) lays down that the provisions of this subchapter are not applicable with respect to any person against whom there is pending a criminal charge, whether by indictment or by information, which has not been fully determined or who is on probation or whose sentence following conviction on such a charge, including any time on parole or mandatory release, has not been fully served, except that such provision is applicable to any such person on probation, parole, or mandatory release if the authority authorized to require his return to custody consents to his commitment.

Certain terms used in subchapter II are defined in Section 3411 as follows:

(a) "Narcotic addict" means any individual who habitually uses any narcotic drug so as to endanger the public morals, health, safety, or welfare, or who is or has been so far addicted to the use of such narcotic drugs as to have lost the power of self-control with reference to his addiction.

(b) "Treatment" includes confinement and treatment in a hospital of the Public Health Service and under supervised aftercare in the community and includes, but is not limited to, medical, education, social, psychological and vocational services, corrective and preventive guidance and training, and other rehabilitative services designed to protect the public and benefit the addict by eliminating his dependence on addicting drugs, or by controlling his dependence, and his susceptibility to addiction.

(c) "Surgeon General" means the Surgeon General of the Public Health Service.

(d) "Hospital of the Service" means any hospital or other facility of the Public Health Service especially equipped for the accommodation of addicts, and any other appropriate public or private hospital or other facility available to the Surgeon General for the care and treatment of addicts.

(e) "Patient" means any person with respect to whom a petition has been filed by a United States attorney (see below).

(f) "Post-hospitalization programme" means any programme, established by the Surgeon General, and providing for the treatment and supervision of a person.

(g) "State" includes the District of Columbia and the Commonwealth of Puerto Rico.

(h) "United States" includes the Commonwealth of Puerto Rico.

(*i*) "Related individual" means any person with whom the alleged narcotic addict may reside or at whose house he may be, or the husband or wife, father or mother, brother or sister, or the child or the nearest available relative of the alleged narcotic addict.

2. *Application:* Section 3412 (Preliminary proceedings) provides that:

(*a*) Except as otherwise provided, whenever any narcotic addict desires to obtain treatment for his addiction, or whenever a related individual has reason to believe that any person is a narcotic addict, such addict or related individual may file a petition with the United States attorney for the district in which such addict or person resides or is found requesting that such addict or person be admitted to a hospital of the Public Health Service for treatment of his addiction. Any such petition filed by a narcotic addict must set forth his name and address and the facts relating to his addiction. Any such petition filed by a related individual with respect to a person believed by such individual to be a narcotic addict must set forth the name and address of the alleged narcotic addict and the facts or other data on which the petitioner bases his belief that the person with respect to whom the petition is filed is a narcotic addict.

(*b*) After considering such petition, the United States attorney must, if he determines that there is reasonable cause to believe that the person named in such petition is a narcotic addict, and that appropriate State or other facilities are not available to such person, file a petition with the United States district court to commit such person to a hospital of the Public Health Service for treatment as provided in this subchapter. In making his determination with respect to the non-availability of such facilities, the United States attorney must consult with the Surgeon General, and other appropriate State or local officials.

(*c*) Upon the filing of any such petition by a United States attorney, the court may order the patient to appear before it for an examination by physicians as provided under section 3413 of this title and for a hearing, if required, under section 3414 of this title. The court must cause a copy of such petition and order to be served personally upon the patient by a United States marshal.

3. *Decision-making authority:* The court must immediately advise any patient appearing before it pursuant to an order issued under subsection (*c*) of section 3412 (see above) of this title of his right to have: (1) counsel at every stage of the judicial proceedings under this subchapter and that, if he is unable because of financial reasons to obtain counsel, the court will, at the patient's request, assign counsel to represent him; and (2) present for consultation during any examination conducted under this section, a qualified physician retained by such patient, but in no event is such physician entitled to participate in any such examination or in the making of any report required under this section with respect to such examination. The court must also advise such patient that if, after an examination and hearing as provided in this subchapter, he is found to be a narcotic addict who is likely to be rehabilitated through treatment, he will be civilly committed to the Surgeon General for treatment; that he may not voluntarily withdraw from such treatment; that the treatment (including post-hospitalization treatment and supervision) may last 42 months; that during treatment he will be confined in an institution; that for a period of three years following his release from confinement he will be under the care and custody of the Surgeon General for treatment and supervision under a posthospitalization programme established by the Surgeon General; and that should he fail or refuse to cooperate in such posthospitalization programme or be determined by the Surgeon General to have relapsed to the use of narcotic drugs, he may be recommitted for additional confinement in an institution followed by additional posthospitalization treatment and supervision. After so advising the patient, the court must appoint two qualified physicians, one of whom must be a psychiatrist, to examine the patient. For the purpose of the examination, the court may order the patient

committed for such reasonable period as it may determine, not to exceed 30 days, to the custody of the Surgeon General for confinement in a suitable hospital or other facility designated by the court. Each physician appointed by the court must, within such a period so determined by the court, examine the patient and file with the court a written report with respect to such examination. Each such report must include a statement of the examining physician's conclusions as to whether the patient examined is a narcotic addict and is likely to be rehabilitated through treatment. Upon the filing of such reports, the patient so examined must be returned to the court for such further proceedings as it may direct under this subchapter. Copies of such reports must be made available to the patient and his counsel.

If both examining physicians referred to above conclude in their respective written reports that the patient is not a narcotic addict, or is an addict not likely to be re-habilitated through treatment, the court must immediately enter an order discharging the patient and dismissing the proceedings under this subchapter. If the written report of either such physician indicates that the patient is a narcotic addict who is likely to be rehabilitated through treatment, or that the physician submitting the report is unable to reach any conclusion by reason of the refusal of the patient to submit to a thorough examination, the court must promptly set the case for hearing. The court must cause a written notice of the time and place of such hearing to be served personally upon the patient and his attorney. Such notice must also inform the patient that upon demand made by him within 15 days after he has been served, he is entitled to have all issues of fact with respect to his alleged narcotic addiction determined by a jury. If no timely demand for a jury is made, the court, in conducting such hearing, determines all issues of fact without a jury.

If the court determines after a hearing that such patient is a narcotic addict who is likely to be rehabilitated through treatment, the court must order him committed to the care and custody of the Surgeon General for treatment in a hospital of the Public Health Service. The Surgeon General must submit to the court written reports with respect to such patient at such times as the court may direct. Such reports must include information as to the health and general condition of the patient, together with the recommendations of the Surgeon General concerning the continued confinement of such patient.

4. *Medical examination:* See paragraph 3 above.

Note: Any physician conducting an examination under this subchapter must be a competent and compellable witness at any hearing or other proceeding conducted pursuant to this subchapter and the information obtained at the examination and statements made by the patient to the physician shall not be held confidential but may be revealed in the physician's report and testimony.

5. *Treatment programme:* Notwithstanding any other provision of subchapter II, no patient may be committed to a hospital of the Public Health Service under this sub-chapter if the Surgeon General certifies that adequate facilities or personnel for treatment of such patient are unavailable.

The Surgeon General is authorized to enter into arrangements with any public or private agency or any person under which appropriate facilities or services of such agency or person will be made available, on a reimbursable basis or otherwise, for the examination or treatment of individuals pursuant to the provisions of this subchapter.

The Surgeon General is authorized to establish, as an integral part of the programme of treatment for narcotic addiction, outpatient services to: (1) provide guidance and give psychological help and supervision to patients and other individuals released from hospitals of the Public Health Service after treatment for narcotic drug addiction, utilizing all available resources of local, public and private agencies; and (2) assist States and municipalities in developing treatment programmes and facilities for individuals so addicted, including post-hospitalization treatment programmes and facilities for the care and supervision of narcotic addicts released after confinement under this or any other Act providing for treatment of drug addiction. The Surgeon General must take into consideration in supplying such services the extent of drug addiction in the various States and political subdivisions thereof and the willingness of such States and subdivisions to cooperate in developing a sound programme for the care, treatment, and rehabilitation of narcotic addicts.

6. *Length of stay:* Any patient committed to the care and custody of the Surgeon General must be committed for a period of six months, and is subject to such post-hospitalization programme as may be established (up to three years post-hospital rehabilitation); except that such patient may be released from confinement by the Surgeon General at any time prior to the expiration of such six-month period if the Surgeon General determines that the patient has been cured of his drug addiction and rehabilitated, or that his continued confinement is no longer necessary or desirable.

7. *Appeal:* In conducting any hearing under subchapter II, the court must receive and consider all relevant evidence and testimony which may be offered, including the contents of the reports referred to in section 3413 of this title. Any patient with respect to whom a hearing is held under this subchapter is entitled to testify and to present and cross-examine witnesses. All final orders of commitment under this subchapter are subject to review.

Any patient with respect to whom a hearing has been set under this subchapter may be detained by the court for a reasonable period of time in a suitable hospital or other facility designated by the court until after such hearing has been concluded.

8. *Periodic review:* The court, upon the petition of any patient after his confinement pursuant to this subchapter for a period in excess of three months, must inquire into the health and general conditions of the patient and as to the necessity, if any, for his continued confinement. If the court finds, with or without a hearing, that his continued confinement is no longer necessary or desirable, it must order the patient released from confinement and returned to the court. The court may, with respect to any such patient so returned, place such patient under a post-hospitalization programme.

9. *Discharge procedure(s):* See paragraphs 3 and 8 above.

United States of America (Massachusetts)

Legislation: The commitment, treatment and rehabilitation of alcohol- and drug-dependent persons are dealt with under three separate chapters of the General Laws.

A. *Chapter 123 of the General Laws: Treatment and commitment of mentally ill and mentally retarded persons.*

Note: Provision for the involuntary commitment of alcohol-dependent persons is made in Section 35. There is no comparable provision for drug-dependent persons.

Section 35 (Commitment of alcoholics; care and treatment) defines "alcoholic" to mean a person who chronically or habitually consumes alcoholic beverages to the extent that: (1) such use substantially injures his health or substantially interferes with his social or economic functioning; or (2) he has lost the power of self-control over the use of such beverages. Any police officer, physician, spouse, blood relative or guardian may petition in writing any district court for an order of commitment of a person whom he has reason to believe is an alcoholic. Upon receipt of a petition for an order of commitment of a person and any sworn statements the court may request from the petitioner, the court must immediately schedule a hearing on the petition and cause a summons and a copy of the application to be served upon the person in the manner provided by section 25 of chapter 276. If the person fails to appear at the time summoned, the court may issue a warrant for the person's arrest. The person has the right to be represented by legal counsel and may present independent expert or other testimony. If the court finds the person indigent, it must immediately appoint counsel. The court must order examination by a qualified physician. If, after a hearing, the court, on the basis of competent medical testimony, finds that said person is an alcoholic and that there is a likelihood of serious harm as a result of his alcoholism, it may order such person to be committed for a period not to exceed fifteen days.

B. *Chapter 111B of the General Laws: Alcoholism Treatment and Rehabilitation Law of 1971, as amended.*

Note: The following terms are defined in Section 3 of Chapter 111B (Voluntary and emergency detoxification):

"Alcoholism" means a medically diagnosable disease characterized by chronic, habitual or periodic consumption of alcoholic beverages resulting in: (1) substantial interference with an individual's social or economic functions in the community; or (2) the loss of powers of self-control with respect to the use of such beverages.

"Facility" means any public or private place, or portion thereof, providing services especially designed for the detoxification of intoxicated persons or alcoholics.

"Halfway house for alcoholics" means an intermediate care centre in a community, providing temporary residential accommodation, guidance, supervision, and personal adjustment services for a group of three or more sober alcoholics, but is not a facility as defined above or a permanent residence.

"Incapacitated" means the condition of an intoxicated person who, by reason of the consumption of intoxicating liquor is: (1) unconscious; (2) in need of medical attention; (3) likely to suffer or cause physical harm or damage property; or (4) disorderly.

"Independent physician" means a physician other than one holding an office or appointment in any department, board, or agency of the commonwealth, or in any public facility.

The Law deals separately with the assistance of an incapacitated person to a facility (Section 8) and with admission to a facility, aftercare, etc. (Section 7).

(*a*) *Assistance of an incapacitated person to a facility*

1. *Grounds:* Any person who is incapacitated.

2. *Application:* Any person who is incapacitated may be assisted by a police officer, with or without his consent, to his residence, to a facility or to a police station.

3. *Decision-making authority:* If any incapacitated person is assisted to a police station, the officer in charge of his designee must notify forthwith the nearest facility that the person is being held in protective custody. If suitable treatment services are available at a facility, the Department of Mental Health must thereupon arrange for the transportation of the person to the facility in accordance with the provisions of Section 7 of Chapter 111B of Massachusetts General Laws (see below).

Note: A person assisted to a facility or held in protective custody by the police pursuant to these provisions, must not be considered to have been arrested or to have been charged with any crime. An entry of custody must be made indicating the date, time, place of custody, the name of the assisting officer, the name of the officer in charge, whether the person held in custody exercised his right to make a phone call, whether the person held in custody exercised his right to take a breathalyser test, and the results of the breathalyser test if taken, which entry must not be treated for any purposes as an arrest or criminal record.

4. *Medical examination:* To determine for the purposes of this Chapter only, whether or not such person is intoxicated, the police officer may request the person to submit to reasonable tests of coordination, coherence of speech, and breath.

Any person assisted by a police officer to a police station has the right, and must be informed in writing of said right, to request and be administered a breathalyser test. Any person who is administered a breathalyser test is presumed intoxicated if evidence from said test indicates that the percentage of alcohol in his blood is 10% or more and must be placed in protective custody at a police station or transferred to a facility. Any person who is administered a breathalyser test must be presumed not to be intoxicated if evidence from said test indicates that the percentage of alcohol in his blood is 5% or less and must be released from custody forthwith. If any person who is administered a breathalyser test and evidence from said test indicates that the percentage of alcohol in his blood is more than 5% and less than 10% no presumption may be made based solely on the breathalyser test. In such instance a reasonable test of coordination or speech coherence must be administered to determine if said person is intoxicated. Only when such test of coordination or speech coherence indicates said person is intoxicated may he be placed in protective custody at a police station or transferred to a facility.

5. *Treatment programme:* A programme of detoxification treatment for no longer than 48 hours.

6. *Length of stay:* No person assisted to a police station pursuant to the above provisions may be held in protective custody against his will; provided, however, that if suitable treatment at a facility is not available, an incapacitated person may be held in protective custody at a police station until he is no longer incapacitated or for a period of no longer than 12 hours, whichever is shorter.

7. *Appeal:* Not stated.

8. *Periodic review:* Not stated.

9. *Discharge procedure(s):* The patient may be discharged at the discretion of the administrator of the detoxification centre or at the request of the patient. The patient is encouraged to consent to appropriate outpatient or aftercare treatment.

(*b*) *Admission to a facility, aftercare, etc.*

1. *Grounds:* Any person who is intoxicated and voluntarily applies for treatment at a detoxification facility or is brought to said facility in accordance with the provisions previously described.

2. *Application:* By person or by a police officer.

3. *Medical examination:* Prior to the admission of any person, the administrator of the facility must cause him to be evaluated by physician-supervised personnel, experienced in alcoholism diagnosis. If there is any concern about the health or the immediate treatment needs of such person, he must be examined by a physician.

4. *Treatment programme:* If upon said evaluation or examination, a determination is made that the person is intoxicated or is an alcoholic, and adequate and appropriate treatment is available, he must be admitted. If any person is not admitted for the reason that adequate and appropriate treatment is not available at the facility, the administrator of the facility, acting whenever possible with the assistance of the director, or his designee, must refer the person to a facility at which adequate and appropriate treatment is available. If a person is not admitted to a facility, and has no funds, the administrator must arrange for the person to be assisted to his residence, or if he has no residence to a place where shelter will be provided him.

5. *Length of stay:* Up to 48 hours (see paragraph 6 below).

6. *Discharge procedure(s):* Any person admitted to a facility must receive treatment at the centre or facility for as long as he wishes to remain or until the administrator determines that treatment will no longer benefit him; provided, however, that any person who at the time of admission is intoxicated or incapacitated, must remain at the facility until he is no longer incapacitated, but in no event may he be required to remain for a period greater than 48 hours.

Note: If any such person is committed for rehabilitative purposes to the Massachusetts correctional institution, Bridgewater or to the Massachusetts correctional institution, Framingham, he must be required to remain for a period of not less than 10 days.

C. *Chapter IIIE of the General Laws: Drug Rehabilitation Law of 24 December 1981*

Note: Under section 8 [(Voluntary) admission to facilities; application; inpatient and outpatient treatment; discharge; readmission], a "drug-dependent person" is defined as "a person who is unable to function effectively and whose inability to do so causes, or results from, the use of a drug other than alcohol, tobacco or lawful beverages containing caffeine, and other than from a medically prescribed drug when such drug is medically indicated and the intake is proportional to the medical need."

1. *Grounds:* Person believes he is a drug-dependent person.

2. *Application:* Any person who believes that he is a drug-dependent person may apply

for admission to a facility. Such application may be made either to the director or to the administrator of a public or private facility.

3. *Decision-making authority:* If the director finds that the person is a drug-dependent person who would benefit by treatment, he may cause him to be admitted to a facility as an inpatient or outpatient.

In determining whether to admit to a facility a person who is reported to be a drug-dependent person who would benefit by treatment, the director must consider the past record of treatment, if any, afforded the person at a facility, and whether or not the person complied with the terms of any prior admission.

4. *Medical examination:* Upon receipt of an application for admission, the director must designate a psychiatrist or if, in the discretion of the director, it is impracticable to do so, a physician to make an examination of the person to determine whether or not he is a drug-dependent person who would benefit by treatment. The psychiatrist or physician must report his findings in writing to the director after the completion of the examination, stating the facts upon which the findings are based and the reasons thereof.

5. *Treatment programme:* The administrator may transfer any inpatient to an outpatient programme if he finds that the patient is a proper subject for such a programme, provided, however, that the administrator may return any such patient to an inpatient programme if he deems it appropriate. A patient originally admitted to a facility as an outpatient must not be transferred to an inpatient programme without his written consent.

Each patient admitted is subject to the supervisory powers of the administrator exercised in accordance with the rules and regulations.

Before causing a person to be admitted to a facility, the director may make a recommendation to the person as to the period deemed necessary to accomplish adequate and appropriate treatment, but in no case may the period exceed one year. The director must also notify the person of the nature of the treatment to be afforded and the facility to which he will be admitted. If the person consents in writing to the admission to the facility, the period deemed necessary to accomplish treatment and the nature of the treatment, he may be admitted to a facility.

If the director decides that the applicant is to be refused admission to a facility because he is not a drug-dependent person who would benefit by treatment or because adequate treatment is not available at an appropriate facility, he must make known in writing to the applicant the basis for his decision.

6. *Length of stay:* Not more than one year.

7. *Discharge procedure(s):* A patient admitted to a facility may receive treatment at the facility so long as the administrator believes that it will continue to benefit him. Any patient may, at any time, notify the administrator in writing that he wishes to terminate treatment. Upon receipt of any such notification the administrator must determine whether further treatment would benefit the patient, and must inform the patient of his determination. If the administrator determines that he would not benefit by such further treatment, the patient must be discharged from the facility. If the administrator determines he would so benefit, he must so advise the patient. If the patient chooses to terminate treatment despite the determination by the administrator that the patient would benefit by further treatment at the facility, the administrator must notify the

director that the patient has caused treatment to be terminated during the recommended period against the advice of the administrator. If the patient applies for readmission for treatment in any facility, the fact that treatment has been terminated during the recommended period against the advice of the administrator may be considered in determining whether or not to readmit him, and, if the patient is readmitted, in determining to which facility he should be readmitted for treatment.

Note: Provisions governing the emergency treatment of a drug-dependent person are contained in Section 9 of Chapter IIIE, as follows:

Any facility may afford emergency treatment to a drug-dependent person or a person in need of immediate assistance due to the use of a dependence-related drug if the person requests such treatment. The term of emergency treatment must not exceed 48 hours without compliance with the provisions relating to procedures for admission to a facility; provided, however, that if prior to the termination of the emergency treatment period the person applies for admission, he may, in the discretion of the administrator, continue to receive treatment at the facility while his application is under consideration.

United States of America (Wisconsin)

Legislation: Commitment for treatment is dealt with by two separate sections of the State Mental Health Act 1972 (Chapter 51).

A. *Section 51.20 (Involuntary commitment for treatment)*

This Section provides that every written petition for examination must allege that the individual to be examined:

1. is mentally ill, drug-dependent, or developmentally disabled and is a proper subject for treatment; and

2. is dangerous because the individual

   (*a*) evidences a substantial probability of physical harm to himself or herself as manifested by evidence of recent threats of or attempts at suicide or serious bodily harm;

   (*b*) evidences a substantial probability of physical harm to other individuals as manifested by evidence of recent homicidal or other violent behaviour, or by evidence that others are placed in reasonable fear of violent behaviour and serious physical harm to them, as evidenced by a recent overt act, attempts or threat to do serious physical harm;

   (*c*) evidences such impaired judgement, manifested by evidence of a pattern of recent acts or omissions, that there is a substantial probability of physical impairment or injury to himself or herself. The probability of physical impairment or injury is not substantial under this subparagraph if reasonable provision for the individual's protection is available in the community, if the individual is appropriate for placement or, in the case of a minor, if the individual is appropriate for services or placement. The individual's status as a minor does not automatically establish a substantial probability of physical impairment or injury under this sub-paragraph.

B. *Section 51.45 (Wisconsin Alcoholism and Intoxication Treatment Act of October 1978)*

Note: It is the policy in Wisconsin that alcoholics and intoxicated persons should not be subjected to criminal prosecution because of their consumption of alcoholic beverages but should rather be afforded a continuum of treatment in order that they may lead normal lives as productive members of society.

"Intoxicated person" means a person whose mental or physical functioning is substantially impaired as a result of the use of alcohol.

"Incapacitated by alcohol" means that a person, as a result of the use of or withdrawal from alcohol, is unconscious or has his or her judgement otherwise so impaired that he or she is incapable of making a rational decision, as shown objectively by such indicators as extreme physical debilitation, physical harm, or threats of harm to himself or herself or to any other person, or to property.

1. *Grounds:* An intoxicated person who has threatened, attempted or inflicted physical harm on himself or herself or on another and is likely to inflict such physical harm unless committed, or a person who is incapacitated by alcohol may be committed to the community board and brought to an approved public treatment facility for emergency treatment. A refusal to undergo treatment does not constitute evidence of lack of judgement as to the need for treatment.

2. *Application:* The physician, spouse, guardian or a relative of the person sought to be committed, or any other responsible person, may petition a court commissioner or the circuit court of the county in which the person sought to be committed resides or is present for commitment under this subsection. The petition must:

   (*a*) state facts to support the need for emergency treatment;

   (*b*) state facts sufficient for a determination of indigency of the person; and

   (*c*) be supported by one or more affidavits that aver with particularity the factual basis for the allegations contained in the petition.

3. *Decision-making authority:* Upon receipt of a petition, the court must determine whether the petition and supporting affidavits sustain the grounds for commitment and dismiss the petition if the grounds for commitment are not sustained thereby. If the grounds for commitment are sustained by the petition and supporting affidavits, the court or court commissioner must issue an order temporarily committing the person to the custody of the community board. A hearing must be held within 48 hours after receipt of petition.

4. *Medical examination:* See paragraph 2 above.

5. *Treatment programme:* "Treatment" means the broad range of emergency, outpatients, intermediate, and inpatient services and care, including diagnostic evaluation, medical, surgical, psychiatric, psychological, and social service care, vocational rehabilitation and career counselling, which may be extended to alcoholics and intoxicated persons, and psychiatric, psychological and social service care, which may be extended to their families. Treatment may also include, but must not be replaced by, physical detention of persons who have threatened, attempted or inflicted physical harm on themselves or

another while in protective custody or undergoing involuntary treatment, or who have attempted or committed an escape while in protective custody or undergoing involuntary treatment.

6. *Length of stay:* Not longer than 48 hours.

7. *Appeal:* Not stated.

8. *Periodic review:* Upon arrival at the approved public treatment facility, the person must be advised both orally and in writing of the right to counsel, the right to consult with counsel before a request is made to undergo voluntary treatment, the right not to converse with examining physicians, psychologists or other personnel, the fact that anything said to examining physicians, psychologists or other personnel may be used as evidence against him or her at subsequent hearings, the right to refuse medication that would render him or her unable adequately to prepare a defence, the exact time and place of the preliminary hearing and of the reasons for detention and the standards under which he or she may be committed prior to all interviews with physicians, psychologists or other personnel. Such notice of rights must be provided to the patient's immediate family if they can be located and may be deferred until the patient's incapacitated condition, if any, has subsided to the point where the patient is capable of understanding the notice. Under no circumstances may interviews with physicians, psychologists, or other personnel be conducted until such notice is given, except that the patient may be questioned to determine immediate medical needs. The patient may be detained at the facility to which he or she was admitted or, upon notice to the attorney and the court, transferred by the community board to another appropriate public or private treatment facility.

9. *Discharge procedure(s):* When on the advice of the treatment staff the superintendent of the facility having custody of the patient determines that the grounds for commitment no longer exist, he or she must discharge a person committed under the Law.

A2.2. DIVERSION TO TREATMENT FROM THE CRIMINAL JUSTICE SYSTEM

Argentina

Legislation: Section 9 of Law No. 20.771 of 9 October 1974.

1. *Grounds:* When a person sentenced for any offence is physically or psychologically dependent on drugs.

2. *Application:* Not stated.

3. *Decision-making authority:* The judge must impose, in addition to the sentence, a "curative safety" measure (see below).

4. *Medical examination:* Not stated.

5. *Treatment programme:* The "curative safety" measure consists of an adequate detoxification treatment and such therapeutic care as may be required for rehabilitation in appropriate establishments, as determined by the judge, but not in outpatient facilities.

6. *Length of stay:* Indefinite, but may not exceed the duration of the sentence. The curative safety measure must be carried out first and counted as part of the time to be served under the sentence.

7. *Appeal:* Not stated.

8. *Periodic review:* Not stated.

9. *Discharge procedure(s):* Treatment is terminated by judicial decision on the advice of experts.

Note: In 1979 the Drug Addict Recovery Centre was established in units of the Federal Penitentiary Service to implement the provisions of Section 9 of Law No. 20.77. This is a restricted facility to which access is gained only through the criminal courts.

Brazil

Legislation: Law No. 6368 of 21 October 1976 enacting measures for the prevention and suppression of illicit traffic in and abuse of narcotic drugs or substances that cause physical or psychic dependence and other provisions.

1. *Grounds:* For persons dependent on narcotic drugs or on substances causing physical or psychic dependence, diversion to treatment may be ordered, as follows:

   (*a*) A dependant who has committed a punishable offence and been sentenced to a term of imprisonment or custodial security measure must undergo treatment in the clinic attached to the penal establishment where he is serving his sentence.

   (*b*) Where the judge finds the accused not guilty, as a result of official expert evidence that his dependence, at the time a criminal act was committed, made him totally incapable of understanding the unlawful nature of his conduct or of acting on such an understanding, he must order the accused to undergo medical treatment.

2. *Application:* Public prosecutor. At preliminary hearing, the judge must ask the accused whether he is a dependant and point out to him the consequences of his statements. An adjudication hearing must take place within 30 days of a medical examination ordered by the court.

3. *Decision-making authority:* Judge of competent court.

4. *Medical examination:* Official expert evidence. In the absence of official experts, the offender must be examined by medical practitioners appointed by the judge.

5. *Treatment programme:* Medical outpatient treatment. Where the person in any way fails to cooperate in treatment provided on an outpatient basis or is brought to trial a second time under the same conditions, the court may order hospitalization. Where the offender has been rehabilitated, the fact must be communicated to the judge, who must hear official expert testimony to that effect and the opinion of the public prosecutor and then decide whether to close the proceedings.

6. *Length of stay:* Not stated.

7. *Appeal:* Not stated.

8. *Periodic review:* Not stated, but see paragraph 9 below.

9. *Discharge procedure(s):* When an offender has been rehabilitated, the judge must hear official expert testimony to that effect and the opinion of the public prosecutor and then decide whether to close the proceedings.

Burma

Legislation: The Narcotics and Dangerous Drugs Rules, 1974.

Note: Convicts who are addicts may if necessary be admitted for medical treatment in prison hospitals. Medical treatment is given under the Government scheme. The Government must, after obtaining all necessary assistance, take steps for the rehabilitation in every way of users of drugs on recovery after medical treatment, to enable them to resume their places in society as useful citizens and to perform their share of the duties of the country.

"Addict" means any person who has the desire to use narcotics and dangerous drugs and who is unable to refrain from taking such drugs and who suffers from withdrawal symptoms when he does not consume the same.

No information is given in the Rules on the treatment provided in prison hospitals.

Egypt

Legislation: Section 37 of Law No. 182 of 1970 relating to psychotropic drugs, as modified by Law No. 16 of 1973.

Note: Paragraph 6 of Section 37 of Law No. 182 stipulates that a drug taker who volunteers for treatment must not be prosecuted. A special committee (whose membership is defined in Section 37 of Law No. 152) alone has the power to decide whether an effective cure has been achieved by treatment prior to discharge.

France

Legislation: Law No. 70–1320 of 31 December 1970 relating to the health measures for the control of drug dependence and the suppression of traffic in, and illicit use of, poisons.

1. *Grounds:* Persons making illicit use of substances or plants classified as narcotics.

2. *Application:* The public prosecutor may order a person who has made illicit use of narcotics to undergo detoxification or to submit to medical surveillance.

3. *Decision-making authority:* Examining magistrate or the juvenile court magistrate. The specialized establishment in which the person concerned must undergo treatment if continuous or part-time hospitalization is necessary is designated by writ of the examining magistrate. If the person's condition does not necessitate continuous or part-time hospitalization, the examining magistrate issues a writ placing him under medical surveillance either by a physician of his choice or by a social hygiene clinic or approved health establishment, either public or private.

Persons who have complied with the medical treatment prescribed for them and have continued the treatment until its termination are not liable to prosecution.

Similarly, proceedings are not initiated against persons who have made illicit use of narcotics where it is established that since their offence they have undergone detoxification or have submitted to medical surveillance.

In the event of a second offence, the public prosecutor determines whether or not criminal proceedings should be initiated.

4. *Medical examination:* Competent health authorities arrange for a medical examination of the person and an investigation into his family, professional and social life.

5. *Treatment programme:* If it appears from the medical examination that the person is an addict, he is ordered by the health authority to attend an approved establishment of his choice or, if he fails to exercise this right, an officially designated establishment in order to undergo detoxification. Once a person has begun the required course of treatment, he must remit to the health authority a medical certificate indicating the date of commencement of care, the probable duration of treatment, and the establishment in which he is to be hospitalized or under whose surveillance he is to undergo outpatient treatment.

If undergone in a specialized establishment, detoxification must involve either continuous or part-time hospitalization or, alternatively, the two types of hospitalization consecutively. Periods of hospitalization may be followed by outpatient treatment.

If undergone under medical surveillance, without hospitalization in a specialized establishment, detoxification must be supervised by an approved physician.

6. *Length of stay:* Not stated.

7. *Appeal:* Not stated.

8. *Periodic review:* The health authority follows the progress of the treatment and at "regular intervals" informs the public prosecutor's office of the medical and social situation of the person.

The physician reponsible for the treatment may at any time propose to the examining magistrate that the conditions of treatment should be modified or the person concerned placed in another establishment better adapted to his needs.

9. *Discharge procedure(s):* Not stated.

Federal Republic of Germany

Legislation: Apart from the Law of 28 July 1981 (see below), the Notice of 2 January 1975 is also relevant.

A. *Law concerning the trade in narcotic drugs (Narcotic Law) of 28 July 1981.*

1. *Grounds:* Under Section 35 (Deferment of execution of sentence) of Chapter VII (Drug-dependent offenders), if a person has been sentenced for a crime to imprisonment for a period of not more than two years and the reasons for judgement state or it has been established otherwise that the offence was committed due to narcotic drug addiction.

2. *Application:* Law-enforcement authority.

3. *Decision-making authority:* The law-enforcement authority may defer, with the approval of the court of first instance, the execution of punishment, residual punishment or institutionalization in drug detoxification centres for a period not exceeding two years, if the person convicted is undergoing appropriate treatment promoting his rehabilitation or promises to undergo such treatment, and it is certain that this treatment will be started. Treatment also includes any stay in a state-approved institution aiming at curing the dependence or at preventing a relapse.

4. *Medical examination:* Not stated.

5. *Treatment programme:* See paragraph 3 above.

At times established by the law-enforcement authority, the person convicted is required to prove that he has begun treatment or is continuing it; the persons treating him or the institutions concerned must inform the law-enforcement authority if treatment has been discontinued.

Note: The law-enforcement authority revokes the deferment of execution if the treatment is not started or continued or if the convicted person does not furnish the proof mentioned above. The revocation can be cancelled if the convicted person subsequently proves that he is under treatment.

Deferment of execution is also revoked where:

(*a*) an aggregate sentence is imposed subsequently and its execution is not deferred as well; or
(*b*) another prison sentence or measure of rehabilitation and prevention involving deprivation of liberty is to be executed.

If the law-enforcement authority has revoked the deferment, it is authorized to issue a warrant of arrest for the purpose of the prison sentence or for institutionalization in a centre for the care of addicts. The revocation can be challenged by appealing to the court of first instance. The continuation of execution is not interrupted by the appeal to the court.

Under the provisions of Section 36:

(a) If the execution has been deferred and the convicted person has undergone treatment in a state-approved institution where his way of life is subject to considerable restrictions, the period of institutionalization served by the convicted person can be credited against the penalty until two-thirds of the sentence have been disposed of by such credit. The decision to credit institutionalization in this way is taken by the court, together with the approval pursuant to Section 35. If two-thirds of the sentence have been disposed of by the credit, or treatment in the institution is no longer required at an earlier date, the court can suspend the execution of the residual penalty on probation as soon as the court is assured by evidence submitted in court that the convicted person is not likely to commit any further crime.

(b) If execution has been deferred and the convicted person has undergone, treatment for his addiction other than that specified here, the court must suspend the execution of the prison sentence or residual penalty on probation, as soon as the court is assured by evidence submitted in court that he is not likely to commit any further crime.

(c) If the convicted person has undergone treatment for his addiction after committing the crime, the court may order, if the requirements specified here are not fulfilled, that all or part of the period of treatment be credited against the sentence, provided that this is advisable given the requirements imposed upon the convicted person by the treatment.

(d) The decisions pursuant to subparagraphs (a) to (c) must be taken by order by the court of first instance without any hearing. The law-enforcement authority, the convicted person and the persons in charge or the institution must be heard. Immediate appeal can be filed against the decision. The caution regarding the suspension of the residual penalty must be given by the court.

Under Section 37:

(a) If an accused person is suspected of having committed a crime as a result of narcotic drug dependence and the penalty to be expected is imprisonment for a period not exceeding two years, the public prosecutor, with the approval of the court competent to open the main proceedings, may provisionally refrain from preferring the public charge, if the accused proves that he has been undergoing treatment for his dependence as specified in Section 35 (a) of at least three months, and that his rehabilitation is to be expected. The public prosecutor must fix the dates on which the accused is to prove the continuity of treatment.

The proceedings must be continued if:

(i) the treatment is not completed as envisaged;
(ii) the accused does not provide the proof required;
(iii) the accused commits a crime showing thereby that the grounds on which the decision not to prefer the public charge was based were not well founded; or
(iv) as a consequence of new facts or proofs, imprisonment for a period of more than two years is to be expected.

In the cases covered by items (i) and (ii) above, the proceedings may be suspended if the accused can subsequently submit proof that he is still under treatment. The person can no longer be prosecuted if the proceedings are not reopened within a period of four years.

(b) If the public charge has already been preferred, the court may provisionally discontinue the proceeding, with the approval of the public prosecutor, until the end of the trial in the course of which the findings of fact can be considered for the last time. The decision is made by way of a court order which is not subject to appeal.

6. *Length of stay:* At least three months.

7. *Appeal:* See paragraph 5 above for appeal procedure in connection with revocation of deferment of execution of sentence.

8. *Periodic review:* At times established by the law-enforcement authority, the person convicted must prove that he has started treatment or is continuing it. The persons treating him or the institutions concerned must inform the law-enforcement authority if treatment has been discontinued.

9. *Discharge procedure(s):* See paragraph 5 above.

B. *Penal code, Section 64 (revised under notice of 2 January 1975).*

Note: Section 64 may be summarized as follows:

Detention in a withdrawal clinic

1. The court shall order that any person convicted of an unlawful act committed under the influence of intoxication or whose crime is a result of habitual intoxication, or any person not convicted of such a crime for the mere reason that he cannot be found responsible for the crime and such person is also found to habitually consume alcoholic or other intoxicating substances in excessive amounts, shall be detained in a withdrawal clinic if there is the danger that he will commit serious unlawful acts in consequence of his habit.

2. No such order shall be made if, before the person is sent to the withdrawal clinic, it appears to the court (usually on advice of probation officers or a medical examination) that such treatment does not offer any prospect of success and the person is likely to relapse to his habitual intoxication.

Hong Kong

Legislation: Drug Addiction Treatment Centres Ordinance (Chapter 244 of the Laws of Hong Kong).

1. *Grounds:* Persons found guilty of an offence punishable by imprisonment otherwise than for nonpayment of a fine and who are addicted to any dangerous drug (as defined in the Dangerous Drug Ordinance). For detention in addiction-treatment centres to be ordered in lieu of any other sentence, the court must be satisfied that, given the circumstances of the case and having regard to the person's character and previous conduct, it is in his and the public interest that he should undergo a period of cure and rehabilitation in such a centre.

2. *Application:* Court.

Note: If the Governor of Hong Kong is satisfied, on application by the Commissioner of Prisons, that a person serving a sentence of imprisonment is addicted to any dangerous drug and, having regard to his health, character and previous conduct, it is in his and the public interest that he should undergo a period of cure and rehabilitation in an addiction-treatment centre, the Governor may order such person to be transferred to and detained in an addiction-treatment centre.

3. *Decision-making authority:* Court.

Note: When a court makes a detention order, no conviction may be recorded against the person in respect of whom the order is made unless, in the opinion of the court, the circumstances of the offence so warrant and the court orders accordingly.

4. *Medical examination:* Before a detention order is made in respect of any person, the court must consider a report of the Commissioner of Prisons on the suitability of such person for cure and rehabilitation and on the availability of places at addiction-treatment centres, and if the court has not received such a report it must, after such person has been found guilty, remand him in the custody of the Commissioner of Prisons for such period, not exceeding three weeks, as the court thinks necessary to enable such a report to be made. The Commissioner must, in his report, inform the Court whether or not a detention order has previously been made in respect of the person.

5. *Treatment programme:* A period of cure and rehabilitation in a treatment centre. If the Governor is satisfied, on application by the Commissioner of Prisons, that a person detained in an addiction-treatment centre is exercising a bad influence on other persons detained in that centre, the Governor may order such person to be transferred to, and detained in a prison for a period not exceeding: (*a*) the balance of the period during which such person might have been detained in an addiction centre; or (*b*) the term of imprisonment to which such person was liable for the offence of which he was found guilty, whichever is less.

6. *Length of stay:* The period of detention (not less than four and not more than 12 months from the date of the detention order) is determined by the Commissioner of Prisons in the light of the health and progress made by the person and the likelihood of his remaining free from addiction to any dangerous drug on his release. After this period, he must be released.

7. *Appeal:* Not stated.

8. *Periodic review:* A Board of Review is established for each addiction-treatment centre. The functions of the Board include reviewing the progress of each person since admission and making recommendations to the Commissioner of Prisons relating to his release.

The Board of Review for an addiction-treatment centre must interview persons: (*a*) during the third month after the date of their admission; (*b*) at least once every two months during the four months following the first interview; and (*c*) thereafter at least once a month.

9. *Discharge procedure(s):* The Commissioner of Prisons may order that a person released from a centre be subject to supervision, for a period of 12 months from the date of release, by such organization or person as the Commissioner may specify. While under supervision the person must comply with such requirements, including medical examination, as the Commissioner may specify. The Commissioner may at any time vary or cancel a supervision order.

The Commissioner may, if he is satisfied that a person against whom a supervision order is in force has failed to comply with any requirement of that order, make a recall order against such person requiring him to return to an addiction-treatment centre, and thereupon such person may be arrested and taken to an addiction-treatment centre and detained there.

If a person in respect of whom a detention order, a supervision order or a recall order is in force is sentenced to imprisonment: (*a*) for a term of two years or less, the detention order, supervision order, or recall order must be suspended until the expiration of his term of imprisonment; (*b*) for a term of more than two years or a new detention order is made in respect of him, the first-mentioned detention order, or the supervision order, or recall order, as the case may be, ceases to have effect.

Indonesia

Legislation: Law No. 9 of 26 July 1976 on narcotics.

1. *Grounds:* Conviction for unauthorized personal use of narcotics. "Narcotics" are defined in the Law.

A "narcotics addict" means "someone who utilizes narcotics and is in a state of dependence on narcotics, physically as well as mentally, resulting from the use or abuse of narcotics".

2. *Application:* Not stated.

3. *Decision-making authority:* Judge pronouncing sentence.

4. *Medical examination:* Not stated.

5. *Treatment programme:* Medication and nursing of narcotic addicts and rehabilitation of ex-addicts is at their expense. It is provided at rehabilitation institutions. The establishment, organization, and function of rehabilitation institutions and branches are determined by the President. Involvement of private and government community agencies is sought.

"Rehabilitation" is an endeavour to make a narcotic addict recover so that he regains his physical and mental health in order to readapt to his living environment and improve his dexterity, knowledge, and skill.

6. *Length of stay:* Not stated.

7. *Appeal:* Not stated.

8. *Periodic review:* Not stated.

9. *Discharge procedure(s):* Not stated.

Note: The official "Explanations" concerning the above-mentioned Law state: "The Judge who pronounces the verdict on a criminal case can:

(*a*) order the offender to be put in a rehabilitation institution for narcotic addicts without punishment, or

(*b*) punish the offender.

This Article 32 is governed by the conception that a narcotic addict, besides an offender, is also a victim of narcotic abuse.

Since treatment and rehabilitation of victims of narcotic abuse do not constitute the task and responsibility of the Government only, but are also a responsibility of the community in general, the existence of rehabilitation institutions is considered necessary.

This Article is intended to secure coordination in the efforts to control and manage narcotic abuse, taking into consideration that this problem relates to various social aspects and functionally involves various governmental agencies and private parties."

Israel

Legislation: The Penal Law of Punishment, 1970.

1. *Grounds:* Person has been sentenced to imprisonment, other than conditional imprisonment, for a term of six months or more, and the court is satisfied, after hearing the opinion of a psychiatrist, that the accused is addicted to dangerous drugs, within the meaning of the Dangerous Drugs Ordinance and that there is reason to believe that he committed the offence for which he has been sentenced in consequence of that addiction, and that the said addiction may lead him to commit further offences. The court may, in its sentence, order that the person be detained in a closed institution to be cured of that addiction.

2. *Application:* Court.

3. *Decision-making authority:* Court.

4. *Medical examination:* Opinion of psychiatrist that the accused is addicted to dangerous drugs.

5. *Treatment programme:* Any person against whom a court order has been made is detained in a "closed institution" under the same conditions (subject to some exceptions) as those for the hospitalization of a "sick person" within the meaning of the Treatment of Mentally Sick Persons Law, 1955.

An order ("detention order") may not be made unless an institution approved by the Minister of Health suitable for curative treatment has stated that it can accommodate the sentenced person for the purposes of the treatment.

The Minister of Health may, with the consent of the Minister of Police, approve a psychiatric ward in a prison as a suitable institution.

6. *Length of stay:* A detention order may not be made for a period exceeding three years or exceeding the term of imprisonment that the sentenced person has to undergo, whichever is the longer.

The period of detention must be deducted from the term of imprisonment of such person unless the court directs that the whole or part of that period may not be deducted. Where the court so directs, it must, after hearing the opinion of a psychiatrist (or a physician), determine whether the period of treatment in a closed institution shall take place before or after the person serves his prison sentence.

7. *Appeal:* Not stated.

8. *Periodic review:* The Attorney-General or his representative must, once every six months, bring the case of the patient before the court that made the detention order, and the court may rescind the order if it is satisfied that there is no justification for the continued detention of the patient in a closed institution.

9. *Discharge procedure(s):* The Minister of Justice must appoint a Board of three persons of whom one is a district court judge and at least one is a psychiatrist.

Where the Board is satisfied that a patient is no longer in need of treatment in a closed institution or is incurable, it may direct his release from the closed institution at any time prior to the expiration of the period of the order. The Board may also in its discretion, from the point of view of the cure or rehabilitation of the patient, direct that he be released for such time or on such conditions as it may think fit.

The person in charge of the closed institution or a person empowered by him in that behalf may grant the patient special leave for a period not exceeding four days.

Release from a closed institution does not relieve the patient of liability to the term of imprisonment that he still has to undergo at the time.

A patient who leaves a closed institution without permission and a person who aids a patient to leave are liable to imprisonment for a term of one year.

Mauritius

Legislation: The Psychotropic Substances Act, 1974.

1. *Grounds:* Any person who fails to comply with or contravenes any provision of the Psychotropic Substances Act of 1974 and is convicted of such offence.

2. *Application:* By court hearing criminal case.

3. *Decision-making authority:* Court hearing criminal case.

4. *Medical examination:* Not stated.

5. *Treatment programme:* The court before which a person is convicted may, if it thinks fit, in addition to any other penalty imposed, order that the accused undergo such treatment, education, aftercare, rehabilitation, or social reintegration as the court thinks appropriate.

6. *Length of stay:* Not stated.

7. *Appeal:* Not stated.

8. *Periodic review:* Not stated.

9. *Discharge procedure(s):* Not stated.

Philippines

Legislation: The Dangerous Drug Act of 30 March 1972.

1. *Grounds:* Either:

   (a) compulsory submission of a drug dependant to treatment and rehabilitation after arrest; or

   (b) voluntary submission of a drug dependant to confinement, treatment, and rehabilitation by the defendant himself or through his parents, guardian, or relative.

   If a person charged with an offence is found by the court, at any stage of the proceedings, to be a drug dependant, the court must suspend all further proceedings and transmit copies of the record of the case to the Dangerous Drug Board.

   If a drug dependant voluntarily submits himself for confinement, treatment and rehabilitation in a treatment and rehabilitation centre and complies with such conditions therefor as the Board may, by rules and regulations, prescribe, he is not criminally liable for any violation of the Dangerous Drug Act. This exemption is extended to a minor who may be committed for treatment and rehabilitation in a centre upon sworn petition of his parent, guardian or relative, within the fourth civil degree of consanguinity or affinity, or of the Director of Health or the Secretary of the Department of Social Welfare, in that order.

   "Drug dependence" means a state of psychic or physical dependence, or both, on a dangerous drug, arising in a person following administration or use of that drug on a periodic or continuous basis. "Dangerous drug" is defined in the Act.

2. *Application:* If the Board determines, after medical examination, that public interest requires that a drug dependant be committed to a centre for treatment and rehabilitation, it must file a petition for his commitment with the Court of First Instance, Juvenile and Domestic Relations Court, or Circuit Criminal Court of the province or city where the person is being held for investigation or is being tried. Any of said courts may receive and act upon a petition for commitment.

3. *Decision-making authority:* A petition is filed with the Court of First Instance, Juvenile or Domestic Relations Court, or Circuit Criminal Court.

4. *Medical examination:* Examination by two physicians who must report to the Court.

5. *Treatment programme:* By court order for commitment to a centre for treatment and rehabilitation.

6. *Length of stay:* Unlimited.

7. *Appeal:* Not stated.

8. *Periodic review:* The director of the treatment centre must report to the court every four months on the patient's progress.

9. *Discharge procedure(s):* The person or a relative or guardian may petition the Court for release. If, after a hearing, the Court orders discharge of the person, it must indicate whether the period of treatment is to be deducted from any criminal sentence, taking into account the person's behaviour during treatment.

Poland

Legislation: Law of 19 April 1969 (Criminal Code).

Note: The full text of the Law of 19 April 1969 (Article 102 of the Criminal Code) regarding treatment of alcohol-dependent offenders reads as follows:

"Where sentence has been imposed for an offence committed in association with the habitual use of alcohol or other intoxicant, the court may commit the offender to an institution for the treatment of dependence before the sentence is carried out.

The period of stay in the institution shall not be fixed in advance; it shall not, however, be shorter than six months or longer than two years; the court shall decide upon discharge from the institution in the light of the results of the treatment."

Senegal

Legislation: Law No. 75–81 of 9 July 1975 repealing and amending Section 8 of Law No. 72–24 of 19 April 1972 on the prevention of contraventions in the field of narcotics.

1. *Grounds:* Any person accused of or charged with illicitly using or attempting to use narcotics may, following an examination, be required by the competent examining court or court passing sentence to undergo detoxification. In such cases, the court may dismiss the charges against the person before he is sent for detoxification treatment.

2. *Application:* Any physician who, while carrying out a diagnosis or a treatment, becomes convinced that a person is illicitly using narcotics must notify the chief medical officer of the region. Where the chief medical officer of a region is notified of a case of a person using narcotics, either by a certificate from a physician or by a report from the Regional Governor or from the Prefect, he must arrange for the person concerned to be medically examined.

3. *Decision-making authority:* The court before which the person is charged, on the basis of medical examination and specific recommendations of the chief medical officer of the region.

4. *Medical examination:* By at least three physicians. The person's family, professional, and social life must also be investigated.

5. *Treatment programme:* Treatment may be in a detoxification centre, or on an outpatient basis under the care of a physician or care establishment under the jurisdiction of the

Ministry of Public Health.

Note: Drug-dependent persons who report voluntarily to a care establishment under the jurisdiction of the Ministry of Public Health with a view to treatment are not subject to the above provisions. Upon written application, such persons may remain anonymous when admitted. Their wish to remain anonymous may be set aside only for reasons other than the prevention of illicit use of narcotics.

6. *Length of stay:* Not stated.

7. *Appeal:* Not stated.

8. *Periodic review:* Not stated.

9. *Discharge procedure(s):* Not stated.

Switzerland (Federal)

Legislation: Federal Law of 18 March 1971 to amend the Swiss Penal Code.

1. *Grounds:* The offender is an alcoholic and the offence committed is related to this condition.

2. *Application:* Judge.

3. *Decision-making authority:* Judge.

4. *Medical examination:* The judge, if necessary, orders an expert appraisal to be made of the offender's physical and mental state and the advisability of treatment.

5. *Treatment programme:* The judge may order the offender to be detained in an establishment for alcoholics, or if necessary in a hospital establishment, in order to prevent further crimes or misdemeanours. The judge may also order outpatient treatment. The competent authority (medical establishment) designates the appropriate establishment for the treatment.

In the case of detention in, or admission to, a health or care establishment, the judge suspends the execution of any sentence involving deprivation of liberty.

In the case of outpatient treatment, the judge may suspend the execution of the sentence if the latter is incompatible with the treatment. In such cases, he may impose rules of conduct to be followed by the convicted person and if necessary place him under protective surveillance.

The establishment for alcoholics must be separate from the other establishments for which provision is made under the Swiss Penal Code.

6. *Length of stay:* If the detainee is incurable or the requirements for conditional discharge are not satisfied after a period of two years, the judge decides, after consultation with the persons responsible for directing the establishment, whether and to what extent any suspended sentences are to be executed. Where the requirements therefor are satisfied, the judge may order the adoption of another measure to protect public safety in place of the sentence imposed.

7. *Appeal:* Not stated.

8. *Periodic review:* See paragraph 6 above.

9. *Discharge procedure(s):* As soon as the competent authority considers the detainee to be cured, it must discharge him from the medical establishment. It may discharge him conditionally and place him under protective surveillance for 1 3 years. It must report its decision to the judge prior to the person's discharge (from the establishment).

The judge decides whether and to what extent any suspended sentences are to be executed on discharge from the establishment or at the end of the period of care. The competent authority must express its opinion on this subject when reporting its decision. The period of detention in the treatment establishment must be deducted from the sentence that was suspended at the time the measure was pronounced.

Thailand

Legislation: Narcotics Law of 1979.

1. *Grounds:* A person who has consumed the (prescribed) narcotics and applied for treatment in a medical establishment before his offence is discovered by competent authority and has strictly complied with the rules and regulations for treatment and the disciplinary rules of the medical establishment and obtained a certificate from the competent official as prescribed by the Minister (in charge and in control of the execution of the law) is exempted from the penalties for the statutory offences provided for in Sections 91 and 92 of the Law, as follows:

   (*a*) *Section 91:* consumption of narcotics belonging to category I (e.g., heroin); or category II (e.g., morphine, cocaine, codeine, medicinal opium) except for the curing of diseases upon authorized prescription by a medical doctor or dentist.

   (*b*) *Section 92:* consumption of narcotics belonging to category V (e.g., marijuana, *kratom* plant).

2. *Application:* Not stated.

3. *Decision-making authority:* Not stated.

4. *Medical examination:* Not stated.

5. *Treatment programme:* Not stated.

6. *Length of stay:* Not stated.

7. *Appeal:* Not stated.

8. *Periodic review:* Not stated.

9. *Discharge procedure(s):* Not stated.

Union of Soviet Socialist Republics
(Russian Soviet Federal Socialist Republic)

Legislation: Decree of 1 March 1974 on the compulsory treatment and occupational rehabilitation of chronic alcoholics.

Note: Any person who has been sentenced to imprisonment for an offence committed in a curative and labour rehabilitation preventorium, or committed prior to admission thereto but after commitment by a people's court for compulsory treatment for chronic alcoholism, is subject (after having served his criminal penalty) to commitment to a preventorium for the period of treatment that has not been completed, where medical findings indicate the necessity of such treatment.

United Kingdom (England and Wales)

Legislation: Criminal Justice Act of 1972. Power of constable to take drunken offender to treatment centre.

Section 34 provides that a constable may, if he sees fit, arrest any person who is drunk and incapable, drunk and riotous or disorderly in his conduct, or drunk and disorderly while in a public place and may take such person to any medical treatment centre for alcoholics approved for such purposes by the Secretary of State; while the person is being taken to the treatment centre he shall be deemed to be in lawful custody. The treatment centre need not admit the person for treatment and use of the authority conferred in this law does not preclude the person being charged with any crime.

United States of America (Federal)

Legislation: Narcotic Addict Rehabilitation Act of 1966, as amended (Public Law No. 89–793).

See p. 161 for a summary of this Act.

United States of America (Massachusetts)

Legislation: Sections 10–13 of Chapter 111E of the General Laws: Drug Rehabilitation Law of 24 December 1981.

A. *Section 10. Defendant charged with drug offence.*

1. *Grounds:* Any defendant who is charged with a drug offence.

2. *Application:* Any defendant who is charged with a drug offence must, upon being brought before the court on such charge, be informed that he is entitled to request an examination to determine whether or not he is a drug-dependent person who would benefit by treatment, and that if he chooses to exercise such right he must do so in writing within five days of being so informed.

   If the defendant requests such an examination, the court may in its discretion determine that the defendant is a drug-dependent person, who would benefit by treatment, without ordering examination. In such event, the court must inform the defendant that he may request assignment to a drug-treatment facility, and advise him of the consequences of assignment and that if he is so assigned the court proceedings will be stayed for the term of such assignment.

3. *Decision-making authority:* The provisions of Section 10 apply to proceedings in the superior court provided, however, that no defendant who has been examined for his drug dependence pursuant to this Section in a district court has the right to a new examination if his case is bound over or appealed to the superior court; provided, however, that a superior court judge may, in his discretion, grant a second such drug examination.

   The court proceedings are stayed for the period during which a request made under this Section is under consideration by the court. If the defendant requests an examination, the court must, unless it has already determined that the defendant is a drug-dependent person, appoint a psychiatrist, or if it is, in the discretion of the court, impracticable to do so, a physician, to conduct the examination at an appropriate location designated by it. In no event may the request for such an examination or any statement made by the defendant during the course of the examination, or any finding of the psychiatrist or physician be admissible against the defendant in any court proceedings.

   The psychiatrist or physician must report his findings in writing to the court within five days after the completion of the examination, stating the facts upon which the findings are based and the reasons therefor.

   If the defendant is also charged with a violation of any law other than a drug offence, the stay of the court proceedings may be vacated by the court upon the report of the psychiatrist or physician, whereupon the report must be considered upon disposition of the charges in accordance with Sections 11 and 12, and the remaining provisions of this chapter do not apply. If the defendant is charged with a drug offence only and if the psychiatrist or physician reports that the defendant is a drug-dependent person who would benefit by treatment, the court must inform the defendant that he may request assignment to a drug-treatment facility, and advise him of the consequences of the assignment and that if he is so assigned the court proceedings will be stayed for the term of such assignment.

   If the defendant requests assignment and if the court determines that he is a drug-dependent person who would benefit from treatment the court may stay the court proceedings and assign him to a drug-treatment facility.

In determining whether or not to grant a request for assignment under this Section, the court must consider the report, the past criminal record of the defendant, the availability of adequate and appropriate treatment at a facility, the nature of the offence with which the defendant is charged including, but not limited to, whether the offence charged is that of a sale or sale to a minor, and any other relevant evidence.

If the court does not assign the defendant to a facility, the stay of the court proceedings is vacated.

Note: The following terms are defined in Section 1 of Chapter 111E:

"Director" means the director of the division of drug rehabilitation.

"Drug" means any controlled substance as defined in Chapter 94-C, or glue or cement, as defined in Section 19 of Chapter 270.

"Drug-dependent person" means a person who is unable to function effectively and whose inability to do so causes, or results from, the use of a drug other than alcohol, tobacco or lawful beverages containing caffeine, and other than from a medically prescribed drug when such drug is medically indicated and the intake is proportional to the medical need.

"Drug offence" means an act or omission relating to a dependence-related drug which constitutes an offence pursuant to Section 21 or subdivision (1) of Section 24 of Chapter 90, Section 8 of Chapter 90B, Chapter 94C, or Section 62 of Chapter 131; provided, however, in the case of a juvenile this definition is applicable if said juvenile is charged with being delinquent by reason of an offence pursuant to said sections.

"Facility" means any public or private place, or portion thereof, which is not part of or located at a penal institution and which is not operated by the federal government, providing services especially designed for the treatment of drug-dependent persons or persons in need of immediate assistance due to the use of a dependence-related drug.

"First drug offence" means that illegal act which stands pending for trial. Persons arrested for prior drug offences in which the case has been terminated favourably to the defendant, are considered as a first drug offender.

"Independent psychiatrist" means a psychiatrist, other than one holding an office or appointment in any department, board, or agency of the commonwealth, or in any public facility or penal facility.

"Independent physician" means a physician, other than one holding an office or appointment, in any department, board, or agency of the commonwealth, or in any public facility or penal facility.

"Private facility" means a facility other than one operated by the federal government, the commonwealth, or any political subdivision thereof.

"Psychiatrist" means a physician who has board certification or board eligibility in psychiatry.

"Public facility" means a facility operated by the commonwealth or any political subdivision thereof.

"Tolerance" means a state in which increased dosage of a dependence-related drug is required to produce the physiological and psychological effects of prior dosages.

"Treatment" means services and programmes for the care and rehabilitation of drug-dependent persons, or persons in need of immediate assistance due to the use of a dependence-related drug, including, but not limited to, medical, psychiatric, psychological, vocational, educational, and recreational services and programmes.

"Withdrawal" means the involuntary physical and psychological reaction or illness which occurs when the intake of a dependence-related drug to which the user has developed a tolerance is abruptly terminated.

4. *Medical examination:* See paragraph 3 above.

Note: If the psychiatrist or physician reports that the person is not a drug-dependent person who would benefit by treatment, the defendant is entitled to request a hearing to determine whether or not he is a drug-dependent person who would benefit by treatment. The court may on its own motion, or upon the request of the defendant or his counsel, appoint an independent psychiatrist, or if it is impracticable to do so, an independent physician to examine the defendant and testify at the hearing. If the court determines that the defendant is a drug-dependent person who would benefit by treatment, the procedures and standards applicable to a defendant who is determined by the court, following the report of the first examining psychiatrist or physician to be a drug-dependent person who would benefit by treatment, apply to the defendant.

5. *Treatment programme:* If the defendant requests assignment and if the court determines that the defendant is a drug-dependent person who would benefit by treatment, and the defendant is charged for the first time with a drug offence not involving the sale or manufacture of dependence-related drugs, and there are no continuances outstanding with respect of the defendant pursuant to this Section, the court must order that the defendant be assigned to a drug-treatment facility without consideration of any other factors.

Before such assignment, the court must consult the facility or the division, to determine that adequate and appropriate treatment is available.

If the defendant requests assignment, and if the court determines that the defendant is a drug-dependent person who would benefit by treatment, and the defendant is charged for the first time with a drug offence not involving the sale or manufacture of dependence-related drugs, and there are no continuances outstanding with respect to the defendant pursuant to this Section, and adequate and appropriate treatment at a facility is not available, the stay of court proceedings remains in effect until such time as adequate and appropriate treatment at a facility is available.

In all other cases, an assignment order may not be made unless, after consultation with the facility or the division, the court determines that adequate and appropriate treatment is available, provided, however, that the court may in its discretion order that the stay of court proceedings remain outstanding until such time as adequate and appropriate treatment is available.

If the stay of the court proceedings remains in effect for the reason that adequate and appropriate treatment at a facility is not available, the issue of the availability of adequate and appropriate treatment at a facility may be reopened at any time by the court on its own motion, or on a motion by the prosecutor, or the defendant.

At any time during the term of assignment, the administrator may transfer any in-patient to an outpatient programme if he finds that the patient is a proper subject for such a programme; provided, however, that the administrator may retransfer the patient to an inpatient programme if he finds that the person is not suitable for outpatient treatment, and provided further that immediately upon such transfer the administrator notifies in writing the assigning court and the director of such transfer.

6. *Length of stay:* An order assigning a person under Section 10 must specify the period of assignment, which must not exceed 18 months or the period of time equal to the maximum sentence he could have received had he been found guilty of every count alleged in the complaint or indictment, whichever is shorter.

7. *Appeal:* In no event may any defendant be assigned pursuant to Section 10 unless the defendant consents in writing to the terms of the assignment order.

8. *Periodic Review:* Throughout the period of assignment at a facility pursuant to Section 10, the administrator of the facility must provide quarterly written reports on the progress being made in treatment by the defendant to the assigning court. Failure to comply may be grounds for suspension of the facility's licence. At the end of the assignment period, or when the patient is discharged by the administrator, or when the patient prematurely terminates treatment at a facility, whichever occurs first, the administrator must notify in writing the assigning court and the director of such termination, and state the reasons for such termination, including whether the defendant successfully completed the treatment programme.

In reaching its determination of whether or not the defendant successfully completed the treatment programme, the court must consider, but not be limited to, whether the defendant cooperated with the administrator and complied with the terms and conditions imposed on him during his assignment. If the report states that the defendant successfully completed the treatment programme, or if the defendant completes the form of treatment ordered by the court, the court must dismiss the charges pending against the defendant. If the report does not so state, or if the defendant does not complete the term of treatment ordered by the court, then, on the basis of the report and any other relevant evidence, the court may take such action as it deems appropriate, including the dismissal of the charges or the revocation of the stay of the court proceedings.

9. *Discharge procedures:* Any patient assigned under Section 10 may apply in writing to the assigning court for discharge or transfer either from inpatient or outpatient treatment or from one facility to another; provided, however, that not more than one such application may be made in any three-month period. Upon receipt of an application for discharge or transfer, the court must give written notice to the patient of his right to a hearing and to be represented by counsel at the hearing.

Within ten days of the receipt by the court of an application for discharge, the administrator and an independent psychiatrist, or, if none is available, an independent physician, designated by the court to make an examination of the patient must report to the court as to whether or not the patient would benefit from further treatment at a facility. If the court determines that the patient would no longer so benefit, the patient's application for discharge must be granted. If the court does not so determine, the application must be denied.

B. *Section 11. Defendant charged with other than drug offence.*

Note: The full text of this Section reads as follows:

"Any person found guilty of a violation of any law other than a drug offense, who prior to disposition of the charge, states that he is a drug dependent person, and requests an examination shall be examined by a psychiatrist or, if, in the discretion of the court, it is impracticable to do so, by a physician, to determine whether or not he is a drug dependent person who is a drug addict who would benefit by treatment or a drug dependent person who is not a drug addict but who would benefit by treatment.

"If the defendant has previously been examined, pursuant to a request for an examination made in accordance with Section 10, the report of the physician or psychiatrist who conducted the examination shall serve at the examination provided for under this Section.

"The examination shall be conducted at any appropriate location upon appropriate order of the court. In no event shall the request for such examination or any statement made by the defendant during the course of the examination or any finding of the psychiatrist or physician be admissible against the defendant in any criminal proceeding. The psychiatrist or physician shall report in writing to the court within five days after the completion of the examination, stating the facts upon which the report is based and the reasons therefor.

"If the report states that the defendant is a drug dependent person who would benefit by treatment, and if the court orders that the defendant be confined to a jail, house of correction, prison, or other correctional institution, the court may further order that the defendant be afforded treatment at a penal facility for the whole or any part of the term of imprisonment; provided, however, that the court shall determine the term of treatment to be afforded with the advice of the administrator of the penal facility; and provided, further, that the court shall not order that the defendant be afforded treatment at a penal facility unless the defendant consents to the order in writing. The administrator may terminate treatment of the defendant at such time as he determines the defendant will no longer benefit by treatment.

"If the report states that the defendant is not a drug dependent person who would benefit by treatment, the defendant shall be entitled to request a hearing on whether or not he is a drug dependent person who would benefit by treatment. If the court determines that he is a drug dependent person who would benefit by treatment, and if the court orders that the defendant be confined to a jail, house of correction, prison, or other correctional institution, the court may order that the defendant be afforded treatment at a penal facility in accordance with the standards and procedures set forth in this Section.

"If the court does not order that the defendant be confined to a jail, house of correction, prison, or other correctional institution, the court may order that the defendant be afforded treatment pursuant to Section 12 (probation of drug-dependent persons)."

C. *Section 12: Probation of drug-dependent persons.*

Note: The full text of this Section reads as follows:

"Any court may, in placing on probation a defendant who is a drug-dependent person who would benefit by treatment, impose as a condition of probation that the defendant receive treatment in a facility as an inpatient or outpatient; provided, however, that the court shall not impose such a condition of probation unless, after consulting with the facility, it determines that adequate and appropriate treatment is available. The defendant shall receive treatment at a facility for so long as the administrator of the facility deems that the defendant will benefit by treatment, but in no event shall he receive treatment at the facility for a period longer than the period of probation ordered by the court. A periodic program of urinalysis may be employed as a condition of probation to determine the drug free status of the probationer. The cost of the administration of such program shall be borne by the commonwealth. If at any time during the period of treatment the defendant does not cooperate with the administrator or the probation officer, or does not conduct himself in accordance with the order or conditions of his probation, the administrator or the probation officer may make a report thereon to the court which placed him on probation which may consider such conduct as a breach of probation.

"Throughout the period of probation at a facility pursuant to this Section, the administrator of said facility shall provide quarterly written reports on the progress being made in treatment by the defendant to the defendant's probation officer."

D. *Section 13. Juveniles and youthful offenders.*

Note: The full text of this Section reads as follows:

"The division shall accept for referral juveniles and youthful offenders referred to the division by the department of youth services. Application by the department of youth services for such referral shall be made to the director.

"Upon receipt by the director of a request for referral from the youth service board, he shall, unless the person has been examined pursuant to Section 10, designate a psychiatrist or, if in the discretion of the director it is impracticable to do so, a physician, to make an examination of the person to be referred to determine whether or not he is a drug dependent person who would benefit by treatment. The psychiatrist or physician shall report his findings in writing to the director after the completion of the examination, stating the facts upon which the findings are based and the reasons therefor.

"If the director finds that the person is a drug dependent person who would benefit by treatment and that adequate treatment is available at an appropriate facility he may recommend to the department of youth services that the person be admitted to the facility as an inpatient or an outpatient.

"In determining whether to admit to a facility a person who is reported to be a drug dependent person who would benefit by treatment, the director shall consider the past record of treatment, if any, afforded the person at a facility, and whether or not the person complied with the terms of any prior admission.

"If the director decides to admit to a facility a juvenile or youthful offender pursuant to this Section, he shall recommend to the department of youth services the period deemed necessary to accomplish adequate and appropriate treatment but in no case shall the period exceed one year.

"The director shall also notify the department of youth services of the nature of the treatment to be afforded and the facility to which the person will be admitted. If the department of youth services consents in writing to admission to the facility, to the nature of the treatment to be afforded, and to the period deemed necessary to accomplish treatment, the person shall be admitted to the facility.

"If the director decides that the referral to the division is to be refused because the juvenile or youthful offender is not a drug dependent person who would benefit by treatment or because adequate treatment is not available at an appropriate facility, he shall make known in writing to the department of youth services the basis for this decision.

"The referral to the division shall terminate at the conclusion of the period of treatment to which the department of youth services consents or upon a determination by the director that the juvenile or youthful offender will no longer benefit by treatment, whichever first occurs. If the director determines before the conclusion of the period of treatment to which the department of youth services consents that the juvenile or youthful offender will no longer benefit by treatment, he shall make known in writing to the department of youth services the basis for his decision.

"Juveniles and youthful offenders referred to the division pursuant to this Section shall remain subject to the jurisdiction and control of the department of youth services for all purposes, including, but not limited to, discharge and release; provided, however, that the treatment to be afforded the juvenile and youthful offenders referred to the division shall be within the jurisdiction and control of the division. In no event, however, shall a juvenile or youthful offender be referred for a period longer than the period during which he is subject to the jurisdiction and control of the department of youth services."

A2.3. COMPULSORY REPORTING, CENTRAL REGISTRIES, LABORATORY TESTING AND COMMUNITY SURVEILLANCE

Burma

Legislation: Narcotics and Dangerous Drugs Rules, 1974.

1. *Reporting:* See paragraph 2 below.

2. *Registration:* Addicts to narcotics and dangerous drugs are required to present and register themselves at the medical treatment centres nearest to their place of residence. The medical officer in charge of the centre must enter on the Register of Addicts to Narcotic and Dangerous Drugs (a prescribed form) the names of the addicts who present themselves for registration. The Register is to be kept confidential "so as to protect the dignity of such addicts". The medical officer in charge must issue a Registration Card (a prescribed form) to any such addict immediately after the name of the addict has been entered in the Register.

When a registered person moves permanently from one township to another, the person must notify the medical officer in each township.

When "it has been validly found" (no standard or procedure stated in the legislation) that any person whose name has been entered in the Register is, as a result of "medical treatment" (not specifically defined), in such a condition as "to require no further consumption of narcotic and dangerous drugs" (this presumably means that withdrawal symptoms no longer occur), the Drug Addicts Registration and Medical Treatment Supervision Board has discretionary authority to delete the name of the person from the Register. All documents relating to such person are then destroyed. For occasional users of narcotic and dangerous drugs, separate records containing full particulars (name, occupation, address, etc.) must be completed and kept confidential for use in the taking of health statistics. No Register is established for "occasional users".

"Addict" means any person who has the desire to use narcotics and dangerous drugs and who is unable to refrain from taking such drugs and who suffers from withdrawal symptoms when he does not consume the same.

"Occasional user" means any person who consumes narcotics and dangerous drugs occasionally and who, in spite of non-consumption of the same, is still free from withdrawal symptoms.

3. *Laboratory testing:* Not stated.

4. *Community surveillance:* Not stated.

Colombia

Legislation: Decree No. 1188 of 25 June 1974 promulgating the National Statute on Narcotic Drugs.

1. *Reporting:* Doctors treating patients who need drugs or substances that produce physical or psychic dependence in quantities greater than therapeutic doses are required to inform the competent health authorities, supplying the following particulars: the name, age, marital status, nationality, and domicile of the patient, how long he has been using the substances, what they are and the daily dose required.

2. *Registration:* The Ministry of Public Health is required to keep a register of drug addicts, which must contain all the data necessary for evaluating, at any time, the trend of this phenomenon in the national territory.

The register is confidential and the data it contains may be used only to prevent illicit traffic.

3. *Laboratory testing:* Not stated.

4. *Community surveillance:* Not stated.

Cyprus

Legislation: The Narcotic Drugs and Psychotropic Substances Law, 1977

1. *Reporting:* The Council of Ministers may (by regulation) require any medical practitioner who attends a person whom he considers, or has reasonable grounds to suspect, to be addicted to controlled drugs of any description, to furnish to the prescribed authority such particulars with respect to the said person as may be prescribed.

2. *Registration:* Not stated.

3. *Laboratory testing:* Not stated.

4. *Community surveillance:* Not stated.

Finland

Legislation: Law No. 96 of 10 February 1961 on the treatment of persons making improper use of intoxicants.

1. *Reporting:* Any person found intoxicated must be reported without delay by the police and military authorities to the social welfare board in the community where the person is resident.

   Medical practitioners shall supply to the social welfare board all information concerning any patient who may be a drunken driver in order that the person may be given necessary treatment.

2. *Registration:* See paragraph 1 above.

3. *Laboratory testing:* Not stated.

4. *Community surveillance:* The social welfare board must order any person needing treatment to be placed under surveillance, and ensure proper periods and methods of surveillance.

   A person needing treatment and placed under surveillance must where necessary, be afforded assistance as far as possible.

   The person subject to surveillance must:

   (*a*) where necessary, undergo medical examination and treatment;

   (*b*) at certain times, or otherwise whenever summoned, report to the social welfare officer or to the authority or supervisor designated by the social welfare board, to supply the information necessary for purposes of surveillance; and

   (*c*) observe the instructions given to him with regard to his place of residence or domicile.

   Surveillance must be so arranged as not to be unduly onerous or inconvenient to the person concerned.

France

Legislation: Law No. 70-1320 of 31 December 1970 relating to the health measures for the control of drug dependence and the suppression of traffic in, and illicit use of, poisons.

1. *Reporting:* Whenever the public prosecutor (*procureur de la République*), in pursuance of Article L. 628-1 of the Public Health Code, orders a person who has made illicit use of narcotics to undergo detoxification (*cure de désintoxication*) or to submit to medical surveillance, he must inform the competent health authority.

2. *Registration:* Not stated.

3. *Laboratory testing:* Not stated.

4. *Community surveillance:* Any person making illicit use of narcotics must be placed under the surveillance of the health authority.

Note: (*a*) *Special provisions applicable to persons reported by the public prosecutor:*

The public prosecutor may order a person who has made illicit use of narcotics to undergo detoxification or to submit to medical surveillance.

A medical examination of the person and an investigation into his family, professional and social life must be conducted by the health authorities. If the health authority considers, on the basis of the medical examination, that the person's condition is not such as to necessitate detoxification, the authority must order him to submit for as long as is necessary to medical surveillance, either by a physician of its choice or by a social hygiene clinic or approved health establishment, either public or private. The health authority must follow the progress of the treatment and at regular intervals inform the public prosecutor's office of the medical and social situation of the person.

(*b*) *Special provisions applicable to persons reported by the medical and social services:*

The case of a person making illicit use of narcotics may be referred to the health authority either by the certificate of a physician or by the report of a social worker. The health authority must then make arrangements for a medical examination of the person and an investigation into his family, professional, and social life.

If it appears from the medical examination that the person's condition is not such as to necessitate detoxification, the health authority must order him to submit for as long as is necessary to medical surveillance either by a physician of its choice or by a social hygiene clinic or approved health establishment, either public or private.

(*c*) *Special provisions applicable to persons attending preventive voluntary or curative establishments of their own accord:*

Drug-dependent persons who of their own accord attend a clinic or hospital establishment for purposes of treatment are not subject to the above provisions. If they specifically request, their identity may be kept secret at the time of admission. Their identity may be revealed only on grounds other than the suppression of the illicit use of narcotics.

Persons who have received treatment under the conditions provided for in the preceding paragraph may ask the physician who treated them for a personal certificate specifying the period(s), duration and purpose of treatment.

Hong Kong

Legislation: Dangerous Drugs (Amendment) Ordinance 1981, and Drug Addiction Treatment Centres Ordinance (Chapter 244).

1. *Reporting:* Reporting agencies (e.g., hospitals, clinics, voluntary agencies, etc., providing services to a "drug abuser") specified in the legislation must disclose certain "confidential information", defined as information recorded by the Registry mentioned

below or a reporting agency in respect of any person and which relates to any one or more of the following:

(a) the use, or alleged use, by that person of a dangerous drug;

(b) the conviction of that person for an offence under the Dangerous Drugs Ordinance;

(c) the care, treatment or rehabilitation of that person by reason of his use of a dangerous drug.

"Drug abuser" means a person who is the subject of any confidential information.

2. *Registration:* Not stated, but a Central Registry of Drug Abuse exists, the purposes of which include:

(a) the collection, collating, and analysis of confidential information supplied by reporting agencies and of information on drug abuse and its treatment supplied by other sources; and

(b) the publication of statistical information on drug abuse and on various forms of treatment of drug abuse.

3. *Laboratory testing:* Not stated, but see paragraph 4 below.

4. *Community surveillance:* The Commissioner of Narcotics may order that a person released from a centre be subject to supervision, for a period of 12 months from the date of release, by such organization or person as the Commissioner may specify. While under such supervision the person must comply with such requirements (e.g., medical examination) as the Commissioner may specify. The Commissioner may at any time vary or cancel a supervision order. If a person in respect of whom such an order is in force is addicted to any dangerous drug or has failed to comply with the order, a further detention order may be issued by a magistrate on application by or on behalf of the Commissioner. If a magistrate is satisfied that a person detained in a centre is exercising a bad influence on other inmates, he may, subject to certain conditions, order his transfer to prison.

Indonesia

Legislation: Law No. 9 of 1976 on narcotics.

1. *Reporting:* Parents or guardians of an under-age narcotic addict are required to report him to an official assigned by the Ministry of Health and to bring him to a hospital or to the nearest physician to receive necessary medication and nursing. Medication and nursing are carried out in rehabilitation institutions. The establishment, organization, and function of rehabilitation institutions and branches are determined by the President. Involvement of private and government community agencies is sought.

2. *Registration:* Not stated.

3. *Laboratory testing:* Not stated.

4. *Community surveillance:* Not stated.

Note: For definitions of "narcotic addict" and "rehabilitation" under this Law, see p. 140.

Italy

Legislation: Law No. 685 of 22 December 1975 on control of narcotic drugs and psychotropic substances, prevention and care of dependence on such drugs or substances and rehabilitation of persons dependent on them.

1. *Reporting:* Any physician who attends or assists a person using narcotic drugs or psychotropic substances for personal, non-therapeutic purposes must report the fact to one of the centres (hospitals, clinics, medical, or social centres) established for the care and rehabilitation of persons using narcotic drugs. Before notification is made, the physician must ask the person concerned if he intends to undergo treatment, either anonymously or otherwise. In cases where the person does not voluntarily undergo treatment, or interrupts a course of treatment, the physician is required to report the fact immediately to the nearest centre.

The police must inform the nearest of the aforementioned centres and the local magistrate of all cases coming to their attention of persons who use narcotic drugs or psychotropic substances for non-therapeutic purposes.

The police must accompany to the nearest office any person who may be found in a state of acute intoxication presumed to result from the use of narcotic drugs or psychotropic substances.

2. *Registration:* Not stated.

3. *Laboratory testing:* Not stated.

4. *Community surveillance:* Not stated.

Japan

Legislation: Narcotic Control Law (Law No. 14 of 17 March 1953), as amended.

1. *Reporting:* Formal reports must be made as follows:

   (*a*) A medical practitioner, if he has diagnosed as a result of a medical examination that the medical examinee is a narcotic addict, must report the name, domicile, age, sex of such person and other matters to the governor of the Metropolis, Hokkaido or Prefecture having jurisdiction over such person's place of residence, as expeditiously as possible. The governor of the Metropolis, Hokkaido or Prefecture must, upon receipt of the information, report it to the Minister of Health and Welfare.

   (*b*) A narcotic control officer, a local narcotic control official, a police official, or a maritime safety official, if he has found any narcotic addict or any person who is suspected to be a narcotic addict, must communicate the name, domicile, age, and sex of such person, and the reason why such person is considered or suspected to be a narcotic addict to the governor of the Metropolis, Hokkaido or Prefecture having jurisdiction over such person's place of residence as expeditiously as possible.

(*c*) A public prosecutor, where a person is a narcotic addict or is suspected to be a narcotic addict, or where the judgement of the court (excluding judgements in which penal servitude, imprisonment or detention has been imposed without probation) has been determined with respect to the accused who is a narcotic addict or who is suspected to be a narcotic addict, must communicate the name, domicile, age, and sex of such person to the governor of the Metropolis, Hokkaido, or Prefecture having jurisdiction over such person's place of residence as expeditiously as possible.

(*d*) The chief of a correctional institution (prison, reform, and training school, juvenile detention and classification home, or woman's guidance home), if he releases an inmate who is a narcotic addict or who is suspected to be a narcotic addict, must communicate the name, place of return, age, and sex of such person, date of release, the name and domicile of the caretaker of such person, and the reason why such person is considered to be a narcotic addict or a person who is suspected to be a narcotic addict, to the governor of the Metropolis, Hokkaido, or Prefecture having jurisdiction over such person's place of return (indicating the location of the correctional institution concerned, if such person has no place of return or it is unknown).

2. *Registration:* Not stated.

3. *Laboratory testing:* The governor of the Metropolis, Hokkaido, or Prefecture may, if he considers it necessary with respect to a narcotic addict or a person who is suspected to be a narcotic addict, order a medical examination (i.e., urine test) of such person.

4. *Community surveillance:* Not stated.

Malaysia

Legislation: The Dangerous Drugs Act (No. 234 of 1952) (revised 1980).

1. *Reporting:* A registered medical practitioner must notify the Minister of Welfare Services of persons who are being treated or rehabilitated by him as drug dependants.

2. *Registration:* Not stated.

3. *Laboratory testing:* Not stated, but any social welfare officer or any police officer not below the rank of sergeant or an officer in charge of a police station may take into his custody any person whom he reasonably suspects to be a drug dependant and must within 24 hours produce such person before a magistrate. If the magistrate has reasonable cause to believe that the person so brought before him is a drug dependant, he may order such person to be remanded and be medically examined or observed by a medical officer at a detention centre.

4. *Community surveillance:* A drug dependant admitted to a rehabilitation centre must,

after his release from that centre, be under the aftercare of a social welfare officer or of such other person as the rehabilitation committee may appoint on the advice of the social welfare officer for a period of two years.

Any person who is subject to aftercare on release from a rehabilitation centre must, while under such supervision, comply with such conditions as may be stated in the aftercare order by the Board of Visitors of the rehabilitation centre.

Mexico

Legislation: Regulations of 23 July 1976 concerning narcotic drugs and psychotropic substances.

1. *Reporting:* Qualified medical personnel who treat cases of drug addiction must report such cases to the nearest office of the Ministry of Health and Welfare within eight days of the date on which the case comes to their attention, enclosing their diagnosis and opinion on the need for intervention by the Ministry.

2. *Registration:* Not stated.

3. *Laboratory testing:* Not stated.

4. *Community surveillance:* Not stated.

Norway

A. *Law No. 42 of 8 June 1979 amending Law No. 7 of 12 December 1958 on prisons.*

1. *Reporting:* Not stated.

2. *Registration:* Not stated.

3. *Laboratory testing:* The director of a prison is authorized to order the taking of urine tests, breath tests, and such other examinations as can be performed without danger or significant discomfort in order to detect whether an inmate has consumed an intoxicating or psychotropic substance. A physical search may also be carried out if it is suspected that an inmate has hidden such a substance in his body (such a search may be carried out only by health personnel).

4. *Community surveillance:* Not stated.

B. *Law of 1932 concerning temperance committees, as amended.*

1. *Reporting:* See p. 147.

2. *Registration:* Not stated.

3. *Laboratory testing:* Not stated.

4. *Community surveillance:* The temperance committee must without delay investigate cases of persons residing or living in the municipality who, by reason of the use of liquors or other intoxicating or tranquillizing substances, are an obvious danger to themselves and their surroundings. The committee may also on its own initiative take action against such persons.

Pakistan

Legislation: The Drug Act of 1957 (Opium Rules of 1957).

1. *Reporting:* Not stated.

2. *Registration:* Registration of opium addicts.

Any person not below the age of 25 years who is addicted to opium may apply to the Superintendent of Excise for registration as an addict after having been examined medically by the Civil Surgeon, Karachi, who must also note the number of units per month recommended by him for the consumption of the addict in the space reserved for that purpose in the prescribed form.

The Superintendent of Excise must, on receipt of such application, enter the particulars in the register and issue an opium card, valid up to the end of the financial year.

The ration card should bear a photograph and the signature and thumb impression of the addict duly attested by the Superintendent of Excise. The registered addict may then have the opium ration card registered with any authorized opium vendor in the Federal Capital and purchase opium during that financial year from that vendor.

The card may be registered with another authorized opium vendor only with the prior permission in writing of the Superintendent of Excise.

If an addict wants to have his opium ration card transferred from one licensed shop to another for any reason, the transfer, if considered reasonable, may be ordered by the Superintendent of Excise. If opium is not available in the licensed shop at which the opium ration card of an addict is registered, the addict may, with the prior permission of the Superintendent of Excise, purchase opium from the nearest alternative shop where opium may be available, until opium again becomes available at the shop where his opium ration card is actually registered.

If a person addicted to opium visits the Federal Capital from outside and desires to have opium for his personal use, he may at any time during his stay in the Federal Capital apply for the "grant of addict certificate". The period of validity of such certificate must be shown in red in the opium ration card. Upon the expiry of the period of validity, the addict may either have it renewed for a further period of his stay in the Federal Capital, or surrender it to the Superintendent of Excise.

3. *Laboratory testing:* Not stated.

4. *Community surveillance:* Not stated.

Philippines

Legislation: The Dangerous Drug Act of 30 March 1972.

Note: See p. 182.

Senegal

Legislation: Law No. 75-81 of 9 July 1975 repealing and amending Section 8 of Law 72-24 of 19 April 1972 on the prevention of contraventions in the field of narcotics.

1. *Reporting:* Any physician who, while making a diagnosis or providing a treatment, becomes convinced that a person is illicitly using narcotics, is required to notify the chief medical officer of the region.

2. *Registration:* Not stated.

3. *Laboratory testing:* Not stated, but where the chief medical officer of the region is notified of a case of a person using narcotics, either by a certificate from a physician or a report from the Regional Governor or from the Prefect, he must arrange for the person concerned to be medically examined by at least three physicians and must in addition conduct an investigation into the person's family, professional, and social life.

4. *Community surveillance:* If, on the basis of a medical examination, it appears that the condition of the person concerned merely requires that he be placed under medical surveillance, the chief medical officer of the region must order him to submit to medical surveillance either by a physician or by a care establishment under the jurisdiction of the Ministry of Public Health.

Drug-dependent persons who report voluntarily to a care establishment under the jurisdiction of the Ministry of Public Health with a view to treatment are not subject to the above provisions.

Upon written application, drug-dependent persons may remain anonymous when admitted. Their wish to remain anonymous may be set aside only for reasons other than the prevention of illicit use of narcotics.

Singapore

Legislation: The Misuse of Drugs Act of 16 March 1973 (No. 5 of 1973, as amended) to provide for the control of dangerous or otherwise harmful drugs and for purposes connected therewith.

1. *Reporting:* A medical practitioner who attends a person whom he considers, or has reasonable grounds to suspect, is a drug addict must, within seven days of the attendance, furnish to both the Director of Medical Services and the Director, Central Narcotics Bureau, the following information concerning that person: (*a*) name; (*b*) identity card number; (*c*) sex; (*d*) age; (*e*) address; (*f*) the drug to which the person is believed to be addicted.

2. *Registration:* Not stated.

3. *Laboratory testing:* The Director of the Central Narcotics Bureau may require any person whom he reasonably suspects to be a drug addict to be medically examined or observed by a Government medical officer or a medical practitioner.

Any officer of the Central Narcotics Bureau, immigration officer or police officer not below the rank of sergeant may, if he reasonably suspects any person to have smoked, administered to himself or otherwise consumed, a controlled drug (an offence under the Misuse of Drugs Act), require that person to provide a specimen of his urine for a urine test.

A person who, without reasonable excuse, fails to provide a specimen of his urine within such time as may be required by any of the named officers is guilty of an offence.

Any person who has been required to provide a specimen of his urine for a urine test may, within such manner as may be prescribed, apply for a second test of the specimen of his urine which is kept for that purpose.

If as a result of any second urine test it is found that there is no controlled drug in the specimen of his urine, he must be immediately discharged from any approved institution in which he is detained.

4. *Community surveillance:* Not stated.

Somalia

Legislation: Law No. 46 of 3 March 1970 concerning the production of, trade in, and use of narcotic drugs.

1. *Reporting:* A medical practitioner who attends or examines a person suffering from chronic addiction produced by narcotic drugs must report the case within 48 hours to the police and to the Central Narcotics Bureau.

Any person who infringes this provision is liable to a fine, and in the event of a second or subsequent offence to imprisonment for not more than one year and to suspension from the exercise of his profession for a period equal to that of the sentence imposed, starting on the date of his discharge from prison.

The police authorities, regional directors and district medical officers must notify the Central Narcotics Bureau immediately of all cases of drug addition that come to their attention.

2. *Registration:* Not stated.

3. *Laboratory testing:* Not stated.

4. *Community surveillance:* Not stated.

Sweden

Legislation: Law of 1 January 1982 on care of alcoholics and drug abusers.

1. *Reporting:* It is the duty of public authorities whose duties bring them into regular contact with alcoholics and drug abusers to notify the County Administration if it comes to their knowledge that any person is presumably in need of care under this Law. This does not apply, however, to health and medical authorities except as described below.

It is the duty of a physician whose activities bring him into contact with an alcoholic or drug abuser presumably in need of care to notify the County Administration unless the person thus in need of care can be given satisfactory care or treatment by the physician or otherwise through the medical services.

It is the duty of the public authorities referred to above to supply to the County Administration all particulars that may be relevant to inquiries pursuant to this Law.

2. *Registration:* Not stated.

3. *Laboratory testing:* Not stated.

4. *Community surveillance:* See paragraph 1 above.

Switzerland (Federal)

Legislation: Federal Law of 18 June 1968 on the prevention and control of alcohol abuse.

1. *Reporting:* Not stated.

2. *Registration:* Not stated.

3. *Laboratory testing:* Not stated.

4. *Community surveillance:* A special comission, known as the Commission for Surveillance of Convicted Alcoholics, is to be responsible for the surveillance of persons commited by a decision of a penal court to institutions for alcoholics or to hospitals. The Commission is authorized:

(*a*) to order a person's discharge as soon as he is regarded as cured;

(*b*) to order conditional discharge and to place the person on probation;

(*c*) to order, where necessary, the person's readmission to the institution or hospital. The provisions concerning surveillance cited above are applicable in such cases, and the probation period may be extended to three years.

Switzerland (St Gallen)

Legislation: Law of 18 June 1968 on the prevention and control of alcohol abuse.

1. *Reporting:* Every individual is entitled to report cases of alcoholism to the welfare centre or guardianship authorities. Official agencies, persons holding official posts and civil servants are subject to the same obligation as part of their duties.

2. *Registration:* Not stated.

3. *Laboratory testing:* Not stated.

4. *Community surveillance:* Not stated.

Tunisia

Legislation: Law No. 69-54 of 26 July 1969 prescribing regulations concerning poisons.

1. *Reporting:* The State Secretariat for Public Health must inform the National Bureau of Narcotics of all cases of prescriptions for, and consumption of, narcotics that are, in their view, indicative of abuse. Physicians must inform the Bureau of cases of drug dependence that they detect in the practice of their profession.

The Bureau forwards the documents and information submitted to it under the above provisions, as well as details of any other suspected cases of drug dependence, to the Commission on Drug Dependence, which includes three physicians nominated by the Secretary of State for Public Health. The Commission is empowered to compel any drug addict to undergo detoxification in a specialized establishment, under the conditions to be laid down by Order of the Secretary of State for Public Health.

2. *Registration:* Not stated.

3. *Laboratory testing:* Not stated.

4. *Community surveillance:* Not stated.

Union of Soviet Socialist Republics
(Russian Soviet Federal Socialist Republic)

Legislation: Decree of 21 August 1972 approving the Order on the Commission to Combat Drunkenness.

1. *Reporting:* Not stated.

2. *Registration:* See paragraph 4 below.

3. *Laboratory testing:* Not stated.

4. *Community surveillance:* The Commission to Combat Drunkenness under the auspices of the Council of Ministers of the RSFSR is responsible for harmonizing and directing activities aimed at the prevention of drunkenness, alcoholism, and contraventions committed under the influence of alcohol, and at the elimination of the factors responsible for these phenomena.

The Commission to Combat Drunkenness may establish sections to deal with the following aspects: educational work and publicity aimed at reducing the consumption of alcohol; registration of persons misusing alcohol and suffering from chronic alcoholism, and the surveillance of such persons on the part of the community; therapeutic and prophylactic measures; and the organization of control measures to ensure compliance, on the part of undertakings in the food retailing and catering industries, with the regulations in force governing trade in spirits. The Commission may likewise establish other sections.

United Kingdom (England and Wales)

Legislation: Misuse of Drugs Act 1971.

1. *Reporting:* Under the provisions of this Act, the Secretary of State may by regulations make such provisions as appear to him necessary or expedient for preventing the misuse of controlled drugs.

Regulations under this Act may in particular make provisions for requiring any doctor who attends a person whom he considers, or has reasonable grounds to suspect, is addicted (within the meaning of the regulations) to controlled drugs of any description to furnish to the prescribed authority such particulars with respect to that person as may be prescribed.

2. *Registration:* Not stated.

3. *Laboratory testing:* Not stated.

4. *Community surveillance:* Not stated.

United States of America (Massachusetts)

Legislation: Section 12 of Chapter 111E of the General Laws: Drug Rehabilitation Law of 24 December 1981.

1. *Reporting:* Not stated.

2. *Registration:* Not stated.

3. *Laboratory testing:* The full text of Section 12 reads as follows:

"Any court may, in placing on probation a defendant who is a drug-dependent person who would benefit by treatment, impose as a condition of probation that the defendant receive treatment in a facility as an inpatient or outpatient; provided, however, that the court shall not impose such a condition of probation unless, after consulting with the facility, it determines that adequate and appropriate treatment is available. The defendant shall receive treatment at the facility for so long as the administrator of the facility deems that the defendant will benefit by treatment, but in no event shall he receive treatment at the facility for a period longer than the period of probation ordered by the court. A periodic program of urinalysis may be employed as a condition of probation to determine the drug free status of the probationer. The cost of the administration of such program shall be borne by the commonwealth. If at any time during the period of treatment the defendant does not cooperate with the administrator or the probation officer, or does not conduct himself in accordance with the order or conditions of his probation, the administrator or the probation officer may make a report thereon to the court which placed him on probation, which may consider such conduct as a breach of probation.

"Throughout the period of probation at a facility pursuant to this section, the administrator of said facility shall provide quarterly written reports on the progress being made in treatment by the defendant to the defendant's probation officer."

4. *Community surveillance:* See paragraph 3 above.

Zambia

Legislation: Dangerous Drug Act, 1967.

1. *Reporting:* Any medical practitioner who considers it necessary, for the purpose of the treatment by him of any patient, to prescribe a dependence-producing drug or preparation for a period exceeding four months, must report the case to the Permanent Secretary (defined as "the Permanent Secretary responsible for the Department of the Government for the time being administering the Dangerous Drug Act, 1967").

Except as otherwise provided, no medical practitioner may supply or administer to, or prescribe for any person, a drug or preparation merely for the purpose of addiction.

A medical practitioner who considers it necessary, for the purpose of the treatment or care of a patient who is a drug addict, that he should receive supplies of a drug or preparation must report the case to the Permanent Secretary.

2. *Registration:* Not stated.

3. *Laboratory testing:* Not stated.

4. *Community surveillance:* Not stated.

Annex 3

Bibliography

WHO publications and documents

Changing patterns of drug dependence in two WHO regions. *WHO Chronicle*, **34**: 413 (1980).

CURRAN, W. J. & HARDING, T. W. *The law and mental health: harmonizing objectives.* Geneva, World Health Organization, 1978.

Drug dependence: WHO's strategies and activities. *WHO Chronicle*, **34**: 71–75 (1980).

EDWARDS, G. ET AL. *Alcohol-related disabilities.* Geneva, World Health Organization, 1977 (WHO Offset Publication, No. 32).

EDWARDS, G. & ARIF, A., ed. *Drug problems in the sociocultural context.* Geneva, World Health Organization, 1980 (WHO Public Health Paper, No. 73).

EDWARDS, G. ET AL. Nomenclature and classification of drug- and alcohol-related problems: a WHO Memorandum. *Bulletin of the World Health Organization*, **59**: 225–242 (1981).

KRAMER, J. & CAMERON, D., ed. *A manual on drug dependence.* Geneva, World Health Organization, 1975.

MOSER, J., ed. *Problems and programmes related to alcohol and drug dependence in 33 countries.* Geneva, World Health Organization, 1974.

MOSER, J. & ROOTMAN, I. *Community response to alcohol-related problems, Phase I, Final report.* Geneva, World Health Organization, 1981.

Treatment of drug addicts: a survey of existing legislation. *International digest of health legislation*, **13**: 4–46 (1962).

WHO Technical Report Series, No. 131, 1957 (*Treatment and care of drug addicts:* report of a Study Group).

WHO Technical Report Series, No. 273, 1964 (*Addiction-producing drugs:* thirteenth report of the WHO Expert Committee).

WHO Technical Report Series, No. 343, 1966 (Fifteenth report of the WHO Expert Committee on Dependence-Producing Drugs).

WHO Technical Report Series, No. 363, 1967 (*Services for the prevention and treatment of dependence on alcohol and other drugs:* fourteenth report of the WHO Expert Committee on Mental Health).

WHO Technical Report Series, No. 618, 1978 (Twenty-first report of the WHO Expert Committee on Drug Dependence).

WHO Technical Report Series, No. 650, 1980 (*Problems related to alcohol consumption:* report of a WHO Expert Committee).

* WORLD HEALTH ORGANIZATION. *Alcohol consumption and alcohol problems: development of national policies and programmes.* Geneva, 1981 (unpublished document).

* WORLD HEALTH ORGANIZATION & ADDICTION RESEARCH FOUNDATION. *Report of an ARF/WHO scientific meeting on adverse health and behavioural consequences of cannabis use.* Toronto, 1981.

* WORLD HEALTH ORGANIZATION. *WHO Interregional Workshop on Prevention and Treatment of Drug Dependence, Alexandria, 16–21 October 1978* (unpublished document).

* WORLD HEALTH ORGANIZATION, REGIONAL OFFICE FOR THE EASTERN MEDITERRANEAN. Group Meeting on mental health and mental legislation, Cairo, 12–17 June 1976 (unpublished document).

WORLD HEALTH ORGANIZATION, REGIONAL OFFICE FOR EUROPE. *Public health aspects of alcohol and drug dependence: Report on a WHO conference.* Copenhagen, 1979 (EURO Reports and Studies, No. 8).

Other books and articles

ACUERDO SUDAMERICANO SOBRE ESTUPEFACIENTES Y PSICOTROPICAS, SECRETARIA PERMANENTE. *Legislación vigente en materia de estupefacientes y psicotropicos en los estados partes del Acuerdo Sudamericano sobre Estupefacientes y Psicotropicos, Primera parte.* Buenos Aires, 1981 (document ASEP/SP/3).

ADDICTION RESEARCH FOUNDATION, *Alcohol, society and the state,* Toronto, 1981.

Alcohol abuse and the law. *Harvard law review,* **94**: 1660–1712 (1981).

---

*Persons wishing to obtain copies of these documents should write to: Division of Mental Health, World Health Organization, 1211 Geneva 27, Switzerland.

Alcohol control policies in public health perspective. Helsinki, Finnish Foundation for Alcohol Studies, 1975.

Alcohol, drugs and driving. Canberra, Government of Australia Publishing Service, 1976 (Report No. 4).

ASUNI, T. Socio-psychiatric problems of cannabis in Nigeria. *Bulletin on narcotics,* **16** (2): 17–28 (1964).

Australian Royal Commission into Drugs. Canberra, Government Publishing Service, 1980.

BABAÏAN, E. Control of narcotic substances and prevention of addiction in the USSR. *Bulletin on narcotics,* **31** (1): 13–22 (1979).

BABOR, T. ET AL. The early detection and secondary prevention of alcoholism in France. *Journal of studies on alcohol,* **44**: 600–616 (1983).

BASSIOUNI, C. *International drug control.* (Working paper, Sixth World Conference on World Peace through Law, Abidjan, Côte d'Ivoire, 1973.)

BOGAARD, W. Limits to national penal policies concerning narcotic drugs as set by the international treaties: the Dutch example. *Journal of international law and economics,* **10**: 747–760 (1975).

BROTMAN, R. & SUFFET, F. The concept of prevention and its limitations. *Annals of the American Academy of Political and Social Science,* **417**: 53–65 (1975).

BRYON, C. & CRAWSHAW, P. Law and social policy. In: *Core knowledge in the drug field,* Ottawa, Ministry of Supply and Services, 1978.

CALIFANO, J. A. *Drug abuse and alcoholism in New York. A report to Governor Hugh L. Carey, June 1982.* Albany, NY (unpublished report).

CAMPOS, M. Drug abuse and the law. *Philippine law journal,* **50**: 553–576 (1975).

CERSTEIN, D. & MOORE, M. *Alcohol and public policy: beyond the shadow of prohibition.* Washington, DC, National Academy of Sciences, 1982.

CHATTERJEE, S. The WHO Expert Committee on Drug Dependence. *International and comparative law quarterly,* **28**: 27–51 (1979).

COHRSSEN, J. *Organization of the United Nations to deal with drug abuse,* Washington, DC, The Drug Abuse Council Inc., 1973.

COUNCIL OF EUROPE, EUROPEAN COMMITTEE ON CRIME PROBLEMS. *Penal aspects of drug abuse.* Strasbourg, 1974.

COUNCIL OF EUROPE, EUROPEAN PUBLIC HEALTH COMMITTEE. *Treatment of drug dependence: Final report.* Strasbourg, 1980.

CURRAN, W. J. Comparative analysis of mental health legislation in forty-three countries: A discussion of historical trends. *International journal of law and psychiatry,* **79**: 92 (1978).

CURRAN, W. J. & SHAPIRO, E. D. *Law, medicine and forensic science,* 3rd ed., Boston, MA, Little, Brown & Co., 1982.

DAOUD, F. Drug abuse in Jordan: An exploratory study. *Drug and alcohol dependence,* **6**: 175–185 (1980).

DI GENNARO, G. *Comparative research on the effectiveness of socio-legal preventive and control measures in different countries on the interaction between criminal behaviour and drug abuse: preliminary design of the research.* Rome, United Nations Social Defence Research Institute, 1981 (unpublished document UNSDRI 349).

DILLON, J. Compulsory treatment for heroin addiction: British Columbia opens and closes the doors. *Health law in Canada,* **1**: 1, 14–18 (1980).

DIXON, W. Narcotics legislation and Islam in Egypt. *Bulletin on narcotics,* **24** (4): 11–18 (1972).

GALANTER, M. Improving medical education on alcoholism: A national program. *Currents in alcoholism,* **2**: 225–232 (1977).

GOVERNMENT OF HONG KONG, ACTION COMMITTEE AGAINST NARCOTICS. *Hong Kong narcotics report, 1980: a decade of achievement, 1971–80.* Hong Kong, 1981.

GOVERNMENT OF HONG KONG, CENTRAL REGISTRY OF DRUG ABUSE, NARCOTICS DIVISION, GOVERNMENT SECRETARIAT. *Ninth report, September 1976–December 1981.* Hong Kong, 1982.

GOVERNMENT OF HONG KONG, CENTRAL REGISTRY OF DRUG ABUSE, NARCOTICS DIVISION, GOVERNMENT SECRETARIAT. *Subsequent reporting history of discharges from prisons proper and dates.* Hong Kong, 1982.

GOVERNMENT OF HONG KONG, CENTRAL REGISTRY OF DRUG ABUSE, NARCOTICS DIVISION, GOVERNMENT SECRETARIAT. *Evaluation study on the Alumni Association of the Society for the Aid and Rehabilitation of Drug Abusers (SARDA) 1977–1979.* Hong Kong, 1982.

GOVERNMENT OF HONG KONG, CENTRAL REGISTRY OF DRUG ABUSE, NARCOTICS DIVISION, GOVERNMENT SECRETARIAT. *Study on SARDA Sek Kwan Chau Treatment and Rehabilitation Centre discharges.* Hong Kong, 1982.

GOVERNMENT OF HONG KONG, NARCOTICS DIVISION. *International Working Group on the Single Convention on Narcotic Drugs, 1961, Toronto, Canada, 20–24 September 1982: The Hong Kong experience.* Hong Kong, 1982.

GRAD, F. *Alcoholism and the law.* New York, Oceana Publications, 1971.

HARDING, T. & CURRAN, W. Mental health legislation and its relationship to program development: An international review. *Harvard journal on legislation*, **18**: 205–230 (1980).

INSTITUTE OF MEDICINE, NATIONAL ACADEMY OF SCIENCES. *Report of a study. Alcoholism, alcohol abuse, and related problems: opportunities for research.* Washington, DC, 1980 (Publication IOM 80–04).

INSTITUTE OF MEDICINE, NATIONAL ACADEMY OF SCIENCES. *An Inter-American Workshop: Legislative approaches to prevention of alcohol-related problems.* Washington, DC, 1982.

JAYASURIYA, D. C. The regulation of drug abuse in developing countries. *International digest of health legislation*, **31**: 709–750 (1980).

JERI, F. Guidelines for the prevention of drug dependence in Peru. *Revista de la sanidad de las fuerzas policiales*, **42**: 48–67 (1981).

LUKS, A. Forced treatment grows. *Legal issues*, **14**: 12–14 (1982).

MAREK, A. & REDO, S. Drug abuse in Poland. *Bulletin on narcotics*, **30** (1): 43–53 (1978).

MORAWSKI, J. [*Combating alcoholism: a compilation of the most important legal provisions.*] Zbiorwazniejszych Przepisow Pzawnych, Warsaw, 1977.

MINISTRY OF HEALTH AND WELFARE. *A brief account of drug abuse and counter-measures in Japan.* Tokyo, 1981.

MOSER, J. *Prevention of alcohol-related problems: an international review of preventive measures, policies and programmes.* Toronto, Addiction Research Foundation, 1980.

NARGEOLET, H. & VAILLE, C. Effort to promote European regional coordination of action against drug addiction. *Bulletin on narcotics*, **25** (2): 1–7 (1973).

NEWMAN, R. Planning drug abuse treatment: critical decisions. *Bulletin on narcotics*, **30** (2): 41–48 (1978).

NEWMAN, R. *Methadone treatment in narcotic addiction.* New York, Academic Press, 1977.

NOLL, A. "Drug abuse and its prevention" as seen by the international legal profession. *Bulletin on narcotics*, **27** (1): 37–47 (1975).

NOLL, A. Drug abuse and penal provisions of the international drug control treaties. *Bulletin on narcotics*, **29** (4): 41–57 (1977).

RETTERSTÖL, N. Drug dependency in Norway: use and abuse of dependency-producing drugs, treatment facilities; follow-up studies, prophylactic measures. *Bulletin on narcotics*, **28** (4): 27–44 (1976).

SPENCER, C. *Drug abuse in East Asia*. London, Oxford University Press, 1981.

SMART, R. & MURRAY, G. *Drug abuse and preventive programmes in twenty-three WHO Member Countries*. Toronto, Alcoholism and Drug Addiction Research Foundation, 1981.

SWEDISH NATIONAL BOARD OF HEALTH AND WELFARE, NARCOTICS SECTION, COMMITTEE ON HEALTH EDUCATION. *Summary of the report: The treatment of drug addicts*. Stockholm, 1974.

SWEDISH NATIONAL BOARD OF HEALTH AND WELFARE. *Health and social care for alcoholics in Sweden: problems and future prospects*. Stockholm, 1981.

THE AMERICAN CORRECTIONAL ASSOCIATION. *Drug abuse testing: successful models for treatment and control in correctional programs*. College Park, MD, 1979.

THE PARLIAMENT OF THE COMMONWEALTH OF AUSTRALIA, SENATE STANDING COMMITTEE ON SOCIAL WELFARE. *Drug problems in Australia: An intoxicated society?* Canberra, 1977.

THE WHITE HOUSE. *New directions in international health cooperation: a report to the President*. Washington, DC, 1978.

THE WHITE HOUSE. *Annual report on the Federal Drug Program, 1980*. Washington, DC, 1980.

UELMAN, G. & HADDOX, V. *Cases, text, and materials on drug abuse and the law*. St Paul, MN, West Publishing Company, 1974.

UNITED KINGDOM, DEPARTMENT OF HEALTH AND SOCIAL SECURITY AND THE WELSH OFFICE *The pattern and range of services for problem drinkers: Report by the Advisory Committee on Alcoholism*. London, HMSO, 1980.

UNITED KINGDOM, THE HOME OFFICE, ADVISORY COMMITTEE ON DRUG DEPENDENCE. *The rehabilitation of drug addicts*, London, HMSO, 1968.

UNITED NATIONS. *Commentary on the Single Convention on Narcotic Drugs, 1961*. New York, 1973.

UNITED NATIONS. *Commentary on the Convention on Psychotropic Substances.* New York, 1976.

UNITED NATIONS CONSULTATIVE GROUP ON NARCOTICS PROBLEMS IN ASIA AND THE FAR EAST. *Bulletin on narcotics,* **17** (2): 39–46 (1965).

UNITED NATIONS, INTERNATIONAL NARCOTICS CONTROL BOARD. *Report of the International Narcotics Control Board for 1981.* New York, 1981 (document E/INCB/56).

UNITED STATES DEPARTMENT OF HEALTH, EDUCATION, AND WELFARE. *First special report to the US Congress on alcohol and health.* Rockville, MD, 1971 (DHEW Publication No. (ADM) 74–68).

UNITED STATES DEPARTMENT OF HEALTH, EDUCATION, AND WELFARE, NATIONAL INSTITUTE ON DRUG ABUSE. *Drug abuse treatment and the criminal justice system: three reports.* Rockville, MD, 1977 (DHEW Publication No. (ADM) 78–575).

UNITED STATES DEPARTMENT OF HEALTH, EDUCATION, AND WELFARE, NATIONAL INSTITUTE ON DRUG ABUSE. *Research issues 23: International drug use.* Rockville, MD, 1978.

UNITED STATES DEPARTMENT OF HEALTH, EDUCATION, AND WELFARE, NATIONAL INSTITUTE ON DRUG ABUSE. *Criminal justice alternatives for disposition of drug abusing offender cases.* Rockville, MD, 1978 (DHEW Publication No. (ADM) 79–745).

UNITED STATES DEPARTMENT OF HEALTH AND HUMAN SERVICES, PUBLIC HEALTH SERVICE. *Police referral to drug treatment: risks and benefits.* Rockville, MD, 1981.

UNITED STATES DEPARTMENT OF HEALTH, EDUCATION, AND WELFARE, PUBLIC HEALTH SERVICE. *Alcohol and drug abuse in medical education.* Rockville, MD, 1980 (DHEW Publication No. (ADM) 79–891).

UNITED STATES DEPARTMENT OF STATE. *The global legal framework for narcotics and controlled substances.* Washington, DC, 1979.

VAILLE, C. A model law for the application of the Single Convention on Narcotic Drugs, 1961. *Bulletin on narcotics,* **21** (2): 1–12 (1969).

WEISS, P. Narcotics control in Switzerland. *Bulletin on narcotics,* **16** (2): 1–16 (1964).

WESTERMEYER, J. The pro-heroin effects of anti-opium laws in Asia. *Archives of general psychiatry,* **33**: 1135–1139 (1976).

WESTERMEYER, J. Social events and narcotic addiction: The influence of war and law on opium use in Laos. *Addiction behavior*, **3**: 57–61 (1978).

WESTERMEYER, J. & BOURNE, P. A heroin epidemic in Asia. *American journal of drug and alcohol abuse*, **4**(1): 1–11 (1977).

WHO publications may be obtained, direct or through booksellers, from:

ALGERIA: Entreprise nationale du Livre (ENAL), 3 bd Zirout Youcef, ALGIERS

ARGENTINA: Carlos Hirsch, SRL, Florida 165, Galerías Güemes, Escritorio 453/465, BUENOS AIRES

AUSTRALIA: Hunter Publications, 58A Gipps Street, COLLINGWOOD, VIC 3066 — Australian Government Publishing Service *(Mail order sales)*, P.O. Box 84, CANBERRA A.C.T. 2601; *or over the counter from:* Australian Government Publishing Service Booshops *at:* 70 Alinga Street, CANBERRA CITY A.C.T. 2600; 294 Adelaide Street, BRISBANE, Queensland 4000; 347 Swanston Street, MELBOURNE, VIC 3000; 309 Pitt Street, SYDNEY, N.S.W. 2000; Mt Newman House, 200 St. George's Terrace, PERTH, WA 6000; Industry House, 12 Pirie Street, ADELAIDE, SA 5000; 156–162 Macquarie Street, HOBART, TAS 7000 — R. Hill & Son Ltd., 608 St. Kilda Road, MELBOURNE, VIC 3004; Lawson House, 10–12 Clark Street, CROW'S NEST, NSW 2065

AUSTRIA: Gerold & Co., Graben 31, 1011 VIENNA I

BAHRAIN: United Schools International, Arab Regional Office, P.O. Box 726, BAHRAIN

BANGLADESH: The WHO Programme Coordinator, G.P.O Box 250, DHAKA 5

BELGIUM: *For books:* Office International de Librairie s.a., avenue Marnix 30, 1050 BRUSSELS. *For periodicals and subscriptions:* Office International des Périodiques, avenue Marnix 30, 1050 BRUSSELS — *Subscriptions to World Health only:* Jean de Lannoy, 202 avenue du Roi, 1060 BRUSSELS

BHUTAN: *see* India, WHO Regional Office

BOTSWANA: Botsalo Books (Pty) Ltd., P.O. Box 1532, GABORONE

BRAZIL: Biblioteca Regional de Medicina OMS/OPS, Unidade de Venda de Publicações, Caixa Postal 20.381, Vila Clementino, 04023 SÃO PAULO, S.P.

BURMA: *see* India, WHO Regional Office

CANADA: Canadian Public Health Association, 1335 Carling Avenue, Suite 210, OTTAWA, Ont. K1Z 8N8. (Tel: (613) 725–3769. Telex: 21–053–3841)

CHINA: China National Publications Import & Export Corporation, P.O. Box 88, BEIJING (PEKING)

CYPRUS: "MAM", P.O. Box 1722, NICOSIA

CZECHOSLOVAKIA: Artia, Ve Smeckach 30, 111 27 PRAGUE 1

DEMOCRATIC PEOPLE'S REPUBLIC OF KOREA: *see* India, WHO Regional Office

DENMARK: Munksgaard Export and Subscription Service, Nørre Søgade 35, 1370 COPENHAGEN K (Tel: + 45 1 12 85 70)

ECUADOR: Librería Científica S.A., P.O. Box 362, Luque 223, GUAYAQUIL

EGYPT: Osiris Office for Books and Reviews, 50 Kasr El Nil Street, CAIRO

FIJI: The WHO Programme Coordinator, P.O. Box 113, SUVA

FINLAND: Akateeminen Kirjakauppa, Keskuskatu 2, 00101 HELSINKI 10

FRANCE: Librairie Arnette, 2 rue Casimir-Delavigne, 75006 PARIS

GABON: Librairie Universitaire du Gabon, B.P. 3881, LIBREVILLE

GERMAN DEMOCRATIC REPUBLIC: Buchhaus Leipzig, Postfach 140, 701 LEIPZIG

GERMANY FEDERAL REPUBLIC OF: Govi-Verlag GmbH, Ginnheimerstrasse 20, Postfach 5360, 6236 ESCHBORN — W. E. Saarbach GmbH, Tradis Diffusion, Neue Eiler Strasse 50, Postfach 900369, 5000 COLOGNE 1 — Buchhandlung Alexander Horn, Friedrichstrasse 39, Postfach 3340, 6200 WIESBADEN

GHANA: Fides Enterprises, P.O. Box 1628, ACCRA

GREECE: G.C. Eleftheroudakis S.A., Librairie internationale, rue Nikis 4, ATHENS (T. 126)

HAITI: Max Bouchereau, Librairie "A la Caravelle", Boîte postale 111-B, P-PRINCE

HONG KONG: Hong Kong Government Information Services, Beaconsfield House, 6th Floor, Queen's Road, Central, VICTORIA

HUNGARY: Kultura, P.O.B. 149, BUDAPEST 62 — Akadémiai Könyvesbolt, Váci utca 22, BUDAPEST V

ICELAND: Snaebjørn Jonsson & Co., P.O. Box 1131, Hafnarstraeti 9, REYKJAVIK

INDIA: WHO Regional Office for South-East Asia, World Health House, Indraprastha Estate, Mahatma Gandhi Road, NEW DELHI 110002

INDONESIA: P.T. Kalman Media Pusaka, Pusat Perdagangan Senen, Block 1, 4th Floor, P.O. Box 3433/Jkt, JAKARTA

IRAN (ISLAMIC REPUBLIC OF): Iran University Press, 85 Park Avenue, P.O. Box 54/551, TEHERAN

IRAQ: Ministry of Information, National House for Publishing, Distributing and Advertising, BAGHDAD

IRELAND: TDC Publishers, 12 North Frederick Street, DUBLIN 1 (Tel: 744835–749677)

ISRAEL: Heiliger & Co., 3 Nathan Strauss Street, JERUSALEM 94227

ITALY: Edizioni Minerva Medica, Corso Bramante 83–85, 10126 TURIN; Via Lamarmora 3, 20100 MILAN

JAPAN: Maruzen Co. Ltd., P.O. Box 5050, TOKYO International, 100–31

JORDAN: Jordan Book Centre Co. Ltd., University Street, P.O. Box 301 (Al-Jubeiha), AMMAN

KUWAIT: The Kuwait Bookshops Co. Ltd., Thunayan Al-Ghanem Bldg, P.O. Box 2942, KUWAIT

LAOS PEOPLE'S DEMOCRATIC REPUBLIC: The WHO Programme Coordinator, P.O. Box 343, VIENTIANE

LEBANON: The Levant Distributors Co. S.A.R.L., Box 1181, Makdassi Street, Hanna Bldg, BEIRUT

LUXEMBOURG: Librairie du Centre, 49 bd Royal, LUXEMBOURG

MALAWI: Malawi Book Service, P.O. Box 30044, Chichiti, BLANTYRE 3

WHO publications may be obtained, direct or through booksellers, from: